The Vital Mystic

A Guide to Emotional Strength and Spiritual Enrichment

by
T.Collins Logan

Excerpt of "Castrating an Ego" from *The Subject Tonight is Love*, Copyright Daniel Ladinsky, Pumpkin House Press, 1996; and excerpts of "That Full, Fragrant Curl," "Manic Screaming," "What Happens?" and "Someone Should Start Laughing" from *I Heard God Laughing: Renderings of Hafiz*, Copyright Daniel Ladinsky, Sufism Reoriented, 1996. Reprinted with the permission of Daniel Ladinsky.

Excerpts of "The Guest House," "Enough Words," and "Two Days of Silence," from *The Essential Rumi*, Copyright Coleman Barks, Harper San Francisco, 1997. Reprinted with the permission of Coleman Barks.

THE VITAL MYSTIC, A GUIDE TO EMOTIONAL STRENGTH AND SPIRITUAL ENRICHMENT, Second Edition, March 2009

Copyright © 2003 T. Collins Logan

ISBN 0-9770336-2-7

Published by Integral Lifework Center, PO Box 221082, San Diego, CA 92192

"Learning is finding out what you already know. Doing is demonstrating that you know it. Teaching is reminding others that they know just as well as you."

Richard Bach, *Illusions*

This book is as much from as for the following people:

My parents, my sisters Karin, Kirsten and Michelle, my brother Sam, my friends and inspirations Ann Z., Mark F., Lisa D., Robin B., Kristen H., Jim C., Shauna B., Carol L., Ted M., Joyce C., Dale T., Wendy T., Tim C., Joan L., Tim K., Jock B., Jutta E., Rick F., Marjorie M., Steve G., Anne T., Geral M., Milo H., David Z., Riley R., Tony H., my biological and adopted grandparents, and the many other teachers of my past and present.

Special thanks to my friends Anne, Lisa and Robin for their invaluable feedback on early drafts; Tim C. for introducing me to Daniel Ladinsky and other great writers; Deborah and Stephan for their help with the Insight and Esteem evaluation; David Caruso for his assistance in my research of Emotional Intelligence; and of course Coleman Barks and Daniel Ladinsky for their generous permission to reprint portions of their work.

Table of Contents

Introduction

My Beliefs

Having beliefs similar to mine – or any spiritual beliefs at all, for that matter – is not a prerequisite for appreciating this book. Nor is it my objective to convert people to my particular flavor of spirituality. On the contrary, my hope is that the insights and practices here will benefit people of all religions, and of no religion at all, strengthening the beliefs they already hold. However, you will see my flavor of spirituality reflected in much of this writing, so I will briefly summarize my views.

I am a mystic, in that I believe in a spiritual perception that is a part of our experience, and accessible to all. Within this mystical awareness, I believe we have great capacity to recognize and process information that our rational and emotional faculties can't comprehend, and thereby come to know the Sacred intimately and immediately. As to what the Sacred actually is, I don't claim any special knowledge, or even that I am able to express in words what my heart feels and spirit knows. However, the notions of holiness and divinity, of spiritual forces constantly at work in the Universe, and the potency of individual will have become as natural as breathing to me.

I also believe in a timeless soul, and that all human experience has the inherent and foremost purpose of evolving that soul.   That is why this book describes things as *spiritually healthy* or *spiritually unhealthy*: that is, profitable or unprofitable for the soul's evolution. Are we reincarnated again and again until our soul learns what it is intended to learn? I think we are. Beyond our refinement in this earthly experience, I won't speculate on our next destination, but I remain open – excited, even – to whatever comes. As to various religions and philosophical systems, I would not assert that any has unique primacy in this journey, but that every tradition shares the same core values with every other. Although these belief systems sometimes differ in methodology and language, their objectives are universal: to provide comprehensive enlightenment and a means of perceiving the nature of things; to cultivate a deep and persisting compassion for ourselves and others; and to enhance our ability to do good in the world.

The deeper I delve into mystical matters, the more all of the separate ideas and experiences become one endless, interconnected ocean of being through which individual consciousness swims as but an illusion of self. However, I still consider our unique identity to be a useful, perhaps even necessary contrivance, as we each follow our own path through progressive stages of being. Individuality adds value – both to our own journey and to the good of All – through the contrasting perspectives, creative contributions and diversity of culture and experience it provides. Although I consider all of us to be more alike than different, I still enjoy celebrating those differences.

A Beginning

I have tried to condense years of reflection into a relatively brief format, hoping to hold your attention while I revisit many ideas that may be familiar to you, and introduce some innovative concepts and practices from which I have benefited. I hope you will enjoy all of it. Concepts and processes are presented in many different ways because I expect readers to come from many different backgrounds, with varying exposure to each of these subjects. In my attempt to wrap words around the abstract, you will find everything from poetry and inspirational quotes to real-life examples. All of it converges on a central idea: that wisdom and profound spiritual insight are not the provenance of an elite or uniquely initiated few, but are accessible to all – within each and every one of us. In fact, this book contains little of the definitive truth many might seek, and only maps a suggested course to realizations each of us must arrive at on our own.

In terms of the practices described here, I continually renew my commitment to them. Observing my life, one person might see me as struggling through a fog of my own inadequacies, while another might say I am full of Love and Light. I would not deny or justify either, but ascribe both conditions to being human. I cannot claim to be an authority on anything, but I have found the truth of what is in this book by living it. In preparing for Christian ministry, I spent four years opening my heart and home to the poor, the physically disabled, the socially outcast, the homeless and those struggling with substance abuse. In a decade of managing people, in environments ranging from public education and non-profits to a Fortune 100 company, I have counseled, encouraged and mediated for countless individuals, both in their professional and personal lives. In my ongoing volunteerism, I have overseen successful conflict-resolution and built consensus around community change.

Yet although much of what you will read here has been tested in service to others, the concepts and disciplines have emerged from two additional threads of experience seemingly far removed from that service. On the one hand, there is my own counseling. I saw my first therapist when I was eight years old, and over the past thirty years have spent hundreds of hours in therapy addressing the aftermath of a challenging childhood. From psychoanalysis to Codependents Anonymous, anger management to marital counseling, hypnotherapy to Hakomi, and Ritalin to Zoloft, I've been exposed to a broad range of techniques and philosophies. My progress has been slow and at times painful, but if I am proficient in anything, it is the consumption of psychological care.

Another significant contribution to this work is my own spiritual awakening and ongoing mystical journey. I have had contact with the mystical since I was very young. When I was three, I awoke from an extraordinary dream, a potent vision of self-transformation that I vividly remember to this day.   Since then, my dream-life has transported me to indescribable places, overwhelmed my senses with wonder, and infused my life with wisdom and contentment. Unbidden, and at first hard to understand, these experiences have both inspired me and changed me. Because of them, and aided by a natural curiosity and longing, I began a lifelong search for explanations. Over the last twenty years, this search has immersed me in many different spiritual traditions, resulting in a strong affinity for the beliefs and teachings of Christianity, Wicca, Taoism, Buddhism, Sufism, Vedanta and other systems of Yoga, Hermetic disciplines, the mystical Kabbalah and many others.

Techniques from every one of these traditions have introduced me to a new spectrum of spiritual perception, continually deepening my humility and joy, and inviting me to partake of the Divine. My spirit is awake. The flow of mysterious forces in and around me has captured my heart and expanded my understanding. With discipline and diligence in mystical practice, I have found a tiny haven of clarity; finally, a lot of things make sense that never have before. At the heart of this illumination is neither a selective combination of spiritual concepts, nor an additive syncretism of religious systems, but a paring down of differing approaches to their central substance, penetrating the quintessence of the mystic's way.

This, then, is a resting point in that journey, a time to reflect and share what I have learned, hoping it might be helpful to others. As soon as I reach the final sentence of this book, I am certain dozens of new ideas will present themselves, and a whole new perspective will emerge from the ordered pages I have left behind. Spiritual life is too dynamic to put on paper!   Understandably, this book will be a departure into the unknown for some, while for others it may only be recharting familiar territory. Any shortcomings you find here are sure to be the result of my own imperfect knowledge or inadequate prose, for although approaches may vary, the objectives and benefits of mysticism are universal and the principles and practices described in this work are sound. I only hope that this will encourage and inspire you to pursue your own unique path through the mysterious forest of personal discovery and to nourish the spiritual spark within.

> "The raft is used to cross the river. It isn't to be carried around on your shoulders. The finger which points at the moon isn't the moon itself."
>
> Thich Nhat Hanh, *The Miracle of Mindfulness*

How to Read This Book

Although organized so that each chapter builds on the preceding one, there certainly is no right or wrong way to read this book. If you are like me, and tend to be non-linear in how you digest information, I have some suggestions that hint at a mystical approach to exploration and understanding:

- Let words draw you where your heart wants to go. If you see a chapter heading that intrigues you right away, go there first, then expand out.
- When you hit a speed-bump, such as a description or idea that doesn't make any sense to you, skip over it. Move on and come back later.
- Read small amounts, and – especially if it is new information to you – mull over what you've read for a couple of days before absorbing any more. It likely won't be as beneficial to rush or force your way through this book.

- Try being random: just open up and read a paragraph or two, then close the book, think about what you've read, and repeat the exercise.
- Find someone with whom you can discuss each topic or chapter, if only because synergy and synchronicity are much less likely in a vacuum.

Although I would encourage you to take an unorthodox approach to your reading, there is nevertheless an overlying organization. Chapters are grouped under the following sections:

1. **Charting a Course** – A proposed starting point for mystical inquiry

2. **Restructuring Mind & Heart** – The essential tools of the mystic

3. **Practical Applications** – Principles of a "spiritually healthy" life

4. **Navigating the Thorns** – How to recognize and cope with challenges along the way

At the end of each chapter are questions you may find useful. You could read the questions first, and work your way through the chapter with the questions in mind, or just use them for review. Better yet, come up with your own questions! Challenge every assertion made here, test them in the forge of your own heart, then shape them with the hammer of your spirit and the anvil of your mind.

One recurring theme you will encounter is that emotional strength and spiritual enrichment take time and committed effort. This book is therefore unlikely to be satisfying as a "quick fix" for spiritual or emotional challenges. There are certain to be sudden moments of realization or change in perspective that are the natural result of the practices described, but the most reliable and long-lasting method of self-transformation is what I call "herding wind across stones." It is delicate and slow-going, requiring dedication and patience – which are themselves the first fruits of compassionate effort. If you stick to it, you will be herding wind with skill and joy.

Usage of Quotes

There are many quotes throughout, from musicians, poets, writers, thinkers, religious texts and other sources. Where the authors are more obscure, I have included the time period in which they wrote and their school of thought. Each quote is intended to add a perspective or clarify ideas, and is not meant to convey my grasp of the author's work or make my own words more authoritative. This, in combination with a deliberate modernization and reinterpretation of some of the older writings, makes it fairly likely that I will depart from how others may view these sources. Rather than accepting the context in which I present them, I encourage you to reflect on the meaning of the quotes in the original source material. In all cases, I believe your own path of investigation and discovery will enhance your understanding of all that you encounter here.

A Note to Scholars

This is not an apology of mysticism or any particular school of mystical philosophy or practice. You will find language that reflects everything from perennialism to constructivism, and phenomenology to assertions of absolute reality. *The Vital Mystic* is replete with apparent paradoxes mainly because it offers an encounter with immutable truths through embracing subjective experiences. The cultural, religious and philosophical contexts for interpreting such experiences are, in my view, relevant only external to mystical practice, and except for some widely shared assumptions I have tried to avoid them. However, as we continually invent language to ascribe meaning and value to any belief, it becomes increasingly difficult to escape circular affirmations; mysticism is no exception in this regard, other than by proposing a process of direct, unfiltered spiritual apprehension.

There are certainly physiological, cognitive and behavioral events surrounding and inhabiting the mystical process which deserve careful analysis, and although such analysis is not the subject of this book some observations have been made in passing. One of them is the common thread of emotional transformation and contemplative advancement throughout most, if not all, mystical traditions, and this is addressed in some detail. There is, however, much about mysticism that undermines purely intellectual inquiry. For example, mysticism is antithetical to traditional scientific methods not in that it cannot be observed or readily duplicated, but because it is holistic. Emotions, intentions, an inward contemplative focus, and something more – something I have named *spiritual cognizance* – are concentrated into synergistic and synchronistic phenomena that are both intensely personal and, as a chiefly mystical claim, convey universal wisdom. Further, I believe that the ultimate objectives of mysticism cannot be artificially induced; that is, a nondual consciousness without the foundation of structured introspection and reformed intentions simply will not produce the same results. *The Vital Mystic*, therefore, contains little discussion of the psychological, neurological or other causal mechanics of spirituality, for it is primarily concerned with defining the benefits of mysticism, the concepts commonly shared across cultural and ideological boundaries, and a "best practices" approach to engaging a powerfully transformative discipline.

Lastly, it has been my earnest intention not only to avoid promoting one mystical methodology above any other, but also to take Thomas Merton's criticism to heart, and spurn the "loose and irresponsible syncretism which, on the basis of purely superficial resemblances and without serious study of qualitative differences, proceeds to identify all religions and all religious experiences with one another...." [1] Instead, I propose what I believe to be the essential elements of a mystic's way to spiritual understanding, suggest some criteria for an integrative approach, and outline meditative techniques which can be

---

[1] *Mystics and Zen Masters*, Farrar, Straus & Giroux, 1967

tailored to individual requirements. Of greatest interest are the individual journey of the heart and mind, and entertaining a sufficiently dynamic ontological framework for that journey. As with much writing on metaphysical topics, to fully appreciate all that is proposed here requires a modicum of spiritual curiosity, an open mind and heart and a paucity of assumptions. The dialectics are not always orderly or concrete, and the syntheses offered live more in the realm of intuition than exposition.

Definitions and Concept Grouping

Clear communication depends in large part on a shared understanding of language and usage. In Appendix A, you will find lists of key words and definitions that explain how each idea differs from others in the same concept grouping.

Part One: Charting A Course

1. IDEALISM, FAITH and PRAGMATISM

Many years ago, when I first moved to Seattle, Washington, I attended a seminar on success. The speaker, Lou Tice, told a story that I often recall and which is a wonderful metaphor for faith at work. He envisioned building a new brick house for his family, but the exorbitant cost of the bricks seemed out of reach. Despite this, he persisted in practicing what he called *opportunity thinking*; that is, not ruling out an option just because he couldn't conceive of how to get there. As he was driving through Seattle one day, he spotted a construction site where they were demolishing an old brick building. He turned off the road and asked the foreman at the site what would happen to the leftover bricks when the building was razed. The foreman told him the bricks would be hauled off to a dump somewhere, and that the disposal was an expensive aspect of the overall construction. The opportunity thinker, reaching for his dream, asked if the bricks could be delivered to his own future home site instead. The foreman enthusiastically agreed, and offered to deliver the bricks at no charge.

What happened here? What forces were at work to fulfill this man's vision? Was this a manifestation of his will? An act of some Higher Power? Was it serendipity at work? Or is the source of whatever forces aligned the opportunity thinker's vision and intent with a pile of bricks...irrelevant?   Let's examine the attitude of positive expectation that was being practiced. He kept his mind and senses open and did not limit himself by thinking "I must work harder to achieve greater financial success so that I can buy bricks to build my home." Equally restrictive would be a passive attitude of "well, if the Universe wants my family to have a brick home, we'll receive some blatantly obvious sign, and then we can decide."   Why is this restrictive? Because if we don't begin with a clear and directed vision of what we intend, subtle signs will come and go, and we will overlook them as we insist on a more obvious indication of our fate. Instead of either of these extremes, this story exemplifies an optimistic attitude of openness and expectation, with a joyful readiness to act. When I imagine a change in my life, I offer a clear vision to the Universe with the attitude, "let it be for the good of All, as an act of compassion and gratitude." Then I let my dream go, and remain alert for whatever comes. In this way the first kernels of faith take shape.

> Pleased that he had mortified the mullah and was making an impression on the crowd, the scoffer said, "For instance, show us an apple from the garden of Paradise." Nasruddin immediately picked up an apple and handed it to the man. "But this apple is bad on one side," said the man. "Surely a heavenly apple would be perfect." "A celestial apple would, indeed, be perfect," said the mullah. "But given your present faculties, this is as near to a heavenly apple as you will ever get." [3]

Another example of faith came later on in my life, when I encountered an unsettling surprise during my early Christian experience. I had begun my assessment of the teachings and life of Jesus with a healthy armload of skepticism. I initially began an investigation without a desire to develop beliefs of any kind, being content with my own existential agnosticism. But as I explored various texts, two things happened: I found myself agreeing with much of what Jesus taught, and the evidence seemed to be mounting

---

[3] Mullah Nasruddin story, excerpt from Anthony De Mello's *Song of the Bird*

in support of this man's existence and validating some of the miracles he had performed. I was shocked...and appalled, because the deeper I went, the more intellectually cornered I felt by everything I encountered. Could it be that Jesus really said and did those things? And if that was true, could the miraculous signs and wonders he is reported to have performed be confirmation of his divinity or the existence of a benevolent Creator? What, then, was an appropriate response? And so I continued down the path of collecting and evaluating evidence, all the while straining against any firm conclusions.

Then, one day, some Christian evangelists came to my door. They wanted to explain their faith, and, little did they know, I was ripe for the picking. I asked questions, and they expounded on their positions. It all seemed very reasonable, and they kept coming to meet with me week after week. I must have been broadcasting my own spiritual openness at the time, for over the next few months, I kept meeting people everywhere I went who wanted to introduce me to their beliefs. I was exposed to nearly every religious group Seattle had to offer: Unificationists, Mormons, Jehovah's Witnesses, Scientologists, and the ambassadors of a dozen pseudo-Christian organizations; I was even roped into an Amway rally! Looking back, I am still amazed at the overwhelming synchronicity of that time. In any case, one day, while listening attentively to my weekly evangelists' exegesis on why smoking cigarettes was "an abomination to the Lord," I had an epiphany: on many points, I just didn't think the doctrine of these particular Christians agreed with the teachings of Jesus. In fact, it seemed that they distorted Jesus' views on just about everything in their tradition to suit what I felt were puritanical and controlling attitudes. And then it hit me: I didn't just *agree* with what Jesus taught, I *believed* it!

I then began my first experience of deepening faith, although an idealistic one. I feel blessed to have encountered Christian believers during this time who practiced authentic and unconditional love for each other and for me. My experience of Christianity was reinforced by personal growth, the demonstrated power of prayer, and faith-reinforcing evidences I continually collected through my studies. Subjectively, I experienced a narrowing of my "gap of faith;" that is, the gap between what I reasonably believed to be true, based on credible evidence and fairly sound reasoning, and what the Christian tradition expected of me. And now we come to my crisis. One evening, while discussing the Gospel of John with a philosophy major, I made a bone-chilling discovery: no matter how small my gap of faith was, or how persuasive the evidences, I could never reach a seamless union of proof and absolute truth – no matter what I believed, that gap would never close. Human perception, after all, is flawed. Human reasoning can be mistaken. Descartes' maxim of *cogito ergo sum* is itself a lethal trap for all conclusive logic: if my existence, and the meaning of that existence, is dependant on my ability to think and reason, then what I see with my eyes and hear with my ears is, by its very nature, always open to interpretation. All I could ever have was the illusion of conclusions, the frailty of my own assumptions, and an imperfect understanding of the world.

Anyone who has been through a major physical, emotional or psychological crisis will likely identify with the principle I wish to convey – that when we discover a limitation in our own abilities, or when some capacity we took for granted is taken away from us, all of our assumptions about who we are, and what we can become, are challenged. And so that evening I faced the bald and irrepressible truth of my own intellectual constructions. To be confident in my conclusions, regardless of supportive proof or personal experiences of success, was a fallacy of my own ego. All the explanations I could spew forth in response to the difficult questions of Christian doctrine were a fortress built on sand. Suddenly, my convictions seemed unsupportable, frail and weary. What would I do now?

Thank goodness for philosophy majors! My philosophical friend and I are still in touch to this day, and the depths of *not knowing* which we explored that evening were like a stinging salve for my wounded faith – painful, but healing. It was my first inkling of the principle that freeing myself from all of my previous suppositions could be a comfort instead of a threat. I could embrace the process of exploration with which I began my search for truth, but suspend my desire for the safe haven of absolute conclusions; it was unnecessary, a bulky albatross of intellectual pride, and my spirit of inquiry and adventure did not need to settle for mere absolutes. So I began to learn a more pragmatic sort of faith, the kind of faith that remains open to new ideas, and expects the best of them to percolate to the top over time. This requires much more patience than the hurried, decisive logic I was used to, but the roots of this kind of faith grow much deeper, its branches spread to welcome light through less rigidly prescribed formulae, and its supple leaves absorb and transform what eyes and ears cannot.

> "Those who trust obtain supreme knowledge. By mastering the senses and attaining understanding, they quickly achieve perfect peace. The ignorant and untrusting and self-doubting are lost. Neither this world, nor that beyond, nor happiness itself is for those who doubt themselves."
> Bhagavad-Gita 4.39-40

Chapter Questions

1. What areas of your life have you already experienced opportunity thinking?
2. What standards of proof do you require for something to be true?
3. What events or people in your life have been major catalysts for the evolution of your beliefs?
4. What moments in your life have challenged your assumptions about *what really is*, or how the Universe works?
5. From what do you derive your greatest satisfaction and contentment?
6. For all of the questions above, *why* do you believe what you believe?

2. STAGES of BEING: WHAT MAKES US HUMAN

Before delving into the intricacies of mystical practice and the many ways it can enhance our well-being, I would like to propose a model that describes what "being human" might really mean. How do our thoughts and emotions influence the relationship we have with our environment, and how does our environment change us? What makes us "spiritual?" Is there a universal progression for spiritual evolution? If so, what are the characteristics of such a journey? These are some of questions mysticism attempts to answer, and this chapter explores a suggested framework within which we can interpret and evaluate a mystical approach. In the end, my objective is not to promote a specific worldview or spiritual practice above any other – for we must each come to our own conclusions and discover the methods best suited to us – but to introduce one of many practical ways to cultivate spiritual priorities in an otherwise materialistic world.

Growing Up

As children, we have little responsibility for our actions. All boundaries are externally defined. Rules classify what is right and wrong, and fear – or avoidance of pain – sets the only hard limitations for our behavior. Consequences are often a surprise, felt fully in the present. Family, the default relationships we acquired when entering the world, are our only relevant relationships, and define our childhood self as much as any external influence can.

Early on, family structure and permissiveness also delineate our personal power, and we therefore seek approval and reinforcement from our family when we are young.

As we grow, we begin to understand and accept the idea of personal responsibility, as well as the tension between externally imposed governance and internally generated goals. Boundaries for action are increasingly redefined by learned skills and abilities, internal definitions of freedom, and emotional maturity...all of which often contradict the confinements of ongoing family-imposed boundaries, and thus often induce familial conflict in the course of our challenging those boundaries. For most, this tension peaks in adolescence. As the patterns, logic and motives behind traditional external rules become more evident to us, we question them. Perceived limitations for behavior become more flexible, more self-defined, and instead of living by fear and avoidance, we develop an awareness of broader consequences and objectives outside of the immediate moment.

This transition from external to internal definitions and boundaries naturally results in an intense self-absorption. As every structure that has been externally imposed comes under our scrutiny, rebellious, contrary attitudes and behaviors seem almost reflexive for us. The exploration of our new limits of personal power can be reckless, sometimes even self-destructive. Experimentation on many different levels of thought, emotion and action is a constant. Instead of family, peers often become our primary relationships. Our friendships evolve into a "family of choice," and a new environment for self-definition and personal empowerment. Because of this emphasis on peer-approval, we are still not completely free of external influence, and new boundaries are partly defined by fear of rejection or disapproval in this new set of relationships.

Adulthood, when it finally arrives, is a complete acceptance of personal responsibility for our life, a divestment of dependency on others for sustenance or imposition of emotional boundaries. We realize our own limitations, strengths and potential, and choose a direction for our efforts in this life. A self-defining identity, an internalization of everything we have learned so far during our existence, asserts its autonomy from external influence. As we mature, the quest for personal power so important in our adolescence becomes less important, and our focus naturally shifts to empowering others. For some, this manifests through a career or avocation, while for others, creating a family or close community expresses this change. Boundaries for our action are now framed exclusively by conscience, conviction and fulfillment of personal goals rather than any fear of punishment or desire for approval. We now govern ourselves through self-examination and discipline, instead of submitting to reflexive want or reactive impulse.

This process of growing up has parallels in our spiritual existence, as well as in society as a whole, as cultural maturity tends to be rooted in a critical mass of individual maturity. And just as the evolution of a culture may take hundreds of years, our own spiritual journey likely progresses over lifetimes, reflecting the same stages of development as our passage from childhood through adolescence to adulthood. I call these milestones of spiritual growth *stages of being*, and the following section describes the distinct physiological, experiential, and spiritual interdependencies that characterize that evolution.

Greater than the Sum of Our Parts

Are we more than nerve impulses and chemical interactions? Is there some element of our being that transcends physical existence? It is an old argument, exhaustively proofed on both sides by the greatest thinkers throughout history. As a mystic, I am less concerned with a purely intellectual debate, and more with a direct, personal experience of the answers – satisfying all of my faculties instead of just one. From that experience, I would assert that there is indeed a wealth of self beyond the biophysical, and anyone who travels far enough along the mystic's way will uncover the truths about their own humanity which far surpass rational understanding. A convenient position, to be sure, when faced with analytical skepticism; however, my objective is not to persuade the skeptics but merely to testify from personal insight and universal mystic experience.

The following Pyramid of Self is a proposed arrangement of both the concretely and mystically observable elements of our being. I would suggest further that the dynamic changes in the tendencies and interactions within this Pyramid of Self determine not only our quality of life, but also our overall spiritual evolution. Why? Because as we bring the disparate and often competing aspects of our being into harmony with each other, we not only achieve ever-increasing insight into – and influence over – the flow of our lives, but also reach deeper into the roots of our existence and the startling essence of our underlying Self. This, in turn, begins to remove the common illusions and distractions of our passage, revealing a more profound reason for being. Therefore, understanding these components and their dynamic interaction is crucial to our spiritual evolution. How we manage and advance through this process steers our direction through this life, encourages our capacity for supersensory experience, and assembles a cohesive and resilient character from a scattering of intentions and desires. As will be seen, examining this process provides practical metrics for our daily experience in everything from personal relationships to our contribution to society.

Figure 1: Pyramid of Self

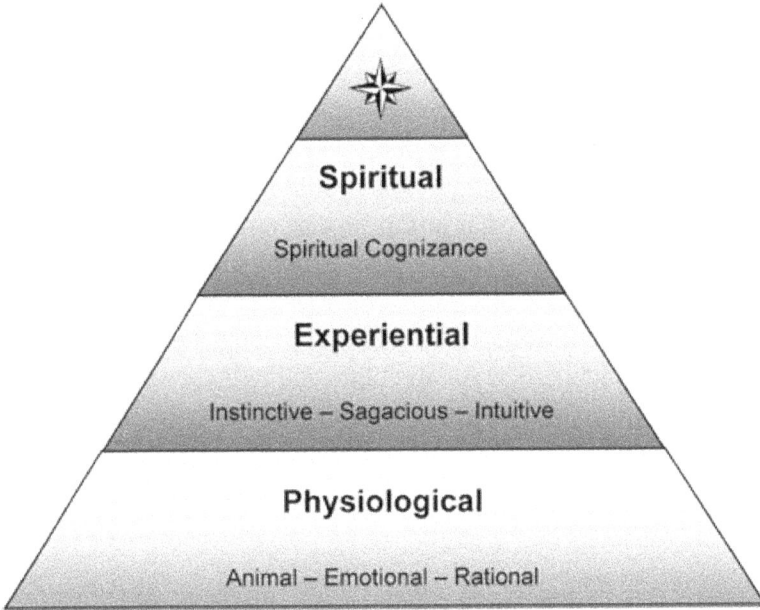

PHYSIOLOGICAL – This is our material being – the basic biochemical creature – and the simplest definition of self. This can be further broken down into:

> **Animal** – The basic physical requirements for sustaining life and the primal impulses to fulfill them. Hunger, thirst, fatigue, sex drive, aggressiveness and competitiveness make up the Animal. These are unthinkingly reactive.

> **Emotional** – Dominated by basic emotions such as fear, excitement, attachment, anger, greed, guilt and other emotional preservation impulses. Though initially raw and reactive, these become more constrained, complex and subtle as we mature. The

Emotional also competes with the Rational, introducing complexities in self-awareness and other-awareness – a grayness that contradicts the Rational's preference to see only in black-and-white. The potential synergy between these two is the beginning of a more sophisticated perception and understanding of self and the world.

Rational – Basic black-and-white logic. A simple comprehension of actions and consequences, observing transparent patterns and relationships, and applying linear problem-solving. The Rational is bent on fulfilling Animal impulses and requirements and is still very attached to our most primitive needs. The Rational also assigns meaning to things. It desires reasons for its own existence and tends to embrace absolutes, especially where right and wrong are concerned. As the Rational advances, however, it begins to challenge these assumptions. In order to resolve such questions, an inherent tension with the Emotional prods us to evolve.

EXPERIENTIAL – This is the information we gather through living and exploring our environment. From our experience, we learn to define ourselves in relationship to others and the world and create boundaries for our will. This level of the pyramid has these components:

Instinctive – The reflexive reactions of fundamental Experiential conditioning and innate somatic knowledge, such as seeking higher ground when lost, running away from a burning building, seeking help when in pain, and following the crowd. One could argue that some of these are genetically programmed behaviors, but even so, without reinforcement through our experience, we would stop responding to them. However, the Physiological still has influence through these instinctive "rules of engagement" with our existence.

Sagacious – Here we begin to have wisdom through observation of our experience, and a more complex, comparative reasoning takes place. Abstract correlations and patterns begin to appear, and the insights we assemble tend to override more primal, Physiological impulses in our decision-making. Self-control becomes easier and our self-awareness expands. We appreciate understated distinctions, departing from black-and-white logic to embrace larger, less rigid concepts such as patience, tolerance and exceptions to rules. We become more comfortable with irresolvable contradictions. "Right" and "wrong" are no longer such extreme absolutes. We realize that we don't – and perhaps can't – know anything with certainty. Strict deduction therefore begins to be complimented by Intuitive insight and spiritual discernment.

Intuitive – Something subtle and multifaceted emerges in the Intuitive. We comprehend truths that aren't necessarily logical, but which seem "right" against the backdrop of accumulated knowledge of our life experience and the innate wisdom of our soul. Although these insights are similar to Emotional reasoning, they draw from a deeper sense of *spiritual* preservation and a broader awareness of life's dynamics. Instead of raw fear, there is practical forewarning. Instead of anger, there is sadness and acceptance. Instead of trying to control, we are inspired toward love and compassion, increasing our empathy and awareness of others. In the Intuitive, the seeds of the Spiritual Self and mystical awareness take root and the lush environs of creativity are established.

SPIRITUAL – This is the purely mystical element of self with which we come to know the Sacred, intensely connecting with our own soul, with spiritual intelligence and with the collective energy of all life. The Spiritual is made up of three forms of spiritual cognizance:

Shared Understanding – The knowledge common to all souls – the instinct of the spirit, if you will – and a window into the nature of our existence. Here we comprehend more deeply that selflessness and discipline are the foundation for building a spiritual life, and that spiritual objectives are a worthwhile pursuit. We also perceive the temporal, impermanent nature of Physiological needs and wants, and embrace kindness, empathy and compassion above all other measurements of morality. Shared Understanding has no ego, no reactively defensive sense of self, and thrives on the interconnectedness of all things. Here we differentiate between the Physiologically/Experientially defined self and our Spiritual nature. Shared Understanding does not discriminate between *self* and *other*.

Moments of Epiphany – Here we make great leaps of comprehension, and our realizations carry with them a powerful emotional, intellectual and spiritual certainty. Such epiphanies may occur in a dream, or as we view a valley from a mountain top, or fall in love, or lose our closest friend, or pray, or meditate, or struggle through a deep depression. Although simple intellectual leaps of understanding can sometimes be predicted or engineered – as when solving a problem or puzzle, for instance – achieving spiritual epiphanies is less formulaic. Our most reliable route is to develop a rich inner life, a life of spirit, which is receptive to such moments and their meaning. These events are so removed from all other aspects of our experience that we know what they are without knowing what they are. Some call them revelations, or prophetic visions, or inspiration, or illumination, and often they seem to strip away all of our previous assumptions. When we choose to listen to our epiphanies and allow them to shape us, these moments powerfully inform and advance our evolution.

Mystical Awareness – The Sufis call this "tasting" the Divine. Mystical Awareness is as solid a sense of the spiritual world as taste, smell or hearing is of the physical world. This is where we directly apprehend underlying realities and mature the wisdom of our souls. Someone in the throes of existential angst might touch on this level of perception-cognition, as might someone lost in meditative concentration, or someone following the promptings of their spirit without fear, or someone who is overwhelmed by a powerful Epiphany. Anyone can access

Mystical Awareness, and the long-established disciplines of various spiritual traditions greatly assist our cultivating this faculty. What is most noticeable about this facet of self is its detachment from both our Physiological and Experiential makeup, and its growing identification – and intimate union – with the Source of All. This is where spiritual discernment is perfected, our most essential life lessons are processed, and our sense of purpose and completion is achieved. Living in balance with a fully realized Mystical Awareness is also described as a "harmonized existence," in equilibrium with the All. That is, when we have fully understood and successfully integrated spiritual cognizance with our many other aspects of self, directing those aspects consciously and in concert with each other while continually nourishing and nurturing All Things…then our existence is truly harmonized.

What awaits us at the apex of our pyramid? The Divine Spark, the True Self, the Self in All, the very essence of our soul and the bedrock of personal reality. Seen by some traditions as the primary objective of mystical practice, and by others as milestone inherent to pursuing what they consider loftier goals, our True Self is both the source and culmination of all other levels of development and experience. By noting the progression of our emotional awareness, mental discipline, and refinement of spiritual cognizance through each of these levels, we can appreciate more clearly where we are in our individual evolution; that is, which stage of being we inhabit at any given time.

Stages of Being

> "Enlightenment is a symptom of growth: and growth is a living process, which has no rest."
>
> Evelyn Underhill, *Mysticism, A Study in the Nature and Development of Spiritual Consciousness*

It is important not attach any importance to our current level of spiritual development, or to where we presume anyone else is in their journey. As trite as it may sound, it really *is* the journey that matters. But for the sake of self-discovery, and the inevitable benefits from that investment, there are many ways we can evaluate this transformation. It often seems as though our evolution moves through the same stages many times over; we appear to cycle through moments of impulse, knowledge and spiritual perception almost constantly. By the nature of our physicality, how could we avoid doing so? I have an idea, and then I have completely forgotten it. I feel deeply, and then that feeling becomes only a fading memory. I learn some crucially important fact about the Universe, only to realize later that my understanding is still very incomplete. So goes the adventure, and thus our humility grows with us.

At any given moment, therefore, we will experience different combinations of our Physiological-Experiential-Spiritual makeup. When I am debating some trivial thing with a friend, for instance, and my ego becomes attached to winning the argument, I may become 60% Physiological, 38% Experiential and 2% Spiritual. But then, only a few moments later, in a state of reflection and openness, I might become 20% Physiological, 30% Experiential and 50% Spiritual. At first, noticing such inner convolutions can be uncomfortable, because it challenges the habits we have developed to cope with self-perception, egoism and our current interpretation of reality. But the longer we are able to observe and maintain a more evolved state – where our Physiological habits become less important than our

Spiritual expression – the more purposeful, powerful and fulfilling our life becomes. One objective, then, would be to elevate the internal balance of my being to be mostly Spiritual, because I believe that evolving toward that end is why I exist; without such a belief, it certainly would be easier to revert to the purely Physiological, and root around for tubers in the muck. Perhaps it is because this reversion would be so easy that I choose not to succumb.

As a byproduct of this perpetual tug-of-war, there are likely many more distinct phases and interdependencies in the evolution of the soul than those in the following list. "Spiritual" advancement is difficult to quantify and is as diverse as humanity itself; however, there are some watershed events that practitioners of many different schools of thought and practice have observed along the way. One byproduct of the perpetual physiological/experiential/spiritual tug-of-war within us is that we often find ourselves cycling through these evolutions over and over again. Our only real achievement may be in how conscious we are of the stages we are passing through at any given moment, or in the varying amount of effort required to rectify a regressive drift. Sometimes, we plateau at one stage for months – or even years – before continuing on. In my own belief system, the soul's progress may take many lifetimes. I have found it helpful to revisit these descriptions repeatedly, even after years of mystical practice.

1. **Childhood** – The starting point of ignorance. Here we are concerned mostly with primitive urges and self-gratification, with barely a hint of spiritual perception. This is a fairly self-protective phase, while at the same time impulsively adventurous. We are dependent on externals and recklessly reactive, seeking pleasure and ego reinforcement above all else.

2. **First Questions** – We now start sincerely questioning what is, and engage our first insightful surprises about our environment and ourselves. We experience awe and inspiration, and new questions keep arising in us. We suspect there is more to life than stimulation and pleasure, and more to ourselves than animal impulses. This can be unsettling and bewildering, and

we may reach out for someone or something to guide us – a mentor, a cultural tradition, or a structured system of belief.

3. **First Awakening** – We are now exposed to our first knowledge beyond the materially obvious – perhaps as a spiritual epiphany or as an unexpected sense of healing or wholeness – and we often react to this with willful resistance. After first tasting awe, we may disregard the raw and powerful insights and emotions triggered by the implications of Spirit. Fear and other primitive impulses quickly assert themselves. As a result, we may rebel against our current beliefs, guides or mentors and seek distraction and solace in more primitive behaviors.

4. **Commitment to Exploration** – Given some time to rebel and relax, we overcome initial resistance and eventually revisit our enhanced awareness and sense of discovery. We decide to follow through on those nagging impulses to explore Spirit. Instead of fear, we now experience euphoric excitement, even while encountering the same insights, ideas and emotions that once frightened us. A feeling of belonging to something greater permeates us, and we investigate with eagerness.

5. **Challenge to Character** – Now we encounter seemingly insurmountable obstacles, causing us to stumble and flounder. We suddenly realize this journey may be more difficult than we expected. Disappointment causes hesitation, and, beleaguered by uncertainties, we might even give up for a time. Spiritual observations and internal shifts of perspective may become too disorienting or seem completely absurd. We may grow numb, or tired, and once again lose our tolerance of risk and our thirst for insight. We may abandon many of our initial hopes about the world and ourselves. We may resist accepting responsibility for our own spiritual well-being and seek comfort or escape.

6. **Recommitment** – Out of our doubts and wariness we return like prodigal offspring to our journey. We accept the limitations we have uncovered, even as we begin to move beyond them. We take responsibility for the health of our soul and cultivate our first sincere emotional, mental and spiritual disciplines, refining all our senses even as we wean ourselves of

dependence on them. We may grieve over our shedding of innocence and the new weight of accountability we feel. There may be emotional pain or existential anxiety over uncomfortable changes, but still we move forward. And as we learn compassion for ourselves, we also develop stronger empathy for others. This, rather than spiritual thirst, is what drives us now.

7. **Potential Derailment** – A subtle but persistent inflation of ego arises within our newfound spiritual confidence. If left unexamined, this can become arrogance. Our journey may now be derailed by pride and overconfidence, and although we feel increasingly informed and empowered, we are really returning to our earliest stage of self-protective ignorance and attachment to the pleasure of our achievements. Our beliefs become a facade for self-indulgence, and we can substantially lose our way in any number of distractions and delusions.

8. **First Freedoms** – At some point an unexpected event reminds us of humility, allowing us to see, perhaps for the first time, how little we really know, how self-absorbed we are, and how short a way we have actually come. A sense of humor is useful here, so we can chuckle at all the serious certainties we have held so dearly. We begin to *completely* let go, offering the outcome of anything we do to the good of All. Ego doesn't compete for our attention as it once did. We set ourselves free from attitudes of needy attachment and discover authentic compassion and objective affection for self, others and the realms of Nature and Spirit. In humility, we now become more transparent and open to new ways of being, and several forms of spiritual cognizance may erupt simultaneously within us.

9. **Spiritual Self-Sufficiency** – Although we still have our own identity and ego, these lose importance to us as we become less captivated by our ideas of "self." At the same time, we cease searching outside ourselves for truth, wisdom or strength, and our emotional and spiritual self-reliance grows. We can now dwell fully in the present, becoming absolutely comfortable with the current moment. A patient, empathetic and kind

disposition springs forth from us with ease, and a renewed clarity of purpose permeates our day-to-day life. We continue the very difficult work of healing ourselves on the most fundamental levels, often with an unnerving honesty and insight. And we share that healing with others through how we unselfconsciously are – as opposed to what we consciously do. Any lingering urge to be judgmental or even differentiate between people vanishes. We embrace profound respect and admiration for all things, and spontaneously manifest an encouraging and edifying presence for everything and everyone in our lives.

10. **Union and Alienation** – Barriers to our communion with All that Is break down completely. Enduring connection with every aspect of the Sacred – our True Self, the realms of Nature, other people, spiritual intelligences, and even the unimagined and unknowable – becomes simple and transparent to us. Because of this connection, we understand more clearly the characteristics of our shared human condition, the purpose of Spirit, and the patterns of creation all around us. Our wisdom deepens. Our own spiritual directedness is sharpened. This can be isolating, because many of the mundane habits in which we heartily engaged (and which others we care about may still think important) lose their allure. Also, our wisdom and assertions, though clear and obvious to us, might seem like nonsense to others. Because of this, we may feel alienated, sad, or even agitated and angry – despite the wonders and miracles we constantly seem to be witnessing. And so we should pay special attention to nourishing and nurturing ourselves on every level, remaining committed to our spiritual practice and sharing our journey with other spiritually minded people.

11. **The Great Choice** – At this stage we are faced with a decision: to remain engaged with the world – that is, society with its acquisitive and sensual orientation – or to exit the world. In part, this is influenced by our commitments to partnership, family and community. It is nevertheless tempting to sharply reduce interaction with the physical realm, perhaps because we

have become so intensely aware of conditions and forces at work within it, and because there are other ways of being now available to us. For example, we might wish to pursue continuous meditation and reflection, exploring new insights and awakenings without a care for what goes on around us. We might want to hermit ourselves away in the wilderness. We might be tempted to leave the material plane altogether. We realize we have complete freedom at this point (we have always had this potential, but now we fully understand it), but like any other type of personal empowerment, we hope to use our freedom wisely. At this milestone in our evolution we must reshape and renew the primary focus of our lives, even as we question the importance of who we are and what we do.

12. **Compassionate Service** – However we remain in the world, we decide to help transform it, aligning ourselves with all that is healing, loving and creative. How can we encourage the spiritual life of others? How can we bring compassion and healing to the suffering? How can we contribute to works of good for All? We now act from a place of innately apprehending the answers to these questions. At this stage we are still susceptible to drifting from our course and might even revisit old patterns of thought and behavior. Why? Because even though we are more fully actuating our purpose, our commitment to the Sacred still benefits from daily renewal. Also, there can be pain over the continued stripping away of our previous conceptions of *what is*. We may even grieve over losing the spiritual excitement – or intimacy with previous conceptions of the Divine – we once experienced. What helps us most at this time is that although we no longer clutch at accomplishment for our sense of security, we continually actuate our newfound purpose. Paradoxically, this is both a time of challenging and far-reaching decisions and an easy and commanding ability to act. And, of course, there are always a few deep-seated fears and vulnerabilities we continue to address, though fewer than when we began. I think this stage of being is almost like another childhood, where we stand on the threshold of a whole new type of journey, and a whole new

approach to our existence. At the same time, it is the beginning of true spiritual adulthood, where we have at long last learned the value of transcendent selflessness.

13. **Harmonized Existence** – Like cresting a tremendous wave in our passage, we now enter into ever-deepening continuum of unconditional love-consciousness, and with it a comprehensive sense of peace and simplicity. We become like a piece of bread soaked with spiritual honey, perpetually replenished. All our goals and desires are consumed in the effortlessness of passionately and compassionately being. We have both nothing more to accomplish and an endless number of tasks before us, and there is only quiet contentment, unquestioning strength, and sincere humility in the face of the Absolute. Every action becomes a sharing of our essence, which in turn has come to identify itself with the essence of All Things. We more easily maintain a hyperextended, all-inclusive consciousness that prevents disruption or misdirection, and mundane doubts evaporate. Because of a now persistent contentment, infusive joy and overall spiritual health, we often don't think to look further. However, as with many previous stages of being, the next horizon may come upon us suddenly and unbidden, and all that we require to meet it is patience, resolve and courage.

14. **Consummate Acquiescence** – We tend to squirm away from the first glimpses of this stage, just as we may have avoided others early on, because it challenges and dissolves the last vestiges of our identity – both personal and Universal. Even subjective identification with the Absolute is displaced by something more distilled: an ever-present All-Being that pierces the very quiddity of existence. Here we encounter the bedrock of reality where we completely inhabit our own soul; that is, we submerge ourselves in the entirety of the Divine Spark itself, with all its infinite possibilities. We no longer know, or feel, or sense – we *become*. Where previously our lives were infused with unconditional compassion, now the will to love is eradicated within a raw, unadorned presence of the

Most Sacred: there is no will, there are only the foundations of things – of love, and will, and even the Life Force itself – in which we flow and which flow through us. Like a cup of water emptied into a lake, we have utterly forgotten self, becoming both the lake and the empty cup. All barriers are gone – all predispositions, all fears, all aspirations, all measurements; even thought itself is subjugated to completely being. There cannot be differentiation any longer: the farthest reaches of the Universe are equal to the nearest object; a sense of vastness is equivalent to a sense of closeness; the beginnings and ends of space-time have no reference other than elemental continuity; the order and relationship of All that Is melts into an entirety which transcends the cosmos itself. Even nothingness and somethingness – even life and death – share common ground in our awareness. It is no small understatement to say that this letting go is impossible to put into words, nor can the far-reaching spiritual benefit of living from such a state easily be described. But this stage is available to everyone, is a natural occurrence, and, like all that has gone before, it has always been within us.

Is there more? I am certain there is much more. There are undoubtedly aspects of our journey that reach even beyond the Absolute. Perhaps the Universe itself is but a bubble floating on an endless sea, and the Infinite is but one pebble among millions in a transdimensional landscape beyond imagining. We must continually question and remain open. And as our hearts expand in all directions at once to encompass what we can never completely understand, the most incredible and the most ordinary will keep calling to us from the core of our being, echoing an eternal *"Yes!"*

This, then, is the framework within which I will explore mystical experience: that the Pyramid of Self represents the complex expression of our nature, and that universally experienced stages of being reflect our understanding, integration and harmonization of that multifaceted nature. In case I exhibit too much confidence that this association and progression of spiritual milestones is accurate, I will recall a quote from *The Journey Home* by Lee Carroll, a book I recommend for its potent metaphors. In it, Michael of Pure Intent hears the same message over and over: "Things are not always what they seem." A corollary to this truism is: "We are not always as far along as we think." I have found these to be good axioms to remember as I navigate my life.

What remains is to examine the many ways we can identify and advance through each phase of our growth, why this is important in the great scheme of things, and how mysticism provides a unique and particularly well-suited process for such a complex exploration. Mysticism asserts that everything we require to understand ourselves and our relationships to the Universe is readily available within our spiritual center; it is simply a matter of introducing new ways of perceiving and organizing existing information, and quieting counterproductive patterns of thought and emotion which distract us from underlying truths. The next chapter, the Golden Intention, describes what is perhaps foremost in our spiritual toolkit to achieve this end: the compass of purified desire.

Chapter Questions

1. Can you identify which stages of being you have already experienced in your life?
2. When did you first notice a transition from externally generated guidance to internally generated guidance?
3. What is the balance of your physiological-experiential-spiritual make-up right now? What was it yesterday? What will it be tomorrow?
4. Do you think the spiritual evolution of society as a whole is important? Why or why not?

3. HOW to GET THERE: the GOLDEN INTENTION

The only problem with not castrating
A gigantic ego is
That it will surely become amorous
And father
A hundred screaming ideas and kids
Who will then all quickly grow up
And skillfully proceed
To run up every imaginable debt
And complication of which your brain
Can conceive

Hafiz, *Castrating an Ego* [5]

I remember asking someone, a man who had been running one of the largest planned communities in the U.S. for twenty years, what inspired him and kept him going. We were walking in a field of tall grass that had been yellowed by the summer sun, and he bowed his head for a moment, choosing his words carefully. Finally, he said, "My inspiration now is much different than what motivated me as a young man, when I first started out with just an idea. I think my reasons have changed constantly over the years. I don't think I would have continued, if I couldn't keep coming up with new reasons for what we are doing here." Then it was my turn to walk quietly for a time, and think about the implications of his statement. Consider the following situation: You are standing on a street corner waiting for the light to change. A baby stroller rolls by you, and you

---

[5] From *The Subject Tonight Is Love* by Daniel Ladinsky, Pumpkin House Press, 1996

hear someone screaming behind you "Stop the stroller! Save my baby!" Meanwhile, a huge dump truck is barreling down the road, and in a fraction of a second, you realize that you must act quickly to save the child's life. You lunge after the stroller and pull it to the sidewalk just in time. Does this seem like the right thing to do? Most of us would instinctively react this way, but how do we know for certain what the consequences of this action will be? What if the baby grows up to be a devious and immoral person, or invents a new drug that addicts millions, or deliberately kills thousands for some pathological cause? What if this child is, in fact, another Stalin or Hitler?

As unusual as this situation would be, it illustrates the principles of *rationalized motivations* and *unpredictable consequences*. That is, none of us know what our actions will eventually create in the grand scale of things, and most of us must generate our own reasons for acting by trying to predict a specific end. We certainly have some control over the most limited outcomes of our effort, but is relying on these outcomes a dependable justification? The cascading chain of events that any single choice generates in the world around us is beyond our estimation or comprehension; the initial moment of choice, therefore, is the only moment truly under our influence. Keeping this in mind, how can we make any decision at all or wisely choose an appropriate reaction in a given situation?

> "If causality could be understood in terms of a one-to-one temporal sequence as in a simple Newtonian universe, then no social phenomenon could be discussed at all, since no social or individual event can have just one cause."
>
> Agehananda Bharati, *The Light at the Center*

It seems like it would just be easier to let the world flow around us without our intervention. Of course, even non-action is action, for the baby would roll in front of the truck without our interference, resulting in another series of unforeseeable consequences. Thus we can't be confident in the rightness of our inaction, either. Yet if we are in the world, we seem to be bound to the consequences of our actions, even if we aren't certain what the consequences will be. All societies are, after all, predicated on the assumption that everyone is accountable for their own actions. Accepting this, we take responsibility for our lives, and define the framework of our integrity. This, in turn, sets boundaries for our personal sense of purpose, and quantifies our value to society. However, the question of how to make any choice is still unanswered.

The approach I have taken to this riddle is to practice conscious intentions. To thoughtfully and relentlessly examine my own reasons for acting defines the "rightness" of choices for me. For if my own intentions are really all I have control over, I can only trust that the synergy of my actions with the events in the world around me will produce positive results. I can't be certain of the outcome, but I can believe that my own will to do good aligns with the goodwill of others, and even with the enabling life-force of the Universe itself. Are there influences at work in the world other than human will? I have no doubt there are, but it is not necessary to concern myself with the names and categories of those influences, other than hoping that I act in concert with a will to do good which is both part of and greater than my own will. That is, in fact, how I offer up my own prayers "for the good of All," and so my conscious intentions become yet another facet of that intangible realm called faith.

> There was a man in Caesarea named Cornelius, a centurion in the Italian cohort. He was a deeply devout man who revered God, as did all his household. He made many charitable gifts to people, and prayed to God continually. About three o'clock one afternoon, he saw a vision of an angel of God who came into his room and said, "Cornelius!" He stared at the angel in terror and replied, "What is it, Lord?" The angel said, "Your prayers and deeds of charity have gone up to Heaven and are remembered before God!"
>
> New Testament, *Acts 10:1-8*

The story of Cornelius is instructive on many levels, but at this point I am most interested with what made the acknowledgement of Cornelius and his prayers so notable. Though this is taken from the

Christian canon, Cornelius wasn't a Christian, nor was he a Jew – yet his actions and prayers were "remembered" by a Judeo-Christian Deity. Why is this significant? Because Cornelius represented all that was oppressive and divisive to Christians and Jews of that time. The Romans were the occupiers of the Holy Land, gentiles and defilers, murderers of Christians and Jews alike, and the crucifiers of Jesus. In this context, it is incredible that this story becomes a pivotal event in the life the Apostle Peter and the early Christian Church, breaking down barriers between Jews and gentiles of the 1st Century, and showing that, as Peter later says to Cornelius and his friends, "God does not discriminate between people."

But there is more here. This Roman soldier also symbolizes consciously purified motives – a heart that seeks to navigate what is right and good in the world, and is filled with devotion and kindness toward people and the Divine. Cornelius may not have conformed to the doctrines any particular religion, but he nonetheless aligned himself with the Source of Life and Light. He was *remembered* by the God of his enemies. I believe this is a meaningful lesson for any spiritual orientation, for Cornelius demonstrates a quintessential flavor of intention that enables us to spiritually mature and progress: a heart filled with compassion and devotion, and a mind illuminated with love-consciousness. I propose that where such compassion or devotion is directed matters much less than the conditioning – or "restructuring" – of heart and mind that is achieved through its practice. In the realm of our own well-being and the good of the Whole, there can be no harm in emulating Cornelius.

In counterpoint to an emphasis on refining motives, I have often heard the warning: "The road to hell is paved with good intentions!" What a strange saying. I think what it really means is: "The road to horrible failure and suffering is paved with willful ignorance." If we are shown a better way to do something, a more enlightened approach to action, and still willfully ignore that knowledge to pursue what expedient to our own satisfaction, how could we be maintaining an interest in the "good of All?" To avoid or condemn new information which revises our assumptions demonstrates either a lack of courage, or lack of integrity. Wise and universally beneficial intentions must, of obvious necessity, be *informed* intentions. That is what I mean by constantly and thoughtfully examining my motives.

For instance, if I go the voting booth because I believe democracy is a good idea – with hopes of making a positive impact on the world – but refuse to educate myself about the candidates or how a new initiative impacts my community, what good have I really done? Will randomly selecting who and what to vote for fulfill my intention to positively influence? Perhaps, when aided by mystical insight or miraculous manifestation of Divine will, a seemingly random vote might actually do some good. But if I am informed, and informed continually, I am accepting responsibility for charting a course toward specific ends, and acting out of sincere conviction instead of lazy ignorance. Clearly, this still does not guarantee any particular external outcome of my effort, but it does focus my intentions and authenticates my effort in what I can authentically claim I believe to be in the best interest of all.

> "You will cross over the sea of wickedness on the raft of knowledge. Just as wood kindled by fire is burned to ashes, the fire of knowledge burns all action to ashes; there is no purifier in the world equal to spiritual understanding. Anyone perfecting themselves in spiritual union will, given time, discover this in their own soul."
>
> *Bhagavad-Gita 4.36-38*

What, then, is the *golden intention*? It is the effort to conform my will and work to the good of everyone and align myself with the life-force that infuses every moment of our existence. It holds to the ideal of putting the welfare of the Whole above the self-gratification of a few, and eventually erases all self-consciousness in action. But how do we determine what is really "for the good of All?" One working definition might be "anything that enables, encourages or enhances healing of the heart and evolution of the soul." Under this charter, we attempt to relieve suffering, encourage empowered and constructive action, and bring peace, spiritual prosperity and joy into the world. Still, how can we know what this means, in terms of

thought and deed, from moment-to-moment?   What informs our
decisions? That is one of many things the mystic's way provides in
its progression through levels of spiritual cognizance and emotional
transformation, and is one reason I was initially drawn to mystical
practice.   From the wisdom of our own soul to the mysterious
workings of the Source of Life and Light, mysticism supplies answers
to these most difficult and universal questions.

Is the objective of golden intentions a kind of devoutly altruistic
attitude? In some ways, yes, but such "selflessness" does not always
take on a self-sacrificial flavor. We may appear very selfish and still
do good work, because we have shaped our ideal of what nourishes
our own well-being around what we also believe nourishes the well-
being of others. For example, if I were to write a poem, and someone
finds the poem inspiring, my self-expression may still appear
indulgent to another person who doesn't enjoy the poem at all. By its
nature, then, the golden intention cannot be consistently externally
validated by others – although, as we will later discover, there *are*
ways of confirming the spiritual fruitfulness of our actions and life-
direction.   The main consideration here is that, in the mystic's
worldview, the generation and exoneration of our motives is chiefly
an internal process, and is not dependant on externals.

> Two birds, always together and strikingly similar, are perched in
> the same tree. One gobbles up the fruits of every different taste,
> while the other looks on without eating.
>
> *Mundara Upanishad, III: 1.1*

Clearly, not all actions flow out of carefully contemplated
consideration. Most of what we do seems to stem from habit.
Without conscious reflection, even what little we accomplish outside
of habit may only be a random impulse or irrational reaction. Is there
a way to break free of this, and become more conscious of our state of
mind and heart, and the quality of our intentions?   Our most
successful avenue will be to activate our spiritual cognizance, and to
learn to trust the accuracy of our mystical senses against the
backdrop of love-consciousness. This will be discussed in detail later

on, but we can begin by simply asking "Why?" Why am I buying these clothes? Why am I eating this food? Why am I planning this trip? Why am I doing any of the things I routinely do each day: brushing my teeth, washing my hands, greeting strangers, going to work, making decisions? Why is any of this important to me? And if something isn't important, why am I doing it? The same line of questioning can be turned on our thought process itself: Why do we think certain thoughts at certain times? Why do we believe what we believe? How many of our thoughts, actions and reactions stem from empty habit, and how many flow from the center of who we really are? Stop reading for a moment, and ask yourself: "Why am I reading this book?"

Once we become more aware of what drives us internally and externally, we often evaluate these motives in terms of moral correctness. We live in a society of rules, restrictions and punishments designed around a lowest common denominator of social cooperation, and our conscience and self-awareness is heavily influenced by these superficial standards. Instead, I have found it is more helpful to distinguish between what is productive and counterproductive, or healthy and unhealthy – rigid moral certitude is simply too severe and judgmental to benefit the open-minded inquiry requisite for a more spiritual orientation. However, this approach may be alienating to someone who has relied on a strict set of rules or black-and-white reasoning to navigate the world. As discussed in Stages of Being, most of us experience this innate reflex at one time or another, but mysticism encourages a relaxation of rigid thinking in order to perceive underlying dynamics and deeper truths. We may ultimately come full circle, returning to conclusions about what is "right" or "wrong" which are similar to our initial judgments, but the mystic's way answers those persisting "whys" of existence with an illumination of our heart and mind, so that we perfect a discernment and inner certainty about what we believe, and how we should live, which dispenses with black-and-white reasoning.

The following table illustrates some emotional conditions which contribute to what I call *spiritually healthy* and *spiritually unhealthy* states of mind.   I use the term "spiritual" because I believe there are developmental consequences for filling one's heart with any emotion, especially to the point of becoming attached or disposed to that emotion, and those consequences directly impact our spiritual evolution. I have contrasted emotions that often appear superficially similar, while being very different in their personal, relational, or societal outcomes. On the other hand, some of these states are both fundamentally and superficially opposite. When looking it over, consider the inner emotional landscape you have experienced in your own life.

Table 1: Spiritual Health of Emotional States

Spiritually Healthy State	Spiritually Unhealthy State
Courage to defend the well-being of self and others, with patience and forbearance	Indignant, self-righteous rage, which is easily provoked and unconcerned about the damage it inflicts
Compassionate desire to nourish others with wisdom and kindness, while at the same time sustaining our own well-being	Compulsive need to rescue others without considering our own well-being or what is truly best for those being "rescued"
Love that has no conditions or expectations attached to it, and that patiently accepts another's shortcomings	A desire to control disguised as attention and devotion, but which impatiently demands specific reciprocation
Self-controlled ordering of effort according to what is most important (via spiritual discernment and intuitive insight)	Impulsive submission to every urgent or self-indulgent whim without a thought for what is important
Patience for, and an attempt to understand, those who oppose or antagonize us	Fear, paranoia and hatred of things we do not understand
Gratitude and forgiveness	Resentment and divisiveness
Acceptance and flexibility with whatever comes our way	Resistance to change and panic when things seem out of control
Honesty and openness	Avoidance, denial and deception
Peaceful and supportive internal dialogues	Chaotic and demeaning internal dialogues
Admiration and encouragement	Jealousy and criticism
Contentment in any situation, rich or poor, because our focus is on human relationships and developing a wealth of spiritual understanding	Greed and avarice: a compelling desire to possess material power and wealth
Guilt and shame, which resolves into humility and a renewed commitment to growth and maturity	Perpetual, unresolved guilt and shame, which injures self-esteem and cripples any ability to change

Vulnerable and joyful sharing of sexual intimacy in the context of responsible relationships	Wanton lust: an immersion in carnality without considering emotional or spiritual consequences
Mutual inspiration to greater achievement through fair-spirited competition – or better yet, cooperation	Egotistical competitiveness, which craves victory at any cost
Confidence with humility	Self-aggrandizing arrogance
Taking pleasure in the success of others	Taking pleasure in the suffering of others
Hope and faith in positive outcomes	Despair and pessimism: presuming doom

Did you identify any spiritually unhealthy emotions or patterns of behavior in yourself? In my own past, nearly all of these states have been represented at one time or another. How should we react to such a discovery? Once again, we may respond defensively or judgmentally to our own shortcomings, but this will likely undermine both our confidence and our ability to change. I propose instead that we acknowledge what is occurring, explore *why* we are thinking, feeling or reacting the way we are, and then let the thought, feeling or emotion go. Why hold on to it? Have compassion for it instead, and set it free. There are many ways to do this, even for very deep and difficult-to-relinquish mental or emotional orientations, though sometimes there is a lengthy healing process in-between acknowledging and releasing deep-seated patterns. But it is always possible, and always spiritually healthy, to accept where we are before we attempt to evolve. Clearly, however, whenever spiritually unhealthy tendencies dominate our life, we are operating outside of the golden intention, and are that much less likely to make decisions that benefit others or fortify our well-being.

Transforming Emotional States

The ability to transform our emotional state from something that is antagonistic and self-limiting to something more positive and productive begins with a conscious decision to do so. Beyond this initial acknowledgement of where we are, and making a choice to change, there are any number of methods, both ancient and conventional, which facilitate a new direction. The language and organization of this transformation process can be complicated and highly "jargonized," depending on the approach and underlying philosophy, but the basic progression looks something like this:

1. **Recognition:** We recognize and acknowledge our current emotional state.
2. **Examination:** Without judgment or overreaction, we examine and accept our emotions.
3. **Admission:** We admit to ourselves that change would be beneficial – that having a different emotional state would be more healthy and productive.
4. **Detachment:** We let go of the counterproductive feelings; that is, relax our emotional state until is greatly diminished or dissipates completely. We may also choose to relinquish some of the underlying beliefs or assumptions that brought this state about.
5. **Equilibrium:** We achieve a state of neutral and objective calms where we can decide on which emotional direction we wish to go next.
6. **Commitment:** We choose a specific new emotional direction and begin to actuate that state.
7. **Action:** We facilitate and support the newly chosen state with reinforcing actions, thoughts, beliefs, experiences, etc.

As an abstract concept, this may seem like a fairly simple process. And yet, for anyone who finds themselves habitually filled with rage, jealousy, strong desire or any other spiritually unhealthy condition, even taking the first steps of transformation can be daunting – especially in the moments of strongest emotion. What we'll discover in the coming chapters is that mystical practice, especially within a framework of self-awareness and self-esteem, will greatly enhance our ability to transform emotional states, as well as identify the most healthy emotional direction moving forward. Without a concerted effort to moderate how we feel, and the tools to facilitate that change, our emotional states are much more likely to unconsciously govern our well-being, quality of life and spiritual direction. Without some sort of consistent and clearly defined approach, the ideal of living "for the good of All" is just a lofty and unattainable fantasy.

To summarize, a concise definition of a golden intention is "a careful and continual examination and reorientation of our motives, expressing the purest form of unconditional love in all that we think, feel and do." But it is easiest to act from sincere conviction when we are truly *in love*, that is, when compassion and kindness are an expression of our very essence rather than merely what our heart feels or our mind reasons. This state of being *in agape* – immersed in an unconditional love-consciousness – can be cultivated through ongoing mystical practice, but only if we recognize the necessity of our own emotional transformation. Placing ego-satisfying achievement above kindness and compassion, or any external goals above the refinement of our internal process, is the antithesis of agape and impedes our spiritual evolution. But when we pursue a mystical understanding of things, and apply that understanding to benefit everyone, our desires are perpetually purified. Over years of practice, this discipline perfects a guileless disposition free of impulses and habits that are injurious to the Whole, or which oppose and undermine the evolution of our soul. I would assert that in some form the golden intention is a major tenet of most spiritual traditions.

The Roots of Us: Past and Present Intentions

There is another commonality of many belief systems that illuminates and enriches our self-perception, which we could call *spiritual roots*. This has been described as karma, a life-contract, a dualistic nature, a sinful condition, spiritual baggage, and many other doctrine-specific labels. I won't distinguish between these different definitions, which have the same essential aim: that we take responsibility for our life and every intention in our present and our past – even past lives. Wherever we are in our journey, there will be recurring themes in our experience that are echoes of these deep spiritual roots. Similarly, we are born into this world with certain innate propensities, and acquire much behavioral conditioning throughout our childhood; but as we mature, we can choose to moderate, enhance or reshape these aspects of our being. Once again, it is important to note that we have a primitive reflex to pass positive or negative judgment on ourselves. Letting go of this reflex is the foundation of compassion and one of the essential components of living the golden intention. But taking responsibility for our intentions is not something we can escape, in this life or the next. Thankfully, our task is not onerous or tedious, for once we take responsibility we obtain the keys to our greatest freedoms.

> "Oh my mind! Why do you hover so restlessly over the changing circumstances of life? Why do you make me so confused and restless? Why do you urge me to collect so many things? You are like a plough that breaks in pieces just as it begins to plough; you are like a rudder dismantled just as it ventures out on the sea of life and death. What is the use of many rebirths if we do not make good use of this life?" – The Buddha

To emphasize, I believe our current existence is not about punishment or guilt over our past, but the progression of our spiritual sensitivities and focus. There are persisting consequences for everything we do, everything we think and feel, and everything that has ever been done to us. I won't claim to understand the causality of it, but have discovered that the more our existence springs from spiritually healthy thoughts, feelings and actions, the more rapidly we advance into higher stages of being. Even if we materially succeed in the world, but somehow ignore our spiritual roots along the way, we will continually be faced with the same obstacles to our spiritual growth, physical health and overall happiness. Just as gravity holds us to the earth, our soul is tethered to our past, present and future intentions. This is the significance of each of our actions, and the spiritual weight of every choice we make.

In the next few chapters, we will explore ways of restructuring our patterns of thinking and feeling that might be inhibiting spiritual growth or occlude our access to universally available truths. We will define some practical steps to achieving deeper wisdom, relying on long-established techniques that encourage mystical processing without necessarily embracing the metaphysical or esoteric components of mysticism. From this beginning, hints of a vaster and more authoritative comprehension will emerge, and a new kind of perception is advanced which pierces the veil of illusion surrounding the reality of Self.

Chapter Questions

1. Have you experienced unpredictable consequences, and how did you react to what happened?
2. Can you separate the *spiritually healthy* emotional states you have felt over the past week from the *spiritually unhealthy* ones? Do you believe you could have chosen different emotional reactions in each situation?
3. What are some ways you can inform your intentions before acting on them?
4. Do you believe the same action by the same person, but with different motives, can have different outcomes?

Part Two: Restructuring Mind & Heart

4. OUR SEARCH for MEANING

Thirty spokes converge
in the hub of a wheel
but the empty part
is where the axle goes.

With fired clay
we make clay pots
but the empty space
is the useful part.

With a chisel we carve out
windows and doors
but the rooms in the house
are the space that we use.

So benefit comes
from the things that we have
but true usefulness comes
from having nothing at all.

Tao te Ching, 11

Consider the possibility that the existence of everything, and the meaning of that existence, is interdependent; that is, that all experiences – as well as the individual meaning of each experience – exist for us only in relationship to each other, and that there is no independent meaning without this context. There are many ways to examine this idea, and it is relevant to nearly all philosophies and spiritual traditions. How can I say this with confidence? Because even when the idea of interdependent meaning isn't stated explicitly – as could be argued for Stoicism, Hinduism, Taoism, and Buddhism

– it is a practical and elegant way to resolve the contradictions inherent to almost every belief system. However, whether you embrace this assertion or not, an interdependent construction of meaning is exceptionally useful in facilitating mystical practice. I'll clarify this idea in what follows.

Here are two different moments during my life:

1. Someone despises me because of a mistake I have made. My physical body is failing me, and there is a possibility I might die. My work environment is oppressive and combative, and is slowly crushing my well-being. In my loneliness, I feel great emotional pain and loss.

2. I am deeply in love with someone – who loves me back! Each day I enjoy delicious meals that delight and sustain me. As I stand on a mountaintop, my awareness extends out to fill the vastness all around me. Joy explodes through my being.

What is different about these two experiences, and why? Does one seem negative, and the other positive? I would contend that, at the most fundamental level of reality, they are both absolutely neutral. Whatever value I assign to these events, I am choosing an interpretation of my experience based on what I have learned during my life. Yet each moment does not, necessarily, have any intrinsic meaning or worth, and whatever importance they have to me *right now* will likely be different than at a later time, just as they might have for another person – or wherever a different set of assumptions, a shift in perspective, or a diverging worldview is present. In essence, each of us projects meaning onto our existence based on our self-referential understanding of the moment, when really we can't be certain there is any meaning at all.

Figure 2: Passive Assignment of Meaning

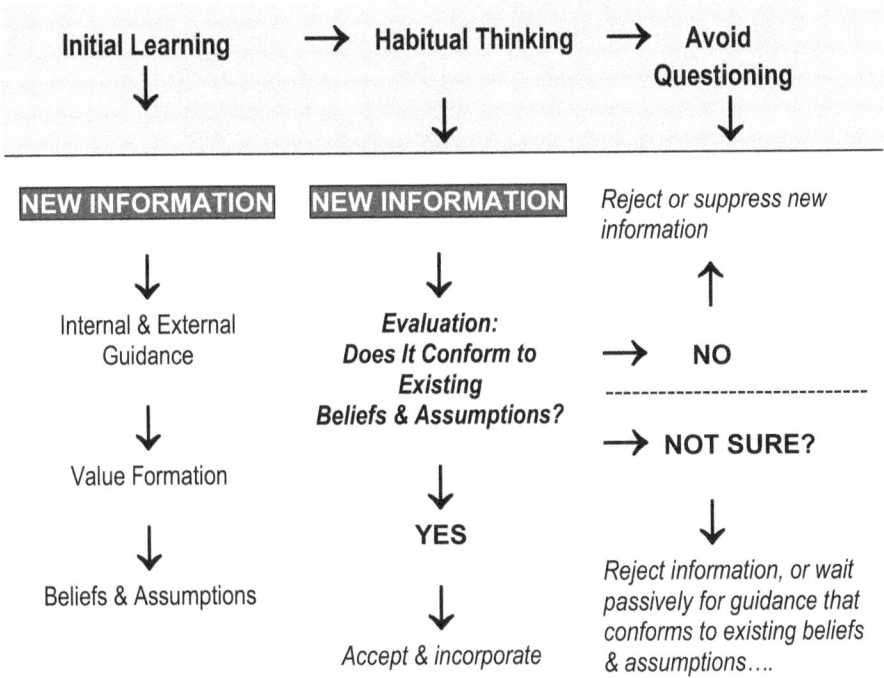

Initial Learning →	Habitual Thinking →	Avoid Questioning
↓	↓	↓
NEW INFORMATION	NEW INFORMATION	Reject or suppress new information
↓	↓	↑
Internal & External Guidance	*Evaluation: Does It Conform to Existing Beliefs & Assumptions?* →	**NO**
↓		-----------------------
Value Formation		→ **NOT SURE?**
↓	↓	↓
Beliefs & Assumptions	**YES**	*Reject information, or wait passively for guidance that conforms to existing beliefs & assumptions....*
	↓	
	Accept & incorporate	

So...what if we let go of our assumptions? What if we pretend, for the sake of stepping into a different perspective, that despite all we have learned we have *no idea* what anything in our life means? To be free of any presumption of meaning would allow us to accept whatever we encounter without prejudice, wouldn't it? That is, we would be able to experience events without confining ourselves to a predetermined valuation of those experiences. And as we greet each experience with unconditional acceptance, a new confidence emerges: that we can *decide* the value of something, instead of accepting what our habitual thinking tells us. Such a state of conscious neutrality – leading first to unconditional acceptance, and then to an intentionally interdependent construction of meaning – empowers us to exit the prison of our own arrogance, and open ourselves to whatever truths are present *in this moment*. This is the key to the door of an ever-expanding mystical perception, because spiritual cognizance explores information outside of our habitual thinking and concrete definitions; in a sense, we must blind ourselves to the ordinary to observe the extraordinary.

Figure 3: Active Assignment of Meaning

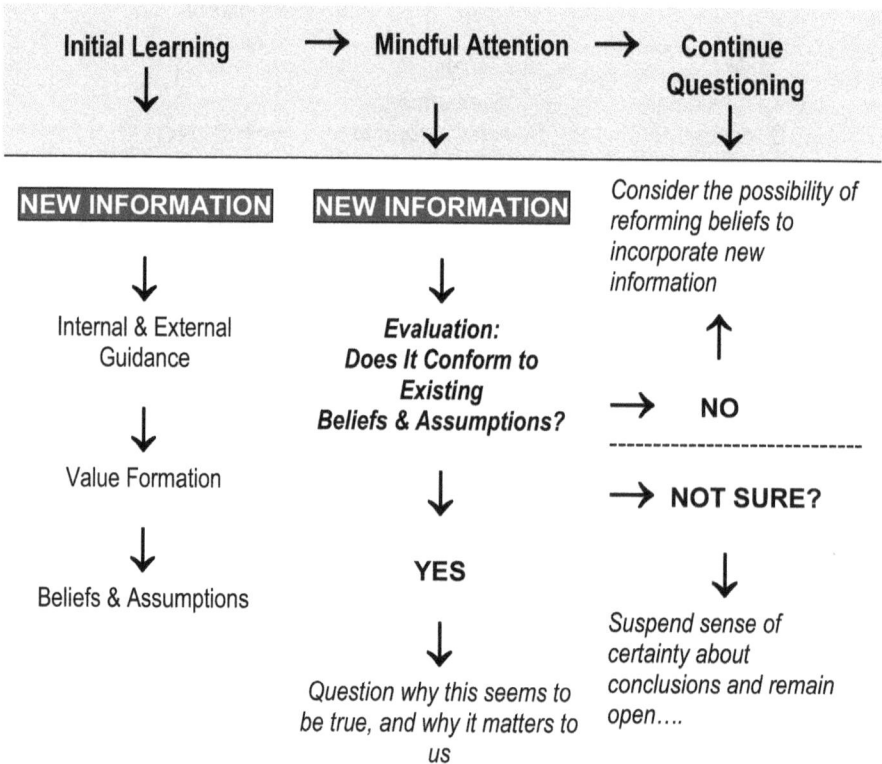

Initial Learning →	Mindful Attention →	Continue Questioning
↓	↓	↓

NEW INFORMATION	NEW INFORMATION	Consider the possibility of reforming beliefs to incorporate new information
↓	↓	
Internal & External Guidance	Evaluation: Does It Conform to Existing Beliefs & Assumptions?	↑
↓		→ NO
Value Formation		-------------------------
↓	↓	→ NOT SURE?
Beliefs & Assumptions	YES	↓
	↓	Suspend sense of certainty about conclusions and remain open....
	Question why this seems to be true, and why it matters to us	

As challenging as it can be to get a handle on this approach, it is that much more difficult to diligently practice it. Most of us have the reflex of assessing value and constructing meaning in an unconscious way. We resist the neutrality of events – that they are simply what they are until we create meaning around them. Mystical practice promotes a state of mind and heart that is detached from automatic interpretations of reality, is secure in itself, and is able to let go of apparent absolutes in favor of more dynamic and subtle relationships. As a preliminary exercise in this conscious shift of perspective, the character Fred in the following example demonstrates one way to escape automatic meaning-generation and explore a more interdependent interpretation of reality.

Fred and the Bubble of Nothingness

Imagine a bubble of nothingness. Absolute nothingness. Not even a thought can penetrate this bubble. Not even an all-powerful Deity, for the non-space and non-time inside this bubble don't even exist and have never existed. It is, in fact, a nonexistence that preceded even our conception of it, in the moment before these sentences were written or read. Inside this bubble of nothingness lives a fellow named Fred. For my own entertainment, I like to imagine him wearing a burgundy sweater and gold wire glasses, sitting at an immense roll-top desk of some richly grained hardwood. Fred is humming to himself and thinking about the essence of his reality as it flows in all directions around him; he does not perceive himself to be in a finite bubble at all. What to us is a non-concept of nonexistence is, in fact, Fred's ever-expanding universe – albeit of "nothingness." Taking a sip of hot chocolate, Fred imagines a realm that utterly contradicts his own: a realm of existence, complete with galaxies, spiritual forces and sapient beings. He even imagines you reading about him right now. But from Fred's perspective, his own universe occupies everything that has meaning and reality for him, and all that exists for you and me is trapped within Fred's bubble of rich – but objectively finite – imagination. Just as we view Fred as a negation of *all that is* for us, Fred views us as a negation of *all that is not* for him.

Then Fred moves on to other thoughts, and you yourself finish reading this description of Fred. Soon, both of you have pretty much forgotten about each other, but a question remains: what is the meaning of Fred to you? And what is the nature of everything in our Universe – everything that we can ever imagine or experience, even

an all-encompassing, all-powerful Deity – to Fred? Clearly, with a
shrug and another sip of hot chocolate, Fred can dismiss everything
that we are, and all that we dream we are, as completely
insignificant, just as we can easily dispense with everything that Fred
imagines he is – Fred doesn't exist, after all! This shows us how the
contrast between our conception of reality and our direct experience
of reality necessitates meaning, and how all meaning is therefore
interdependent – that is, created by the context of one thing relating
to another. This is not only true for the extreme dichotomy of
existence and non-existence, but also for every subtle gradient of
differentiation we perceive both in the external Universe, and in
ourselves. Externally we differentiate a beautiful flower from a
bothersome weed, a refreshing rain from an overwhelming deluge, a
pleasant fragrance from a cloying stench, or an exciting adventure
from a terrifying crisis. Internally we compare and contrast the
inspiring flame of passion and the destructive heat of anger,
overconfident knowledge and humble wisdom, a humorous
observation and a demeaning jibe, a brilliant insight and deluded
insanity. And with each choice to separate and evaluate what we
encounter, we perpetually construct and support all of our most
fundamental beliefs.

As an abstract theory, it may be straightforward for us to entertain
the idea of complete neutrality, in terms of meaning and value, for all
the phenomena that make up our experience. But of course to
function from moment to moment we must also accept and operate
on the relative, interdependent meaning and value we construct.
Why? Because just as there are laws of gravity and
electromagnetism, there are consequences for every action, and for
every emotion and thought. Still, as discussed earlier, those
consequences can be uncertain; ultimately, the outcome of the
Universe itself is a vast unknown. So how can we navigate such a
tenuous reality? Part of our nature is to rationalize our actions, and
hold on tight; we want to justify our decisions, our goals and our
lives. But we have another choice: to suspend judgment of our
experience, and forgive ourselves the necessity of assigning meaning

altogether. Doing this, we plot our course through each moment with only the loving intentions of our heart.

> "Form does not differ from emptiness; emptiness does not differ from form. Form itself is emptiness; emptiness itself is form. So too feeling, cognition, mental formations, and consciousness are emptiness.
>
> All phenomena are empty of characteristics. They are not produced, not destroyed, not defiled, not pure; they neither increase nor diminish. Therefore, in emptiness there is no form, no feeling, cognition, mental formation, or consciousness; no eyes, ears, nose, tongue, body, or mind; no sights, sounds, smells, tastes, objects of touch, or other phenomena....
>
> There is no ignorance or ending of ignorance, up to and including old age and death, or any end of old age and death. There is no suffering, no origin of suffering, no cessation of suffering, no path, no wisdom, no attainment, and no non-attainment."
>
> From the Buddhist *Heart Sutra*

The last chapter suggested a conscious refinement of intentions. In light of indeterminate meaning, we can process our lives from a new starting point: one that is not anchored in inflexible precepts. But neither is it moral relativism. By deciding what ego-free golden intentions are, and opening ourselves to the wisdom of the Universe, we create a structure within which our moral and ethical priorities can be established without absolute meaning while still remaining consistent. What makes this approach so revolutionary is that we are no longer solely dependent on external guidelines for our decisions, but mature within ourselves an insight and immediate cognition that illuminates our understanding, clarifies our purpose, and conditions our conscience. That is one of the primary benefits of mysticism! Through this deliberately conscious self-sufficiency, we take responsibility for our well-being and our contribution to the good of All. Thus we can act wisely, navigating what is to arrive at what – for the good of All – must inevitably be.

Genesis starts with the words, "In the beginning...the earth was formless and void," and this is analogous to our spiritual evolution: we begin in emptiness, and, suddenly and miraculously, there is light. Sometimes, returning to the void, to that sense of neutrality that is free of supposition and attachment to something's significance, purifies our perception. On the bedrock of sincere openness and emptiness, a reshaped context of awareness – an ever-unfolding understanding through spiritual cognizance – can dance unfettered in the gleaming nakedness of continually reexamined truth.

What Happens for a Reason?

Here is one last angle on the idea of interdependent meaning. Because there is really no way to know for certain beyond what we *believe* to be true, it may be that all the minutia of life and every seemingly random occurrence "happens for a reason," for some grand purpose. Or it may be that we somehow choose everything that occurs in our lives, having created a detailed life-contract before we were born, and are perhaps living a dream we ourselves choreographed long ago. Or every event we experience might in actuality *be* completely random. Whatever the case, I would propose that we really don't need to understand why things happen to live a fulfilling, productive and spiritually rich existence. If I pray to a Goddess with love in my heart and a deep and abiding faith that my prayer will be answered, is it a prerequisite I understand the nature of that Deity? If, in fact, I occasionally doubt that such beings exist, is my prayer therefore negated or inadequate? If I acknowledge that my faith is but a construct that depends on a specific ordering of my experiences and perceptions, is my prayer mere vanity and delusion?

I don't think so. Or rather, even if I sometimes think so, it does not matter. For when I pray, my intention is not to invent the Divine as a subjective trick of my mind; my connection and communication with Deity are real to me. Just as when I love someone, it is not my intention to fabricate affection or intimacy with my emotions; my love is honest and straight from the heart. There is no inherent contradiction in questioning and challenging all that is, while simultaneously believing in it. This is, in fact, a healthy tension. For I trust that there are many faces of what we presume to call reality which have not yet been fully understood by anyone, and even eliminating ego and attachment and other obscurations of Truth down to a state of emptiness is itself an interdependent construct of the mind. That is, the conditions of suspended valuation and emptiness originate from the language of thought, which in turn originates from the context and contrast of our experiences. So, to play with words: the reason we have reason is to create reasons, and the creative genius of our species can never escape itself. My faith and my doubt are both endemic to my consciousness, and in fact are dependent on each other. That is why my prayers can be so confident and sincere despite acknowledging my fertile imagination. That is why I can have beliefs and still be comfortable questioning them.

> Those who revel in ignorance end up in blind darkness, but those who devote themselves to knowledge alone end up in an even greater darkness.
>
> *Isha Upanishad, 9*

To conclude, I suggest that if we focus all our efforts on contributing to the best possible outcome for the Whole, instead of trying to interpret the meaning of the events around us within some predisposed notion of truth, our reality will conform to our objectives – it will *become* the truth. That is not to say that we won't have profound insights into the workings of our heart and the world along the way, or discover wonderful surprises about our own powers of observation and influence. We will evolve, and our conception of *what is* will evolve. But in my experience, these enhancements will not change why we are here, or where we are going; they just encourage us to pause a moment and celebrate the supremacy and wonder of being alive. And that is one concrete, non-random explanation behind everything that happens to us, in us and around us.

Closer

Early in the morning
I bet those apostles
were pretty disconcerted
when they found an empty tomb
      they ran up to the entrance
      all out of breath
      and don't you think
      they had mixed emotions
      at finding Jesus gone?
Searching for truth
is like that
      sometimes we run
      eagerly toward the answer
      anxiety and confidence and doubt
      love and hope and terror
      all mingled into one
Only to arrive
      at a new set of questions
      and a new challenge for our assumptions
Maybe if we practiced
running up to a tomb each morning
in such a tremulous state
      we might come a bit closer
      to what really is

In the next chapter, we will examine two potent constructs that influence our identity: self-awareness and self-esteem. How these can be understood and perfected, and how they relate to each other in an interdependent way, becomes a door into how our mind and heart are structured, how we can influence the dynamics of that structure, and the first steps of a mystical journey.

Chapter Questions

1. Have you constructed a familiar, comfortable idea of what reality is, and are you willing to question it?
2. How often have you decided what something meant after it happened, and why did you do that?
3. What event has occurred recently that changed your evaluation of what something or someone has meant in your life?
4. Is returning to a state of "emptiness" a value judgment of the world, or a suspension of any value judgment?

5. STRENGTHENING SELF-AWARENESS and SELF-ESTEEM

What is self-esteem? Is there a relationship between self-awareness and self-esteem? What impact does either have on our spiritual development? Over the last few decades, mainstream U.S. culture has tended to perpetuate an intensive but distorted focus on "loving ourselves." Esteem is often defined as exaggerated self-importance, or as conditional satisfaction over external outcomes. Superficial gratification is offered in many guises: physical beauty; achieving personal goals or social status; assertive empowerment without compassion for others; self-referential values; or immature indulgence. Alongside this misdirection, commercial media never ceases appealing to the lowest common denominators of impulsiveness, narcissism and unrestricted desire. In truth, responding to these motivations actually destroys self-esteem. At the heart of the misconception, I believe, is a marked absence of realistic self-evaluation. When we supplant honest self-awareness with exciting or convenient illusions – confusing needs with wants, for instance – critical needs often go unmet. Without insight into what truly nourishes us, we can quickly lose our way. This is why developing a well-rounded perception of our own thought-process, emotions and behaviors is so critical. Without understanding the whole self, how can we have real affection, compassion or respect for that Self? Beyond a cathartic effort to fulfill confused and impulsive desires, how can we even be sure what love really looks like?

When I was a child, I remember many Christmases spent with relatives I did not know very well. I would agonize for weeks over gift selections for them, sure that I was expected to contribute – and wanting to – but not knowing how. My parents coached me as best they could on what might be appropriate, but they themselves were fairly disaffected from the relatives involved. Not to say that there wasn't love between us all, but tradition, broken family bonds, old antipathies and guilt warred for dominance during the holidays. On one occasion, beside myself with anxiety and indecision, I purchased a gold-plated butane lighter for my grandmother. Little did I know, she was trying to quit smoking at the time, but I considered it a victory to have found a gift she might enjoy. Unfortunately, a similar disconnect was painfully evident between most of the other receivers and givers that Christmas morning, which was ameliorated only by the dry, sardonic humor my family uses to cope with such situations.

Not the rosiest of pictures and perhaps not the most uncommon in today's world. Yet this is exactly how we tend to relate to ourselves, and to our own self-esteem. Without knowing what truly nurtures us, without really understanding the being that yearns to thrive beneath layers of perceived obligation and cultural conditioning, we are nevertheless compelled to be kind to that being, to take notice of its desires and try to satisfy them. We want to care, we just don't know how. So, more often than not, the effort we expend in "loving ourselves" is misdirected or incomplete, becoming little more than a hollow offering. Every now and then, when we finally make the time, we merely end up purchasing another gold-plated lighter to quiet our conscience.

For anyone who has discovered a more self-aware route to well-being, self-esteem has another face, and that is authentic compassion, acceptance and appreciation for who we are – a place from which we derive tremendous resilience and emotional strength. But before heading down that road, let's examine the dynamic between clarity of self-perception and how we feel about what we perceive. Suppose I am "in a funk," but I understand that my dour outlook originates from lack of sleep, a nasty cold, or an argument with a loved one.

Recognizing this, I probably won't put too much stock in those negative thoughts; self-awareness helps me here. On the other hand, if I am unaware of my underlying mood or its source, I may trust my negativity, believe I am inadequate in some way, and be less willing to question that conclusion. If I lack self-awareness, therefore, my mood can undermine my self-esteem. The following SASE Table expands on this interaction of self-awareness and self-esteem, creating four categories of corresponding attitudes and behaviors. Take a moment to evaluate where in the chart you find yourself much of the time.

Table 2: SASE

	high SELF-AWARENESS low	
high **SELF-** **ESTEEM** **low**	**I** The healthiest state. A feeling of successful management of our internal and external life, with consistently renewed insight into how to maintain and improve this equilibrium. A solid and realistic understanding of our own capabilities and limitations, and a tendency to succeed and thrive. An easy integration into our community of peers, without suppressing or altering our identity or sense of self in unhealthy ways.	**II** Feeling confident and successful – and even achieving superficial success – without actually having a solid understanding of our own strengths and weaknesses. A tendency to *overestimate* our capabilities and ignore proven limitations. Unintentional alienation of peers, but with a disowning of responsibility for any negative outcomes of our actions. A strong sense of Self, but an unrealistic one.
	III A clear understanding of our own strengths and weaknesses, but a tenancy to feel insecure and unsuccessful even with this knowledge. Often, we sabotage our own plans, or alienate close friends, or isolate ourselves from supportive communities. We maintain a strong identity, but at great cost to well-being, contentment, and fulfillment of our dreams.	**IV** The least healthy state. Feelings of helplessness and not knowing how to free ourselves from victimizing situations. A tendency to *underestimate* our capabilities and assume limitations that are unproven. We will often subvert our identity to fit in with peers, with the potential of completely disconnecting from our True Self.

Clearly, high self-esteem without equivalent self-awareness leads to considerable pitfalls, as does high self-awareness without adequate self-esteem. This chapter attempts to answer the question of how to develop insight into self, while at the same time feeling good about what we find, thus inspiring us to be both flexible and courageous. How does this tie into spiritual evolution? First, mature self-awareness will aid discernment not only into which stage of being we currently inhabit, but also into what is most beneficial for our spiritual advancement at any given moment. For how could we ever fully appreciate spiritual objectives if we lack awareness of their relevance or benefit to our lives?   Yet even if we have such knowledge, but lack the compassion for Self to act on it, we are much less likely to take the necessary risks to grow, or be able to live the golden intention through all that we do. If we cling to ignorance and self-protectiveness, why would we ever be inclined to let go of our current stage of being? If we are mired in misery, will we sincerely care about "the good of All" or be able to follow through on that conviction?   Thus the tension between insight, self-esteem and overall wellness is constant; the balancing act perpetual. This is yet another example of a complex interdependency that must be thoroughly understood before it has meaning for us – a meaning which can then genuinely inspire us to act.

Figure 4: Cycle of Personal Growth

Increased awareness of our strengths, limitations, and the many facets of self

Improved compassion for self and others due to actions that nourish and support self-esteem

Motivation to work for the good of All out of growing respect, gratitude, and emotional strength

Internal rewards of progressing into higher stages of being, and the spiritual and perceptual expansion inherent to our progress

Paying Attention to Who We Are

> "Watch over your heart with all diligence, for from it flow the springs of life."
>
> *Proverbs, 4:23*

Although the importance of self-knowledge is an underlying assumption of this book, philosophers, spiritual sages and mystics throughout the ages have almost universally promoted the idea. According to Plutarch, the ancient Delphic Oracle had the words "know thyself" inscribed on its walls, words which were later taken up by Socrates as he proposed "an unexamined life is not worth living." Lao Tzu wrote "understanding others, you become knowledgeable, understanding yourself, you become enlightened." Jesus proclaimed, "the Kingdom of God is within you," and "if you do not know yourselves, then you live in poverty, and you are the poverty."[6] Carl Jung put it more ominous terms: "If the demand for self-knowledge is willed by fate and is refused, this negative attitude may end in real death." Many others have joined this chorus into present times, yet self-knowledge is certainly not always a natural condition, nor does achieving it lack difficulty: people can pass through their entire lives without pausing to ask the deeper "whys" of their own existence. But aside from observing our intentions, desires and other patterns of thought and feeling, what are the benefits? Why look within? Because that inner world is where the answers to the most significant of all human inquiries reside: the truth of our identity, purpose and power.

There are certainly myriad non-mystical practices which can help you delve deeper into yourself and see yourself more clearly, and we'll touch on some of those – if only in passing. But our primary objective here is to understand how mysticism, as a holistic system, can achieve the highest level of self-awareness possible. Of course, nearly all self-assessment lacks conclusive validation – both mystical and non-mystical approaches are entirely self-referential, after all –

---

[6] From the *Gospel of Thomas*

and so arguing the objective accuracy of any one method is of necessity beyond the scope of this book. However, I would propose that it is the quality of introspection each avenue inspires which makes it useful to us, and that is something only you can judge for yourself as you experiment with different approaches. Further, in the context of spiritual evolution, it is the overall improvement and depth of self-awareness which allows us to awaken all that we are, and without every aspect of self being fully alive, it is that much more difficult to expand, align and harmonize our existence with the Whole.

Contemplative States Defined

There is a definite and natural progression to contemplating self, and psychology, philosophy and theology have already proposed endless descriptions of deepening self-awareness for us. However, rather than recounting all of the existing theories and systems in detail, I would like to create a loose framework for describing widely used methods of contemplative self-examination that includes a mystical perspective – beginning with the simplest and most common contemplative states, and ending with the more difficult, rare and intentionally "spiritual."

1. **Simple Reflection:** a) We have an experience, thought, feeling or physical sensation; b) we become consciously aware of the phenomena and begin reflecting on them; c) we evaluate them – often unconsciously – according to our current values, beliefs and assumptions; d) we incorporate them into our understanding of the Universe, other people, and ourselves.

2. **Contemplative Self-Awareness:** a) We become consciously aware of the process of *simple reflection* as it occurs in us from moment-to-moment; b) we observe and evaluate the qualities of this process; c) we decide whether we want to interrupt or modify the passive or reflexive aspects of our

valuation of the phenomena in and around us, in order to more actively shape our responses and our understanding.

3. **Suspended Valuation:**   a) We consciously suspend evaluation altogether – that is, we simply observe our experiences, thoughts, feelings and physical sensations without placing them in the context of our values, beliefs or assumptions; b) we consider the qualities of this mental state and reflect on it, but still withhold judgment of even this kind of "thinking about our thinking."

4. **Non-Thought Awareness:** a) We let go of our thoughts and valuations altogether, entering into a state of mental, emotional and sensory quiet – even though we are may still be consciously observing this state in ourselves, we do not reflect on it – at least not while it is happening – but simply allow it to permeate us; b) within this "non-thought" experience, we observe new kind of perception and complex information that can be interpreted as supersensory or spiritual cognizance, and which is difficult to describe in any other way.

5. **Non-Thought Non-Awareness:** a) We stop acknowledging even the supersensory, just as we did the sensory, and directly experience the bedrock of our own existence – that is, the foundations of our sense of self and our relationship to the Universe; b) we tend to react to this experience by reasserting an independent, consciously constructed sense of self that incorporates this new information.

6. **Non-Being Awareness:** a) We cease to discriminate between the state of *non-thought non-awareness* and any independently constructed sense of self – that is, we come to identify ourselves with this state and thus develop a subjective submersion in "non-being;" b) we tend to remain aware of this association of self with non-being, though rarely within the moments of the contemplative experience itself.

7. **Non-Being Non-Awareness:** A suggested end-point in the contemplative progression, where self-awareness and other-

awareness – and any acknowledgement of subject and object – completely evaporate. One result, after emerging from such a state, is that we not only gain addition clarity about every aspect of our existence, but also can direct the many threads of our being through that existence with increasing ease.

You may have noticed a theme in this progression echoed earlier in the emotional transformation process: *letting go.* Letting go of conscious evaluation, letting go of thought and sensory experiences, even letting go of our sense of self. Although it may not always be described as "letting go," this is a critical concept in nearly all contemplative mystical practice. There is also a loose correlation between progressive stages of being and actuation of these states of mind, but use of the mind is not the only path to mystical experience – it is only one of many. However, returning to practical examples, what are some specific contemplative approaches? In this chapter, we will be examining tools that are helpful for achieving the first two of the contemplative states listed, reserving the more advanced techniques for later discussion.

Principles of Meditation

After each of the following sentences, try pausing in your reading for a moment to consider each question; perhaps even grabbing a sheet of paper to write down your thoughts. To begin, what are you feeling right now? Why do you think you are you feeling that way? Are there any extraneous, mundane thoughts racing through your mind? About work, perhaps, or dinner plans – maybe some pressing errands? Look deeper. Are there thoughts beneath the superficial ones? Ask yourself: "What do I really care about at this moment?" And then: "What do I care about in my life?" There may be several answers; write them all down. Now, consider what most frequently bobs to the surface of your mind when you have time alone. What recurring themes have you experienced over the past week? Were they thoughts about the past, the future, or the present? About

people? Work? Tasks? Goals? Wants? Needs? Before moving on
to the next paragraph, did you actually stop reading to think about
these things, or are you rushing on to my conclusion? If you are
rushing onward, why are you doing that?

Such introspective questions and thoughts about thoughts are the
beginnings of contemplative self-awareness. The deeper we look, the
more we challenge our patterns of thinking and feeling and the
assumptions behind them.   Through ongoing inquiry, we gain
increasing clarity about our prevailing motivations, beliefs,
behavioral tendencies, and social masks – those outer shells of Self
we offer the world. This kind of reflective assessment is a very old
technique, and as mode of thought is a critical tool for expanding
human consciousness; perhaps it even inspired human consciousness
itself. It is also the beginning of one type of meditative practice.
Unfortunately, for some of us the term "meditation" raises concern
over awkward sitting positions, complex eastern religions, and
copious amounts of time.   But there are many roads up this
mountain, and though the effort required to reach the summit is not
always easy, the views are truly spectacular.

> "Look within. Let neither the peculiar quality of anything nor its
> value escape you."
>
> Marcus Aurelius, the 2nd Century Stoic, from his diary
> *Meditations*

Meditation can be found within nearly every major belief system, and
is central to most forms of mysticism. In the Christian tradition, there
is contemplative prayer.   In Hinduism, many forms of Yoga
meditation. In Buddhism, concentration meditation and mindfulness
meditation. Shortly we will examine how modern psychology has
also taken on a contemplative approach to understanding ourselves.
And all of these lead to the same place: a more transparent view of
what is going on inside us and around us. By practicing certain
repetitive disciplines, we strengthen a muscle that is frequently
neglected in a world of constant distraction and stimulation: *full
attention.* When we then turn this ability inward, onto our thought

processes and emotions, we develop a piercing honesty into our inner life, revealing both uncomfortable and reassuring realities, and gradually developing a means of shaping all that resides there.

There are, of course, endless forms of meditation, and not all of them are considered "contemplative." Most, however, do fall into five broad categories:

- **Single-Focus Concentration.** The "single focus" might be an external object, an image or concept held in the imagination, an internal process (such as breathing), a repeated word or sound (chanting), or a fixed internal locus (an imagined point inside the body). The objective here is to quiet the mind, body and emotions through deliberate and prolonged concentration, thus eliminating all distractions. Examples of this style of meditation are the many Hindu Yoga utilizing mandalas or mantras, counting breaths (many traditions), and Buddhist *jhana* meditation.
- **Self-Inquiry.** A continuous and often repetitive inquiry into self, looking for different – and more meaningful – answers to the same questions. For example: "Who am I?" or "Where did that thought come from?"
- **Watchfulness.** To examine what is happening within or without with complete attention, and without reaction. To become a truly "aloof" observer of phenomena allows us, over time, to see the true nature of things. When applied to internal processes, watchfulness also enables us change our patterns of thought and emotion over time. Examples of this approach are Sufi *muraqaba* and Buddhist mindfulness.
- **Conceptual Reflection.** In a way, this combines the disciplines of single-focus, self-inquiry and watchfulness – the object of concentration, inquiry and watchfulness being a central idea which, when meditated upon, opens up our mind to new ways of thinking. Zen *koans* are an example of this approach, as is meditating on the body's impermanence (many traditions), or a Christian's contemplation of scripture and concepts like *kenosis* (the Divine becoming flesh).

- **Direct Activation.** To manufacture a specific physical, emotional or mental state through body position and movement, controlled breathing, or force of will. For instance, the Taoist *Tai Chi Chuan,* or fasting (many traditions), or *Hatha* Yoga.

Yet with all this variation, contemplative self-awareness still surfaces as the primary benefactor of each process. For whatever state of mind, body or heart each approach invites, it is always our reflection over that event – our intellectual and emotional interpretation – which makes it meaningful for us.

Sample Meditation

Specific meditative techniques that advance or combine various categories of contemplation will be discussed in following chapters, but for now let's take a look at a simple introductory technique that will quickly enhance your ability to induce contemplative focus.

Pick a thirty-minute slice of your day where you can exit the business of life. If you believe it will be difficult to make this time for yourself, you may want to examine why you have chosen to live this way. Although you could also start with a shorter duration of meditation, and work your way up to thirty minutes, it is better to have a thirty-minute envelope around your practice, regardless of how much time you spend actually meditating. Find a quiet place where you won't be disturbed. Seat yourself comfortably, hands-in-lap, feet flat on the floor. Close your eyes and relax your body. If you find yourself getting sleepy, change your sitting position or open your eyes ever-so-slightly – not enough to see clearly, just enough to let in a little light. Start to breathe in-and-out through your nose – just breathe regularly. Now begin counting your breaths in your mind, focusing on the exhale. In other words: breathe in, breathe out and count one; breathe in, breathe out and count two, etc. Count up to seven, and then begin counting again from one.

One of the things which often happens early-on in meditation training is that our mind will start to wander. You might feel silly, wondering what the point of this exercise is, or become preoccupied with work, relationships, or what you will be doing next. Try to remain focused on your breathing and counting, and let these other thoughts and feelings float off on their own – in other words, don't fight them, just gently turn your focus back to your breathing and counting. If you lose track of your counting, start over. Keep breathing and counting for as long as you can. If you become so agitated or distracted by your thoughts, emotions or physical sensations that you can't continue, then stop for now. Without forcing it to happen, you will find that each day you can concentrate for longer and longer periods, and have fewer and fewer distracting thoughts.

What is happening here? You are training your mind to be able to guide itself, to be open to new experience, and to be placid enough to invite other kinds of perception. If you wish to progress into more complex visualization and meditation techniques, this simple exercise will start you down the path to deepening concentration and direction of your consciousness, and into a much more intimate self-awareness.

Body Awareness and Emotional Vocabulary

In another contemplative approach, we can increase *emotional* self-awareness through observing where we experience feelings in our body, and noting the sensations they produce. For instance, do you find that your hands, arms, legs or feet become restless when you are excited, or perhaps when you are bored? Does your stomach get tight when you are anxious? Does your jaw clench or your neck become tense when you are angry? Where do you physically feel love, fear, joy, or sadness? What happens in your body when you are embarrassed, or when you are disappointed in some way? The more intimately we hone our physical awareness, the more sensitive and unambiguous our emotional consciousness becomes. Try just sitting quietly for thirty minutes and reflecting on some of the intensely emotional experiences of your life, and pay attention to your physical responses to those feelings.

Experimenting with this, you may encounter some unnamed emotions, and might even want to peruse some emotional verbiage to clearly identify what you are feeling. For instance: is the buzzing heat behind your nose anger, frustration, annoyance, tension, fluster, disappointment or fury? Is the empty feeling in the middle of your chest sadness, depression, devastation, or anxiety? Is this joy, contentment, exuberance, wonder, giddiness or ecstasy that makes your heart lurch or throat ache? As an example, use the following chart to compare and contrast your existing "emotional vocabulary." What makes each state unique? Why are there so many words for the same kind of emotion? Exposing yourself to subtle distinctions between similar ideas can awaken whole new worlds of internal comprehension.

Table 3: Emotional Vocabulary Samples

Fearful	Sad	Joyful	Impatient	Tranquil
Jealous, anxious, overwhelmed, concerned, guarded, hesitant, embarrassed, nervous, shocked, offended, ready to run	Crushed, distraught, demoralized, disappointed, downtrodden, tearful, devastated, upset, depressed, grieving, without hope	Appreciative, amused, giddy, amazed, content, pleased, delighted, happy, satisfied, lighthearted, euphoric, bursting with joy	Angry, bored, annoyed, frustrated, furious, irritable, restless, edgy, stressed, explosive, tense, flustered, exasperated, intolerant, out of sorts	Peaceful, patient, relaxed, serene, calm, composed, untroubled, still, restful, impassive, even-keeled, exhausted, spent, relieved, breathing easy, placated, without a care in the world

As one example, when I was very young my father and I were cresting a hill in his old Dodge Dart. Just as we started down the other side, I noticed a young woman riding a bike up the hill with a huge smile on her face. "Why is she smiling?" I asked my dad. "She's not smiling, she's grimacing," he said sagely. And my whole world changed. Suddenly there were entire new categories of related expressions: smirking, smiling, grinning, grimacing, and so on. As I got older, there would be even more gradations, and each one would be turned around in self-perception. When did I smile most sincerely? When was my smirk sardonic? Did I grimace over physical effort differently than when I grimaced over emotional pain? What did it mean to "look determined?" How did I know what it was to *feel* determined? This is how we learn emotional perception and latitude as children...but there is always more to learn.

Evaluation Testing

There is also a more traditionally Western, analytical approach to examining ourselves. In Appendix B, you will find a sample test that measures self-esteem, self-awareness, other-awareness, and emotional aptitude (which I define as the ability to manage and improve self-esteem and self-awareness). I've also provided a means of plotting yourself on the SASE Table at the beginning of the chapter using this evaluation. For additional types of testing, here are some widely available and time-proven methods to satisfy your curiosity:

- **Personality Type.** In terms of assessing general personality traits and making predictions about typical behaviors, the Jung-Myers-Briggs typology approach (also called "Myers-Briggs," "MBTI®" or "Jungian Typology") provides some insightful and dynamic descriptions. This instrument has been used for many years to assess personality *tendencies*. The Myers-Briggs places us into one of 16 different psychological types, comprised of extravert/introvert, sensing/intuitive, thinking/feeling, and judging/perceiving characteristics. However, it is important to distinguish between a *tendency* or *predisposition* and an actual belief or behavior; for me, the Myers-Briggs has only been a useful starting point in a complete personality profile. Versions of this self-evaluation are widely available, both on the Internet, for purchase, and as administered by professionals.

- **Emotional Intelligence.** Another self-awareness tool is measuring *Emotional Intelligence.* One workable definition of EI is our perception and understanding of emotions in ourselves and others, and knowing the best ways to manage those emotions. First introduced by John Mayer and Peter Salovey, and later made popular by author Daniel Goleman, the term "Emotional Intelligence" has gained considerable momentum as an umbrella concept for a broad array of theories and methods. EI alternately includes social awareness, emotional self-management, empathy, relationship management, self-esteem, and all of these things. It should be noted that there is a widening gap between what academic researchers define as EI and the way popular books and human resource consultants are promoting it. Claude Steiner, author of *Emotional Literacy; Intelligence with a Heart,* says it this way: "I fear that emotional intelligence is morphing into yet another corporate, human engineering lubricant with little specific relationship to emotional literacy." I recommend exploring the many resources – including EI self-evaluations – available via the Internet and dozens of popular books. As of this writing, the most widely-used instruments to assess EI are the MSCEIT, the BarOn EQ-i,® and the Emotional Competency Inventory (ECI), all of which are professionally administered at a cost. To my knowledge, only the MSCEIT has so far been scientifically validated.

- **Other Tests.** There are countless self-scoring personality tests available, including thorough and detailed workbooks like the *Berkeley Personality Profile.*[7] If you work at a large company, check with your Human Resources department to

---

[7] by Keith Harary and Eileen Donahue

see what they might have lying around. Also try a search on the Internet; increasingly, tests which formerly cost something are now free and just a mouse-click away at an ever-growing number of websites.

Many Roads

There are many roads up the mountain to perceive and appreciate our physical, mental, and emotional selves, the effort required to gain altitude – and reach a broader, unobstructed view of the landscape inside us and around us – is roughly the same no matter which path we choose. Regardless of our approach, what remains after the initial blossoming of expanded perception is to develop patience and compassion for what we find, and to refrain from judging ourselves. Heightening our introspection can be an upsetting experience if what we encounter contradicts previous self-perception, or highlights well-known but nevertheless discouraging limitations. At the other extreme, if our new insight confirms an aptitude or strength, our challenge will be to avoid arrogance and overconfidence in that area. Whatever we find, our initial responses can be constructive when translated into growth, but we must first try to set any judgmental attitudes aside. Somewhere between the extremes of overconfidence and futile or disabling feelings, we find both the humility to remain diligent, and the confidence to learn new skills. It is on this razor's edge that spiritually constructive self-awareness resides.

> This being human is a guest house.
> Every morning a new arrival.
> A joy, a depression, a meanness,
> some momentary awareness comes
> as an unexpected visitor.
> Welcome and entertain them all!
> Even if they're a crowd of sorrows,
> who violently sweep your house
> empty of its furniture,
> still, treat each guest honorably.

He may be clearing you out
for some new delight.
The dark thought, the shame, the malice,
meet them at the door laughing,
and invite them in.
Be grateful for whoever comes,
because each has been sent
as a guide from beyond.

Rumi, *The Guest House* [8]

Having Compassion for Who We Are

Once we have garnered new information about ourselves, *what will we do with it?* We can appreciate our strengths and learn to trust them. We can respect our weaknesses and limitations, account for them as we move forward, and work to transform them. We can rise to the occasions of life newly empowered – with a realistic understanding of our abilities – to stumble a little less, and succeed a little more. From such beginnings, our core values and future goals are naturally encouraged with every choice we make, because we have clearer insight into what motivates us. And as disciplined self-awareness expands into spiritual cognizance, the additional benefits of an ever-broadening – and integrated – view of self and the Universe naturally arise. However, even if this sounds like a reasonable and healthy course, how can we sustain a positive, hopeful attitude about ourselves regardless of what we encounter? What will inspire us to advance our practice of self-examination with continued diligence and honesty? How can we be brave enough to continue the process of "letting go" in the face of often overwhelming or frightening new information? The answer, I believe, is rooted in our self-esteem.

Self-esteem cannot be an end in itself, but is merely a byproduct of compassionate effort. Thus, "healthy" self-esteem begins with

---

[8] From *The Essential Rumi* by Coleman Barks, Harper San Francisco, 1997

patience, acceptance and loving kindness for our entire being. Our internal attitudes then translate into external actions: we will naturally manifest patience, acceptance and loving kindness toward everyone and everything around us. But how do we first arrive at a capacity to care about ourselves – and care *for* ourselves – and how do we sustain it? Like self-awareness, there are many ways to enhance compassion for self, and also like self-awareness, our approach may of necessity change over time to accommodate evolving perceptions. The key is to continually *nourish and nurture* our being on all levels – physical, mental, emotional and spiritual – and to rework old patterns of thought and behavior, especially those dynamics between ourselves and others that antagonize our well-being. Once again, we will see that mystical practice will provide many of the core components of this holistic nourishment. However, it is helpful to remember, especially when the going gets difficult, that progress in this journey requires steady effort and focus.

The following are some resources and practices to enhance self-esteem as a consequence of improving overall well-being. This enrichment is achieved through a combination of these techniques; practicing some of them in-depth, and a majority of them concurrently, is therefore essential in supporting and fortifying personal growth. Since many are inherent to mystical practice, most of these topics are covered with more depth throughout the book, so I will only summarize them here.

- **Time alone.** As discussed further in Solitude and Self-Sufficiency, this means time apart from our usual relationships and environments. Our objective is to separate ourselves from stimulation that sometimes distracts us from who we are. This might be just a few minutes each day, set aside just for you. Or this may mean taking a vacation from work, or taking a break from an intimate relationship. For me, this has meant camping alone in the wilderness as often – and for as long a duration – as I can. The basic practice is solitude, but the progressive discipline is meditation, reflection, and detachment from all the bustle and demands of our daily lives. Eventually, we will even develop spiritual perception simply by freeing ourselves from busyness, and then learning how to listen to the silence that remains.

- **Quieting the ego, and freeing ourselves from attachments and desires.** Can you be free from your own ideas of what happiness is? Many philosophies and spiritual traditions approach fulfillment with an exhortation to relinquish control – not to abandon interest or appreciation, but to cease being concerned about outcomes. The Buddha once called it "releasing our cows," indicating that goals that we think will fulfill our happiness actually become obstructions to happiness – because we are holding on too tightly. The Bhagavad-Gita describes this as "clinging to immeasurable anxieties...bound by a hundred expectations." In his parable of the seeds, Jesus warned that the "worries of the world" will choke the truth, and he advised: "Don't pile up treasures on earth, where moth and rust can spoil them, and thieves can break in and steal...for wherever your treasure is, your heart will be there too." When we are enslaved to our own impulses and focus our happiness on external events and objectives, we are bound to feel perpetually incomplete. Instead, we can develop wealth within ourselves, and that begins with releasing our attachment to the world, including our own concepts of what contentment and satisfaction really are. As Lao Tzu wrote: "No calamity is worse that being discontented, and nothing brings more sorrow than coveting, but once you learn contentment, you will always have it with you."

- **Meditation.** As meditation helps us observe our inner life and enliven our understanding, it also nourishes our self-esteem. Armed with fresh awareness, we begin free ourselves from false assumptions, confusion, and suffering. Through meditation we won't deny or suppress our experience, but compassionately and thoughtfully consider it. This renovates our ideas about what happiness and fulfillment are, and how to achieve them. Thich Nhat Hanh writes of Buddhist meditation: "When we touch our pain with mindfulness, we will begin to transform it...Mindfulness is the mother who cares for your pain every time it begins to cry." [9] On many levels, a mystic's approach to meditation is about letting go of all preconceptions, and consciously reconstructing our perceptions. The Mystic's Way and Just for Today chapters offer some specific meditative routines, and I encourage you to thoroughly explore this life-affirming discipline regardless of which tradition or specific practice you find to be most appropriate for you.

- **Developing strong intuition and mystical awareness.** For me, these are perhaps the most supportive and nurturing of all practices, and are expanded on throughout the rest of this book. In a progressive spiritual cognizance induced through a variety of techniques, we connect with the inspiring, healing and powerful forces in ourselves and the Universe which otherwise might go unnoticed or ignored. This is what Plotinus, a 3rd Century mystic, has to say about the mystic's way: "In this choral dance the soul sees the fountain of life and the fountain of Spirit, the source of being, the cause of good, and the root of the soul." Sounds pretty good, doesn't it? Intuition and mystical awareness not only lead us deeper into self, but at the same time soulfully affirm what we find.

- **Resolving the injuries of childhood.** For those who had consistent love from their parents growing up, who received trust and approval with no strings attached, and who were otherwise free of psychological, emotional or physical abuse, there may be little here to resolve. Likewise if we had supportive and nurturing peers when we were young, this will be less of an issue. But all of us learned how to be ourselves when we were very small, and any attempt to change misconceptions about Self in the present, and to fully embrace all that we have become, begins with understanding our childhood. For some, this may mean therapy. For others it could mean a long, honest talk with parents or siblings, or

---

[9] From the *The Miracle of Mindfulness*

with others who had a profound influence on us when we were children. Or it could mean learning how to forgive someone we can't reach, or who is unwilling to acknowledge what they have done. However we engage this, we will want to repair any dynamics in our early years that disrupt our ability to have compassion for ourselves in the present. This may be very difficult to do, but it is critically important. See the both A Cognitive-Behavioral Approach and About Suffering sections for more.

- **Physical exercise.** As is popularly cited, daily aerobic exercise each makes a huge difference in our well-being. I remember one story[10] of man in his forties who was so depressed about his life that he wanted to commit suicide. He decided the least suspicious way to die – since he wanted his family to collect his life insurance – was to run as fast as he could until he had a heart attack. So one evening he kissed his family goodbye, and set out to run himself to death. Well, with the tightness in his chest and the burning pain in his limbs, he thought for certain he would succeed. But he didn't. He came home and collapsed, exhausted but alive. The next day he tried again, and felt even worse afterwards. And so it went, until after about a week of running, he found he was feeling much better about everything in his life. Running became his routine, and he lived healthily – and much more happily – for many more years. This is an extreme example of transformation through exercise, and there are certainly less aggressive approaches. One is Hatha Yoga (often called exercise or "posture" Yoga). Another is swimming. I myself enjoy a couple of hour-long walks each day, augmented with hiking, swimming, free weights and Hatha Yoga. Exercise does take up time, but is easily combined with meditation, recreation and socialization. Whatever you can do, get that body moving.

- **Paying attention to what we take in.** I believe a key component to overall wellness is what we routinely introduce

---

[10] From a *Lifewriting* workshop by Steve Barnes

into our physical, emotional and mental being. The food we eat, the entertainment we absorb, the quality of interaction we create with others, the air we breathe. All of this has tremendous influence on our health. If I eat sugary and highly processed foods, drink coffee all day, lounge in front of the TV late into the night, and exercise along a busy street choked with exhaust fumes, how could this not impact my emotional health and spiritual sensitivity? Much of our existence consists of deeply habituated lifestyle choices, and changes will likely take time, especially in areas where we have strong attachments or positive associations from our past. But change we must, so that our median daily "input" presents us with the multifaceted and inherently complex nourishment our body, mind and spirit crave.

- **Immersing ourselves in beauty, wonder and excellence.** I was feeling a bit low one weekend. I couldn't place my finger on what it was that was bothering me, but I felt something was missing from my life. A friend mentioned to me that *Cirque du Soleil* – a troupe of artists, acrobats, actors and musicians from all over the world – was performing in town, and encouraged me to check them out. So I went. Witnessing that kind of artistic excellence fed a part of me that had been starving for a very long time. This experience has been repeated on many occasions: the sun slanting across the alpine meadows of Yosemite; hearing the choir at National Cathedral while otherworldly light from huge stained glass windows spilled across the stone floor; catching an unexpected performance of Shakespeare in the Park; riding the glassy curl of a huge ocean wave; reading an engrossing book while sitting in the sun; walking through the neighborhood garden and stopping to smell the flowers.... Beauty, wonder and excellence are portals into the Divine, and I believe spending time with them brings us closer to the Source of Life and Light. So break your routine, explore your immediate environment, and find something in the world that truly inspires you.

- **Serving our community.** With our time, our income, our skills and knowledge, our compassion – without expectations or attachment to the results. Give with gratitude back to the Universe a tiny fraction of yourself. Without fanfare, or a sense of sacrifice – and certainly without any hint of guilty obligation – enter into the humble joy of service. For anyone who has helped institutionalized patients go on a fieldtrip, or shared a meal with a homeless person, or volunteered for a worthwhile political cause, or any of a thousand opportunities which wait patiently for us to notice them, there is no end to the smile that penetrates right down to our very core, and the intense and lasting lessons we could learn no other way.

- **Experiencing Reiki,[11] or other *Life Force* healing art.** Having someone else administer hands-on healing to us is a great start. Ideally, we can learn these arts ourselves, both for self-administered healing and to share with others. Because many such practices deal directly with Life Force energy (i.e. Reiki, Chi, Prana, etc.), healing and improvement occur on many levels. The immediate results are usually deep physical relaxation and emotional tranquility. I heartily encourage you to explore whatever options are available to you.

- **Attending a retreat or seminar.** Without promoting any particular variety of teaching, the occasional involvement in some sort of organized retreat or seminar can stimulate our spirit. Some examples of the kind of events I'm referring to are Covey training, Mars and Venus workshops, retreats in your own spiritual tradition, artist and writing workshops, and similar events. Many people may not feel they have the means or the freedom to do this, but for those with a devoted interest I have seen the resources miraculously present themselves time and time again. Seek, and you shall find. Admittedly, many such events may have their own self-serving agendas, and it is well worth the effort to do an Internet search on what others have experienced. Also, the

---

[11] For more information on Reiki, see Appendix D.

euphoric sense of discovery can be an addictive short-term high – not to be confused with long-lasting self-transformation. But if you have never attended such a workshop or retreat, or if it has been a long time, just go. Experience some unexpected possibilities.

- **Acknowledging and celebrating the simple fact of life.** We are alive. We can think and feel. What a gift! We should find time to pause, step out of the currents of daily routine, and celebrate. Have a dinner party. Go on a trip. Treat yourself to a favorite activity. Consciously acknowledge and give thanks for everything in your world. As we practice this kind of celebratory gratitude, our spirit is being renewed, while at the same time we nourish the Universe with our joy.

- **Other things:** Surround yourself with people who know how to love unconditionally, and who share your core values. Consider adding a pet to your family. Have plants in your home – or perhaps start a garden – and tend to them lovingly. Find a way to express yourself: a hobby or interest that is uniquely your own. Enrich your life by doing what you love to do. Listen to the longings of your heart, and be kind to them.

Dealing with Fear and Avoidance

There is one major impedance to honest self-awareness and healthy self-esteem that must be addressed head-on: our primitive inclination to avoid the discomfort of growth and change and to preserve familiar self-limiting habits. As alluded to in Stages of Being, the basic instincts of our Physiological self will perpetually reassert themselves throughout our spiritual progress; it is only the varying degrees to which we manage them and replace them with reformed sensibilities and loving intentions, that shifts our consciousness to the Spiritual Self. The following is a brief inventory and categorization of what fear and avoidance look like, with some assumptions and beliefs from which they are frequently derived: [12]

Table 4: Fear Cycles

Driving Assumptions & Beliefs	Fear Category	Avoidance/Fulfillment Behaviors
Beliefs: I'm not lovable. I am weak and vulnerable. **Assumptions:** I won't be attacked or punished if no one notices me; I'll be able to keep coasting along and never feel threatened.	Social Conformance	• Never outshine anyone. • Always do what I'm told. • Never rock the boat. • Don't say what I really think or feel. • Laugh at jokes I don't think are funny.
Beliefs: The world is a dangerous and unpredictable place. I am ashamed (or unsure) of who I am. People aren't trustworthy. **Assumptions:** The social masks (personas) I maintain are all that keep me safe from abandonment or humiliation.	Challenges to Identity	• Be defensive when criticized. • Be quick to accuse others. • Remain the center of everyone's attention. • Constantly seek assurance or approval. • Use or abuse people to get wants met. • Goals and accomplishments become more important than process.
Beliefs: I must control myself. Nothing I do is acceptable. The world is unpredictable. **Assumptions:** If I control things around me, I can control the chaos of insecurities within me.	Changes in Environment	• Keep the same routine. • Don't take risks or try anything new. • Make everything perfect. • Over-plan to avoid the unexpected. • Obsess about financial security. • Always stick to the rules.

---

[12] These originate from my own cognitive therapy, observations and research, and are not clinical definitions to diagnose or treat specific conditions.

Beliefs: I can't handle it anyway. I'm helpless. Assumptions: Ignorance is bliss...because what I don't know, can't hurt me.	Confronting the Unknown	• Deny what I deeply feel. • Tune out when I encounter something difficult or frightening. • Run away from authentic relationships. • Use drugs and/or alcohol to stay numb.
Beliefs: I'm worthless and unlikable. Assumptions: No matter what I do, I will probably fail.	Value and Purpose	• Be very self-critical and pessimistic. • Sabotage success and disappoint people who trust me. • Become emotionally addicted to sex, relationships, work, food, etc.
Beliefs: It's all too complicated, confusing, and difficult. Besides, I'm incompetent, and I end up hurting people or getting hurt. Assumptions: It's better not to try than to succeed and have responsibilities.	Responsibility and Accountability	• Act like nothing matters. • Don't follow through on commitments to myself or others. • Turn everything into a joke. • Be suspicious of people who seem motivated and directed. • Be reactively nonconformist.
Beliefs: Either nothing is my problem to solve, nor is anything my fault; or everything is my problem to solve, and/or my fault. Assumptions: I must either punish or exonerate myself for the shame I feel by reliving, perpetuating, or compensating for the trauma and abuse I experienced as a child.	Pathological	• Be impulsive and self-destructive (eating disorders, self-injury, substance abuse, overspending, seeking abusive partners). • Become phobic, paranoid, irrationally jealous, or have other uncontrollable fears. • Be perpetually narcissistic, controlling and abusive. • Have little to no understanding or management of emotions. • Never have a satisfying intimate relationship, or be antisocial in general. • Be chronically ill. • Think dichotomously: i.e. only in terms of black/white, right/wrong, good/bad.

Upon even casual examination, you will notice that every one of the "driving assumptions and beliefs" *is basically untrue*. They are stories, elaborate rationalizations that we invent to cope with a difficult reality. As tightly as we may want to hold on to them, they are deceptions. Sometimes they represent core beliefs and values upon which we have founded our lives, and sometimes they are the lingering emotional reactions to past events. In either case, it is possible to change them. Take a look at the avoidance behaviors in the chart, and you will see that they can also be reinforcing behaviors: once we start acting in these ways, *we tend make our false beliefs come true*. This validates and perpetuates our fear cycle, and a lifetime of such behavior results in mistaken beliefs being that much harder to give up. Once we have paused for a moment to reflect on what we have invented – likely as a result of how we adapted to our environment as a child – we realize why we are resisting positive change. We can then begin to let go of what we recognize as outmoded and destructive ideas, and replace them with something better. The next section suggests how to do exactly that.

A Cognitive-Behavioral Approach

One of the first fruits of advanced mystical practice is a profound and ever-increasing relief from fear. But to interrupt our avoidance behaviors, and create the initial space and receptivity for progressive contemplative states, we can benefit greatly from the well-established structure of a cognitive-behavioral approach. As represented here, this approach is chiefly defined by the work of Aaron Beck and Albert Ellis over the past several decades. This method, called "cognitive-behavioral therapy" or CBT, emphasizes the cognitive component of our feelings and behavior – that is, habitual patterns of thought that determine how we feel and respond in certain situations. Where do those thought patterns come from? From our assumptions and beliefs. And however we choose to act, our biased worldview interprets the results of our action as reinforcement of those beliefs. In other words, a similar idea to what is described in the Fear Cycles chart: incorrect beliefs = fearful emotions = behaviors and perceptions which reinforce incorrect beliefs.

CBT proposes a simple remedy: if we become conscious of our thought patterns, and uncover the underlying convictions that created those patterns, we can change them. In doing so, we modify our emotional responses and reactions to new situations, and thereby alter which values we reinforce. Although CBT came out of psychoanalysis, and builds on behavioral theorists such as Skinner, Thorndike and Pavlov, many writers on the subject are quick to point out that the principles of CBT have resided in Buddhist teaching and the writings of the Stoic philosopher Epictetus for thousands of years. I would add that they are present in many other spiritual and philosophical traditions as well, and that constructively reforming our thought patterns is an important objective of most spiritual paths; this is, in fact, modern psychology's approach to contemplative self-awareness. CBT is just one more way to change counterproductive thinking, and thereby the negative emotions and destructive behaviors which result from such thinking. This not only ensures our emotional health, but also greatly assists us in our spiritual journey by removing impedances to higher stages of being.

It is important to note how CBT differs from other forms of "therapy." For one, there are self-paced CBT-inspired guides we can work through on our own, including one provided later in this book (see below). And if we are able to relax our ego sufficiently enough to seek professional help, CBT is usually short-term. According to the NACBT,[13] the average number of weekly therapy visits required to produce significant results is sixteen sessions. CBT is also a "use it when you need it, and not when you don't" solution. It is totally unlike an experience of psychoanalysis where, after ninety consecutive visits, a psychologist might still be expecting us to "make the first move" in our own treatment. Such an experience would be very unusual in CBT primarily because it begins and ends as a collaborative and results-oriented relationship: CBT relies on an open, respectful dialogue between therapist and patient to reshape

---

[13] National Association of Cognitive-Behavioral Therapists; see www.nacbt.org

thinking and reach clear, mutually agreed upon outcomes. This is a very exciting process, and I can't recommend CBT highly enough for anyone who wants to chart a new direction for their life. You will encounter many of its principles – and the results of my own success through CBT – throughout *The Vital Mystic*.

In Appendix E, you will find a CBT-inspired outline of how to interrupt fear cycles. Why does a book about "mysticism" include such a process? Because although it differs superficially from more advanced forms of spiritual exploration, CBT is an excellent model for contemplative-emotive progress, and is a highly effective way to prepare for mystical exploration. Should you decide to try these exercises, I recommend you work through them in a private journal, and allow yourself plenty of time and emotional space (i.e. freedom from work, home and relationship demands) along the way. Often, our fear-transformation will entail a fundamental shift in how we view the world. Sometimes it may take weeks – or even months – to relax the tightly cinched net of previous survival behaviors and open ourselves to other options. Sometimes we will run screaming away from our True Self, because of the power and honesty we encounter, to return with more temerity another day. And sometimes we will laugh or cry our underlying fears into the meaningless oblivion from which they came, relinquishing in that moment every desire to define the present with our past. Whatever our experience, once we have begun replacing our self-limiting fear and avoidance with the shining warmth of a new, compassionately nurturing direction, it will be much more difficult for old deceptions to reassert themselves.

For a detailed "workbook" approach to CBT, try *Mind over Mood*, by Dennis Greenberger and Christine A. Pedesky.

For more information on cognitive-behavioral therapy, visit www.aabt.org, iacp.asu.edu/links.htm, or www.nacbt.org.

For advice on shopping for a therapist, see *Appendix C*.

The Logical Conclusion

To love and thrive, or to loath and fail. It can be stated that simply. If a majority of our patterns of thought and emotion are negative, pessimistic, impatient, destructive, antagonistic, cynical, or hateful, we can't help but express them in actions that fail us and those around us. If we choose to turn away from such darkness to the light of kindness, patience, positive encouragement, spiritual nourishment, and persisting joy, our actions will change, and our odds for success in many different arenas will change with them. More than mere "positive thinking," we are choosing what is *spiritually healthy* over *spiritually unhealthy* because we feel authentic compassion for ourselves through vigorous and balanced self-esteem. This is not a matter of believing a possibility, it is a matter of cause and effect.

"It is only because of my compassion that I can be courageous."

Tao te Ching, 67

What will be covered next is, I believe, a necessary prerequisite for understanding the scope of mysticism's influence on the self and in the world. It proposes an interconnection between thought, emotion, will, and the Universe that is both instantaneous and far-reaching. For what is the purpose of reforming our minds and hearts, if the relationship and dynamics between our being and the Universe is not fully understood? Although our comprehension of *all that is* may at first appear to be subjective or limited, our will – as it consciously and unconsciously manifests every one of our intentions – has an immutable impact on how our life is shaped, our own well-being, and the good of All. Thus the shaping of our will is an inherent component of the mystic's way.

Chapter Questions

1. What experiences in your life have revealed that you hadn't yet realized something important about yourself?
2. What could you do today to create a more honest and realistic view of what motivates and sustains you?
3. What are you truly most afraid of, and how does it influence your behavior?
4. How many of the self-nourishing resources and practices listed in the chapter have you experienced? What was the result of each?
5. What have you done this week to nurture yourself on many different levels?

6. THOUGHTS in ACTION: a MANIFESTED LIFE

"If I have the gift of prophecy, and know all mysteries and all
knowledge, and if I have all faith, so as to remove mountains,
but do not have love, I am nothing."

New Testament, *1Corinthians 12:2*

Whether in pursuing the suggested practices outlined in the
following chapters, or through another means of spiritual self-
realization, we will inevitably encounter powers greater than we ever
imagined while traveling our sacred roads. These powers exist as
any other natural force in the Universe, and are bound by certain
laws. Some label them "psychic" abilities, others claim they are the
hand of Deity at work, while others attribute them to other
supernatural agencies or cosmic energies. Regardless of how these
powers are named, spiritually thirsting human beings will either
incidentally encounter them, or be consciously drawn into this realm
of subtle causality. Understanding the nature and management of
such forces, and the very real strength of the human soul, will
therefore become increasingly relevant as you continue through this
book, and this topic seems a reasonable preamble to deeper
exploration of the Mystic's Way in the following chapter. Those who
are uncomfortable with esoterica may have difficulty here, and I
would encourage them skip forward and return at a later time.
Ultimately, as we climb to the heights of spiritual clarity and the true
knowledge of Self, the impulse to gain mastery of these powers, or
control of any specific outcomes, will lose its importance to us. For
the less we desire mysterious knowledge – while still remaining open

to it – the clearer all mysteries become; the freer we are from craving authority or supernatural ability, the easier it will be to enable the miraculous.

I myself could certainly be more diligent, more compassionate, and less attached to results where my own will is concerned. The criticality of such self-examination cannot be overstated, for our will manifests constantly as a result of every thought in what could be called *artifacts of will*. This is perhaps why so many traditions have treated the deliberate actuation of will – beyond mundane deeds in the physical realm – as magickal, deific or occult in nature. When taking this approach, it is easier to separate out the disciplines and inclinations required to focus the mind and heart into a seemingly miraculous result, and thereby distance – albeit superficially – a natural and often arbitrary stream of our consciousness from a "supernatural" expression of Self. In other words, it initially appears simpler to consciously actuate our will in an *un*ordinary way when we have differentiated it from ordinary experience. However, as we spiritually progress, the distinction between such artificially constructed artifacts of will and our ongoing stream of consciousness ceases to exist. We come to live almost exclusively in our most potent and persistent intentions, and our thoughts – and will – are continually directed by them and expressed in every aspect of our lives.

To ruminate over the mechanics of how will manifests is tempting, but it would only be speculation or alignment with some existing tradition. While the Christian faith invokes prayer and *pneumatika* of the Holy Spirit, the Hermetic tradition focuses on meticulous imagination and ritual; to practice Reiki one must receive symbolic attunements from a Reiki Master, and paranormal ability seems a predictable result of advancement in certain Yoga....And so it goes with countless other belief systems. But are these perspectives of "manifested will" so different? As proposed by the golden intention, all actions are sanctified by noble inclinations of the heart, not by the dogma of any particular tradition. The workings of will and spirit are, after all, universal, and as discussed in the following chapter, a plethora of approaches to mystical awareness can achieve nearly identical ends. But instead of debating these issues, it is more practical to present various artifacts of will – that is, the many ways in which our will can manifest itself – as they are actuated unconsciously by everyone, and consciously by anyone with sufficient mental, emotional and spiritual discipline.

As to concerns over the efficacy of this discourse in the context of differing faiths, I believe thoughtful consideration in this area can benefit people of any tradition. Once again, these practices are worth examining precisely because they have a habit of occurring naturally, to varying degrees, in and around anyone sauntering down a spiritual path, and the disciplines involved are closely related to the states of mind and heart that liberate self-perception and induce mystical consciousness. In this area of knowledge, too often obscured or overcomplicated, I think it is better to be informed and prepared than to grope and stumble within a veil of ignorance. For such an exploration to be spiritually profitable, however, all artifacts of will would of course be subject to the golden intention in alignment with the Source of Life and Light. Without a firm grounding in a pervasive love-consciousness, there is truly little more than distraction here – or worse: unpredictable and outcomes that can be harmful to ourselves and others.

Preparation

There are three things essential to generating or managing spiritually profitable artifacts of will, and this preparation, in turn, reflects both the earliest phases of mystical progression, and an ongoing spiritual challenge:

1. Developing an ever-deepening understanding of, and sensitivity to, our connection with the Source of Life and Light, and the spiritual intelligence of our soul.

2. Exploring with equal agility and devotion the unclouded motives of our heart, continually subjecting them to the golden intention.

3. Through patient practice and gentle skill, free from anxiety, compulsion or fixation, continually nudging these two constants into alignment with each other.

The spiritual masters of every tradition have already laid the groundwork for this process; if we listen to them, we can hear the wisdom of the Universe speaking through them all. It is that listening skill which, as part of our spiritual perception, guides us into seeing our inner worlds clearly, and helps us concentrate and focus our will. Ultimately, these three steps become a *way of being*, what I call a "praying without ceasing," instead of a deliberate or awkward effort, and though I'm not sure self-examination ever becomes easy, it inevitably becomes...simpler. We pass through worry and fascination over the results of our effort, and arrive instead in the joy of the process itself. At this point in my journey, I liken it to balancing flowing water and blowing wind on a scale made of fire. Such conundrums make life interesting for us, and though we cannot claim the results to be our own any more than we could claim to have invented the sunrise, we can still be filled with admiration and satisfaction as this delicate balance breathes through us, and its light and color fill the skies of our imagination.

Praying Without Ceasing

Prayer in this context is a specific mode of interaction, a state of mind and heart that is independent of any religion or belief system, and a useful tool regardless of how you define the "Source of Life and Light." How can we describe this state? Primarily, it is one of complete openness. All the barriers of ego, defensiveness, and fear are relinquished, and what remains is the same kind of connection we find in anyone with whom we share a deep and unconditional affection. Although our mind may be engaged in the process, this is primarily a dialogue of the heart, an intimate *reaching and receiving* of emotional content. When I first encountered the concept of "praying without ceasing" in Christianity, I was confused by it. What did it mean? There are many clues in Judeo-Christian writings that hint at a more profound dialogue with the Divine than casual supplication or compulsory gratitude, but my own practice was initially an awkward, intellectual exercise – it lacked *heart*. In my current understanding, I would describe praying without ceasing as constant, conjoining joyfulness across all aspects of my being; a closeness that transcends casual experience. Some of the finest descriptions of this possibility are provided by the Muslim poet, Shams-ud-din Muhammad Hafiz. Consider these lines from Daniel Ladinsky's rendering of his poem, *That Full, Fragrant Curl*[14]:

> Why do I want to get so close to you tonight,
> Dear Master,
> With such a sharp knife in my hand?
> I'll confess.
> I have been eyeing that beautiful curl dangling
> At the end of your tress.
> I have calculated its worth
> Way into the wee hours.
> I have figured
> The price it will bring
> Is the ransom I need to free myself
> From every god my mind and this world
> Have ever erected,
> To free myself from every sterile idol
> That makes me bow to its lies
> And wants to strangle
> My fragile joys and precious winged pen.
> I need to know I am yours, Beloved,
> To untangle my every alliance with Guilt.
> When that cruel net casts itself,
> It can cause even a great one
> To live in sorrow and sadness.

---

[14] From *I Heard God Laughing: Renderings of Hafiz* by Daniel Ladinsky, Sufism Reoriented, 1996

So let me near you tonight, dear Master,
With a sharp knife concealed in my palm.
Let me cut from your favorite garment
A tiny thread
From which I will make a sacred lasso
To encircle the Sun

How do these words touch you? One can find a similar sentiment of emotional intimacy echoed throughout much of Hafiz's work. And that is the essence of praying without ceasing: to abide in a love-consciousness born of intimate relationship, remaining incredibly and confidently close to the Source of Life and Light at all times; to pry open the doors of our innermost Self and welcome the wisdom of the Universe; to live constantly in quiet expectation of the Divine; to acknowledge the attentive gaze of the spirit realm and be fiercely grateful for it; to continually feel a Sacred Presence in the depths of our heart; to perceive the language of Truth in all things; and to entrust every hope and wish to the Ever-Listening Ear. These are the qualities of deep spiritual connection, carefully engendered against the backdrop of our heart's longing and spacious silence. Although nothing but submersion in one's own belief system can perfect such unselfconscious closeness, I feel it is essential for us to explore how this continuous preparation of intimate alignment is achieved, whatever our path. To enter into holistic mysticism, both the heart and the mind must be engaged – and this kind of "prayer" is excellent training for both. Within this discipline, we come that much nearer to being *in agape* at all times; that is, full to overflowing with empathetic understanding and unconditional compassion. This, in turn, generates a beginning and end to our spiritual impact on the world, confidently informing the shape and direction of our will.

"Constant watchfulness helps the soul to be receptive to the finest expressions of life. This watchful silence unties the knots of our psychic being, and makes it responsive to the soul. It also makes it responsive to the currents of life, revealing its divine orientation."

Mahendranath Sircar, from *Hindu Mysticism According to the Upanisads*

The Art of Suspension

With the same constancy and expansiveness as praying without ceasing, and as a combination of the contemplative state of suspended valuation and its counterpart of equilibrium in the emotional transformation process, the *art of suspension* is one way to achieve a calm and steady state of mind, heart and spirit; to be centered and quiescent amid the many possibilities of existence. It is also a way to increase transparency of the artifacts of will acting in and around us, and to express that awareness in our way of being. In the simplest terms, the art of suspension defers conclusions and valuations in order to see beneath the appearances of things to their underlying truths. To illustrate the process, try the following exercise:

1. Imagine you are suspended in space, holding on to a rope attached to a single point: no matter how tightly you hold on, you could still be whipped about in any direction.

2. If you hold on to two ropes, each connected to a different point, you could still be pulled back and forth in a tug-of-war.

3. If you have three ropes leading to different points, you begin to have some stability, even if each of the points is tugging furiously at you.

4. If you have six ropes attached to six separate points, you have even more stability.

5. Now imagine twelve ropes, all tightly strung and well-anchored, and you become a fixed location between them all, a virtual center in infinite space.

Expanding this analogy, every "point" with a rope attached represents an idea or experience, and the rope which leads to each of them is the thought process – or intuitive process – which connects us to that experience or idea. Perhaps some of the points are formative events in our past, or truths we have reasoned out, or epiphanies that transcend logic. Perhaps some of the ropes are values our parents taught us, or the rules we use to interpret events, or our ever-changing perceptions. Some of our anchors may be the hopes we have for the future, or failures we have experienced in the past. Some may be paradoxes. In suspension, the tension each point exerts on us at any given time – i.e. how hard each rope is tugging on our attention – can be balanced by our conscious awareness of all the other points in our spectrum of past and present. Thus, everything we know enters into continuous dialectic with itself, and the more cognizant we are of this interaction, the more centered we become amid the many conceptual and experiential ropes attached to us. This type of directed awareness is the *art of suspension*, and is really a form of contemplative, "watchful" meditation similar to those advanced in many mystical traditions. The idea is to practice suspension until you are no longer subject to any one influence, or pulled unconsciously in any one direction.

Figure 5: Equal Tension On All Points

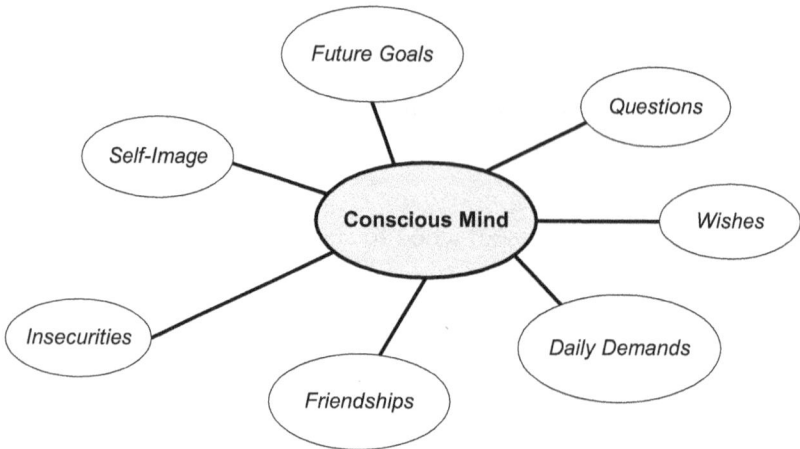

This is a potent kind of watchfulness, because no one idea or experience is allowed to dominate, and competing convictions, emotions, and tendencies of will are held simultaneously without anxiety or drama. There is no sense of conclusion, because we remove ourselves from direct contact with all these simultaneous considerations. We can calmly harness ourselves in a web of *seeming* incongruity and overwhelming information, and still be at peace. In fact, from this suspended state, we will often discover surprising interconnectedness. We see patterns which unify, which show us how diverging ideas or evidences are not as mutually exclusive as they once appeared – for there is almost always interaction and overlap between all forces and fixed points, no matter how far apart they at first appear to be. We discern new relationships, harmonies and coalescences, and when we cannot immediately reconcile one observation with another, the uncertainty does not disturb us. Our assumptions about the meaning and priority of all these experiences are further revised as we add spiritual cognizance to the mix, and in the finest mystical perception we glimpse the underlying fabric of reality transcending initial appearances. Even without deliberate effort to this end, we are taking the first steps toward actuating a state of being from a state of mind, heart and spirit.

As one example, I may comfortably believe these three things simultaneously:

1. That the Universe can take care of itself;
2. That I can relinquish all of my desires, and all of my attachment to outcomes; and
3. That my actions will flow naturally out of my love for others in supportive and healing ways.

But if the Universe doesn't need fixing, why would I try to be supportive and healing? And if I have relinquished all my desires, why would I still desire to do good? In a suspended state, I can view these apparently contradictory positions without cognitive dissonance or any compulsion to justify or resolve them. If, over time, they continue to rationally contradict each other, well…so be it! The Universe is more than capable of simultaneously allowing and expressing these conditions without negating any of them – this is the secret most fully revealed in mystical consciousness. The art of suspension thus welcomes us into this space of all-encompassing neutrality, conditioning our mind for a mystical process whereby everything can be definite, but nothing certain. Take a moment to sit calmly and imagine this possibility, placing yourself at the center of your own existence without reacting to the whirlwind of phenomena within and around you. Try to be an indifferent observer. Can you do this? If you find it difficult to be completely at rest, but are instead drawn into the emotions, meanings and tasks associated with each thread of your attention, the following chapters will provide additional tools to achieve this kind of centered calm.

What is the ultimate result this state? Within our suspension we can be open to every new emotion, experience, idea and spiritual force we encounter without being swept away by any of them. In our awareness of these many points of view – these appearances of what they actually are – and our relationship to them, we are held securely within a single virtual overview without being swayed by even the most compelling interest, even our Self (Self is, after all, just another of the many points of tugging at our attention). Another beneficial outcome of suspension is that our will is not confined or vanquished, but tends to be neutral, and, like our mind, completely at rest. This is an essential prerequisite for directing our will in the most positive ways, as it can then be guided by deliberate, spiritually insightful intentions. It is as if some gigantic planet were suspended in space, unmoving and unaffected by other stellar objects; having relinquished desire for any specific direction, it nevertheless actively attends to all that is around it. Suddenly, in a delicate openness to the subtlest wish, the planet begins accelerating towards a distant star. In my observation, that acceleration far exceeds the speed of light, though measurable results in the physical world often arrive at a much slower pace. And even as these results are actuated, we still rigorously maintain the art of suspension, but the relative position of our consciousness to all our simultaneous considerations – all those fixed points of attention – has changed. This is what I call *wishing without wanting*, and is one way we can act with clarity, purpose, and comprehensive effect. This will be an integral, though briefly visited, milestone in our spiritual progress.

"Someone who believes that anything by its nature is *good* or *bad* is forever disquieted: when they don't have what they think is *good*, they torment themselves, and keep pursuing what they believe to be *good*. But when this is obtained, they are even more disturbed with their irrational and excessive elation, and, dreading a change of fortune, they make every effort to avoid losing the *good* things they have obtained! On the other hand, someone who assumes nothing about what is naturally *good* or *bad* neither shuns nor pursues anything eagerly; as a consequence, they are unperturbed."

Skeptic philosophy, from *Sextus Empiricus,* 3rd Century

Artifacts of Will

In the same spirit, then, as praying without ceasing, and in with a disciplined concentration similar to a watchful state of suspended valuation, our will can be manifested in alignment with the wisdom of the Universe without overreaching effort. Through loving intentions we simply *are*. That is what wishing without wanting means, and that is how nearly all constructive artifacts of will are set in motion. This extremely difficult to describe, and until you observe or experience it for the first time, it may be even more difficult to accept. But as Lester Levenson wrote, "When you are in tune and you have a thought, every atom in the universe moves to fulfill your thought."[15] At the same time, this apparent influence in the world increasingly loses its importance for us: not only do we let go of our attachment to outcomes, we cease to even notice the impact of our will. It just is. Such is the orientation of this state that we do not presume to act at all, but only maintain a steady internal continuum of the golden intention in all things. We may discern the benefit to others of our passing wish, but we do not desire to personally own a positive outcome. Wishing without wanting. Carefully consider that phrase, perhaps spend some time reflecting on it, and see what you

---

[15] As quoted in *Moments of Enlightenment* by Robert Ullman and Judyth Reichenberg-Ullman

can discover about the principle behind the words. Here, then, is an inventory of what our will manifests into being every moment – whether through action or idea, consciously or unconsciously. These are the forces shaped by both worldly and Divine intention.

1. **Meditative neutrality** – Such as the art of suspension or equivalent stillness.

2. **Projection of goodwill on others** – Such as trust, compassion, love, or encouragement.

3. **Invitation of another's goodwill to self** – What politicians, managers, and salespeople often try to do.

4. **Supplication for direction of will** – As with prayerful supplication, or seeking guidance from others.

5. **Subjugation to another's will** – As we do when falling in love, or devoting ourselves to a religious or political cause, or as we might have done as children when we followed our parents or older siblings around like enamored ducklings.

6. **Annihilation of our will** – Such as when we alter our brain chemistry with drugs and alcohol, try to commit suicide, or otherwise permit ourselves to be abused and victimized by external influences.

7. **Integration of another's will and our will** – As with marriage, or a business contract, or playing team sports, or other agreement where there is an assumption of equal participation and investment.

8. **Protecting our will from another's will** – As we do when we withdraw into isolation, or summon the protection of our spiritual tradition, or decline a persuasive request.

9. **Transmutation of another's will** – When we calm aggression, or introduce harmony where there was chaos, or encourage right thinking or right conduct – without actually imposing our will on someone else. That is, we are welcoming another's will, and transforming it. This is often used by skilled counselors, mediators and leaders.

10. **Redirection/Deflection of another's will** – The outcome may be similar to artifacts 2, 8 and 9, and this may have a defensive or corrective intent, where the object of our will may be completely unaware of our influence as the course of their desire is redirected.

11. **Subtraction/Restriction of another's will** – As with physically confining someone, psychologically or emotionally oppressing them, injuring them, or taking their life.

12. **Enhancement/Expansion of another's will** – This is what is happening when we consciously align ourselves with the good of All, or throw our support behind a leader we believe in, or nurture and nourish someone, or procreate.

13. **Creation of Residual will** – In inanimate objects; this has, depending on the intensity of the initial focus and intentions of the mortal creator, a specific half-life – in the case of an Immortal Creator, this raises some interesting questions.

14. **Cascading Propagation of will** – As in mass media, group lectures, political rallies, etc, where intentions and ideas spread throughout large numbers of people via intermediaries. An intriguing theory that describes this process is *memetics*.

Artifacts of will are natural conditions, ordinary consequences of our own intentions. What I am suggesting is that you become so appreciative of these, so conscious of your own direction and disposition – as well as the innumerable forces acting on you at any given moment – that you can actively guide your course through life, instead of being tossed about by circumstance. By considering that course, consulting the wisdom of the Universe via the mystic's way, and aligning yourself with the good of All, you enter harmoniously into the ever-flowing, all-encompassing river that radiates from the Source of Life and Light. Without us even noticing, this matures into a fully harmonized existence of highest spiritual proportion: the limitless, ever-humbling fulfillment of our Divine potential.

"Whoever perceives inaction in action, and action in inaction, is an enlightened person."

Bhagavad-Gita 4.18

Rather than expanding these principles with more examples or explanations, I encourage you to muse over the meaning and application of the artifacts listed above. How have they been revealed in your life? Can you trace past or present experiences to individual artifacts of will, or combinations of artifacts? In the past hour, what artifacts have you manifested as actions from your desires, either intentionally or unintentionally? What do you plan to do during the next hour, and with what level of awareness? The events that result from our intentions are the evidences of our existence: they are the impact we have on the world. Do you want this impact to be conscious and enlightened, or haphazard? That is your choice, and the power inherent to operating from a mindful and mystical state of mind.

Is there a price for miraculously expressing our will? Many ancient and revived traditions address the idea of a cost or sacrifice each time we manifest our will in the world. Some even suppose that when we selfishly enforce our will, a price will be exacted from us – and sometimes that price will greatly outweigh any effect we feel we have achieved. I believe that if this imbalance of energy is occurring, we have stepped out of alignment with the wisdom of the Universe, and are acting out of self-interest, or too self-consciously, or without a clear intention for the good of All. Without the golden intention, and if we avoid relinquishing our ego through wishing without wanting, there is indeed a cost for artifacts of will. We may become sick, or depressed and worried, or experience an oddly debilitating backlash of events – either immediately or over an extended period of time. This is the natural result of desiring anything too much, or pursuing a specific outcome from a spiritually unhealthy state. At the least, this is a sure sign that our heart needs mending. Thus there are consequences for acting outside of the good of All, and deliberately or inadvertently setting our will in opposition to the Source of Life and Light. On the other hand, the only costs of artifacts of will which flow out of compassion, patience, and liberated intent are peaceful satisfaction, joy, and ever-deepening connection.

> "In short, remember this: that whatever you prize which is beyond your will, you have inasmuch destroyed your will."

Epictetus, 1st Century Stoic, from his *Discourses*

Protection

What happens when we open ourselves up to spiritual energies – or to another's will – and do we need to protect ourselves against deliberate or unintentional harm?

Consider this illustration: think of someone sitting in their office, whiling away their time, just waiting for something interesting to happen. Their supervisor walks by and, noticing that this person isn't busy, assigns them a difficult task. Now the employee is extremely busy, maybe even stressed, but not with something they might have chosen to do themselves, but rather with what their boss has told them to do. This is how I see spiritual forces at work in the Universe. If we are spiritually sedentary, lack clear intent, or find ourselves sitting around waiting for inspiration, we will be directed, or lured, or manipulated into some activity which other spiritual or "willful" forces – not necessarily more powerful forces, but simply those which are more directed than we are at the moment – decide we ought to be pursuing. This can also be true for the spaces we inhabit, and even the inanimate objects around us. Thus we might ask ourselves, "Have I consecrated this room to a specific purpose?" "Am I directed and of clear intent in how I use this computer?" "Do I accept responsibility for the immense value and power of this breath of air...?" It is our choice to be conscious and self-directed, or unconscious and the tool of some other influence. This does not mean we should keep ourselves perpetually busy, angst-ridden, driven, or self-conscious...but rather that we should be clear-headed and reflect on where we are, why we are, what are doing, and what we will be doing next.

"Let no act be done without a purpose, or other than according to the perfect principles of art."

From Marcus Aurelius' *Meditations*, 2nd Century

I enjoy seclusion and separation from the frantic emanations of crowded shopping centers or busy restaurants. I find that many people broadcast their intentions and state of being so loudly, I can't help but pick up on them – almost like a strong scent in the air. As you may yourself discover along the mystical path, such sensitivity evokes tremendous empathy for others, and the aura of suffering in a crowded place can be overwhelming, even paralyzing. My instinctive reaction, when too much information is coming at me at once, is to put up mental walls; for there are ways to psychically insulate ourselves from the world, just as we can choose to put in earplugs or wear sunglasses on a bright day. But no matter how carefully we construct barriers to outside influences, or engineer distance from those around us, there is always a way for what is outside to get inside – our environment will always have an impact on who we are, though sometimes in very subtle ways. So part of maintaining well-being and a sense of safety from chaos is to choose environments wisely, and to avoid overextending ourselves in interactions where we consistently lose our peace and equilibrium. Eventually, we may become more resilient, or more able to transform such environments into something positive – though there is certainly no guarantee. We may require spiritual discernment to determine our best course in the moment, but more often honest self-awareness and divestment of ego are all that are required to make sound decisions about how we spend our time.

"What you surround yourself with will either enrich your life, or impoverish you. It will either bring you closer to God's whole world, other people, beauty, and aesthetic enjoyment, or put a barrier between you and these things."

Franky Schaeffer, *Addicted to Mediocrity*

This may be one reason why a Christian's baptism in the Holy Spirit, a Buddhist's taking refuge, or a Wiccan's consecrations, are not – in isolation from consciously directing our will from moment to moment – sufficient to sustain a spiritual life. These traditions themselves warn of outward conformance without inward renewal. Our soul is immensely powerful, and our will can both invite and reject many different forms of conscious and unconscious energy – we might even inadvertently displace, for a moment or a lifetime, the very haven of faith in which we once wholeheartedly invested. So here is what we can do to maintain our spiritual health: if we continually renew our focus, continually clarify our intentions, continually apply ourselves toward the most worthwhile end we can imagine, and continually maintain balance in our lives by nourishing and nurturing every aspect of our being, there is simply no room for anything distracting or destructive to pollute, dilute or redirect our will. And such a position of purposeful fulfillment, such a complete commitment to alignment with the greater good, helps the golden intention flourish in and around us, announcing our loving presence on every plain of existence. This is how we create a beacon in our heart that invites good, and thwarts chaos.

There is, of course, more that we can do. One of the Just For Today meditations says: "Just for today, transforming all things into the good of All." Through this invocation, I create in myself a *transforming filter* through which all forces and events can be changed into good for everyone. In this way, we begin generating Love and Light from the raw materials of the Universe via the transmuting mechanisms of our intentions and will. Whatever comes into our life and interacts with our being can, with continuous faith, be reshaped into a healing and edifying influence – regardless of its source. And as it does with any of our intentions, our will radiates out from us, purifying, transmuting, evolving and interacting with everything it touches. This is our own deliberate and incidental proximity effect. Although I can't explain the underlying science (although I'm sure someday it will be better understood), I have found this to be an efficient method of positive influence and spiritual insulation above and beyond developing barriers, calling down Light, or invoking words or symbols of power. Let your own evolving wisdom guide you here.

Lastly, there are times when we lack the faith, strength or compassion to respond appropriately in stressful situations. We may be too overwhelmed or disoriented to practice transformative filtering, for instance. We may lose our intended focus, or be inundated with new concerns. At such times the world's ancient philosophies and spiritual traditions have some excellent advice for us: step out of the way. Why rage against an overwhelming force, or foolishly sacrifice yourself in some futile effort of self-righteous fervor? Instead, let go, and let the Universe take its course. Practice acceptance, and begin again where and when it is possible to do so. If you are compelled to resist, resist with stillness. Knowing when to act and when to remain still is the difference between wisdom and foolishness, arrogance and humility, and dissipation and effectiveness.

Artifact Exercises & Other Realms

Artifacts of will may at first appear to manifest on different levels of experience, but this is an illusion. For example, when I began exploring the mystic's way, I separated the material, external world from my interior landscape, and thus interpreted artifacts as a projection of will outside myself. In the same way, we may at some point brush against artifacts of will continuously occurring in other realms of existence; that is, on what we perceive to be "higher plains" than the physical realm. But the adage "as above, so below" can also be restated "as within, so without," and the more intimately we encounter the Absolute – the very bedrock of reality – through our spiritual practice, the less we will differentiate between our inner world, the physical plain, and the realm of Spirit. In an ultimate consciousness and appreciation of the grand totality of existence, they are one and the same.

With this understanding, there is still benefit in observing how will manifests in the various appearances of an ultimate reality, to evaluate the symbolism with which our mind translates that abstraction, and to apply the same level of conscious attention to the many worlds – those creative representations of our journey's central themes – unfolding around us. These themes are widely shared among all who enter into the mystical quest, just as dreams of flying through the air or running in place are shared by many young children. They are, in fact, road signs marking our spiritual growth and deepening *gnosis,* and provide still more perspectives and processes to balance within the art of suspension.

Examples are limitless, and recurring representations of these artifacts exist in nearly every spiritual tradition. In the visions of prophets, in the poetry of mystics, and in our own dreams and spiritual epiphanies, we will find both clear descriptions and obscured hints of their variety and thematic consistency. The following are but a sampling of such road signs, and may be helpful in your exploration of mystical practice and manifested living. I won't elaborate on their meaning or function at this time, other than to say that these are but a shifting glimpse of an endless, transdimensional cloud of being, and are more unified in purpose than they at first appear. As with any and all such exercises, these should be explored with sincere humility, complete divestment of ego, and a refined practice of the golden intention. Anyone, at any place along their path, may benefit from their contemplation. Those written in the first person are intended for self-reflection.

- The soul is not the servant of the flesh: the flesh is the servant of the soul.

- I am the mountain, unmoving.

- Drawing many in, converging them, and directing out as one.

- The sword of light is forged within, borne with reverence, for what purpose?

- Intersecting cycles of time, and overlapping circles of space.

- What are the conflicting natures of an oracle?

- Every fear of an external thing is an abstraction of some specific ignorance.

- Embracing the unending darkness, what is my comfort?

- Sincerely befriending, instead of battling, the shadow-self.

- How can I encourage willful spirits to carry out errands of good?

- What guards these realms, and am I prepared to pass through them?

- As I approach thought that is not thought, what will I remember?

- What is this? What is that? Why do I differentiate?

- Can there be love, devotion, compassion, and gratitude that transcend emotion?

- What is broken is complete; the shattered wheel understands its true function.

- Self-absorption destroys true consciousness; true consciousness destroys the self.

- Passing by the first five doors without pausing to enter or even looking in.

- What quality of emptiness resides in the Creator's mind, prior to Creation?

- To reveal a part of myself I have not healed, I need only find someone I believe cannot be helped.

- Why does anything exist?

- There is the essence of pure thought, and the essence of pure love; beyond these, who am I?

Once again, although these may at first seem obscure, if you persistently engage in mystical practice, their meaning will become clear. But how do we begin that journey? And what are the significant milestones along the way? With the preparation of this and all of the preceding chapters, we are now ready to explore the characteristics and actualization of mystical gnosis.

Chapter Questions

1. What is the benefit of observing how your will manifests in the world?
2. How does the art of suspension differ from meditating on emptiness?
3. What type of artifact of will is occurring when you shake someone's hand? When you watch television? When you curse aloud? When you fantasize about a desired future event?
4. What happens to your will when you are asleep and dreaming? When you are sick? When you laugh hysterically?
5. How do you experience love? Where do you think love comes from? How is it transmitted from one person to the next?

7. A MYSTIC'S WAY

I return once again to Daniel Ladinsky's rendering of Hafiz for a beautifully worded insight:

> I have a thousand brilliant lies
> For the question:
> How are you?
> I have a thousand brilliant lies
> For the question:
> What is God?
> If you think that the Truth can be known
> From words,
> If you think that the Sun and the Ocean
> Can pass through that tiny opening
> Called the mouth,
> O someone should start laughing!
> Someone should start wildly Laughing –
> Now![16]

When we let go of all certainty, we open ourselves to answers much larger than we can intellectually grasp or emotionally encompass. That is the mystic's approach to searching for truth. Can we wrangle infinity with logic until we confidently comprehend it? Will endlessly debating the rightness of any perspective make it more right? Mysticism provides us a powerful method of investigating the subtler, more delicate layers of discernment and wisdom behind all

---

[16] "Someone Should Start Laughing" from *I Heard God Laughing: Renderings of Hafiz* by Daniel Ladinsky, Sufism Reoriented, 1996

of our perceptions and constructs, as well as intuiting the complex influences and interdependencies within and around us.

> The softest stuff in the world
> overcomes the firmest.
> The insubstantial enters
> where there is no space.
> By this I know the benefit
> of something achieved by simply being.
> Few in the world can understand
> accomplishment apart from action
> and instruction where there are no words.
>
> *Tao te Ching*, 43

I was first introduced to the idea of spiritual perception when I was a young child. In the fantasy of children's stories, in my most vivid dreams, and the way my mother mused over her tea leaves, there was always something just out of reach, just around the corner – an implied availability of wisdom and a certain flexibility of perception for those who were willing to search and wait. Nature, too, had a powerful influence over me. My parents would let me run alone through the woods and beaches of my early childhood, and there were times when the connection I felt to a tree or rock or animal was astoundingly strong. I cannot, in fact, remember a time when I did not converse with Nature, or feel more at home alone there than in a crowd of people. Magick, strange spirits, and friendship with the wilderness permeated my existence, and were all I knew of normalcy.

Humans were another matter. My mother's warmth and sense of humor saved me countless times from the confusion and discomfort I caused other adults when I was small. If I thought someone was lying about something, I would blurt out my judgments without thinking. When I suspected that someone intended harm, I would boisterously confront them. And so I continued through my early years, presumptuous to a fault, understandably upsetting those around me. I narrowly escaped threats of violence and worse too often to recount. As I matured, I continued to rely on perceptions I trusted but did not understand, and even though I gradually accepted the wisdom of keeping quiet about certain things, I still consider it miraculous that I made it to adolescence.

> There is a pleasure in the pathless woods,
> There is a rapture on the lonely shore,
> There is society, where none intrudes,
> By the deep sea, and music in its roar:
> I love not man the less, but Nature more.
>
> Lord Byron, *Childe Harold's Pilgrimage*

When I was thirteen, at a critical juncture of self-doubt over my own spirituality, a copy of Richard Bach's *Illusions* came my way. It summarized and reinforced everything that had occurred in my life up until then – as well as opening new avenues of thought – and fortified confidence in my fledgling discernment and mystical proclivities. But, like many thirteen-year-olds, I was distracted by a million different impulses at the time. There were new friends, and romantic interests, and music, and cars, and new freedoms, and so much more! Too soon, I would also be seduced by the Cartesian rigors of an increasingly formal education. I would move to Europe, live in a big city, learn a different language and culture, and discard my youthful mysticism in favor of a more constrained, analytical worldview. And thus my childhood, and all its mystery, passed away.

Years flew by. I sampled college, got a job, played folk music, fell in love, and learned a lot about how little I knew. Some time in my early twenties, after a long dry spell of inflexible secularism, I read Madeleine L'Engle's *Walking on Water*. I was just beginning to embrace evangelical Christianity, and my freshly spiritualized experiences were reopening all sorts of windows into less-than-strictly-linear perceptions. There are a lot of great things in Madeleine's book, and though its main topic is what Christian artistry means to her, what stimulated my sleepy soul was how she decided to remain vulnerable, to accept mystery, to temper the habituations of her faith, and *listen to the silence*. From this starting point, the mystic in me blazed back to life, and suddenly I relented my scrupulous exegesis of the Bible, took long hikes alone in the Cascade mountains, released an egotistical confidence in my own spirit-constricting analytical abilities, and once more began listening to that silence.

> That secret depth of fathomless consideration
> That receives the information
> Of all our senses,
> That makes our center equal to the heavens,
> And comprehends in itself the magnitude of the world....

> From Thomas Traherne's *A Serious and
> Pathetical Contemplation of the Mercies of God*

Herding Wind Across Stones

A mystical orientation can be fairly foreign – perhaps even alienating – to someone steeped in conventional Western traditions, and finding a way to characterize mysticism and its benefits for a modern North American audience is challenging. To that end, however, here is a story taken from personal experience that illustrates one way we can draw near to the concepts and practices of mysticism.

Two sisters are hiking up along a stream in the wilderness, hoping to reach a spectacular waterfall they have heard about, which is several miles in. The stream cuts through a steep ravine, with huge boulders, pockets of dangerous quicksand, and no immediately visible path nearby. It looks as if this could be a very long hike indeed. Then one of the sisters, we'll call her Mary, says, "Hey, look! There's a path! It looks pretty easy."

The other sister, Martha, squints through the bright sunshine and shakes her head. "I don't see any path," she says. "Are you sure?"

"Oh, yes," says Mary. "Follow me. C'mon, let's go...."

Martha follows Mary for a while, and they make swift progress up into the hills. They hop along smaller boulders, cross the stream several times, scramble up stretches of loose sand, and walk along channels in the bedrock carved out by eons of rushing water. Still, the trail that Mary is following is not at all obvious to Martha. Then they come to a huge stone that blocks their path. There is no way around it, but Mary says, "Oh, I see," and begins to slide down into a dark, narrow gap at the bottom of the boulder.

"Mary!" Martha cries out, "What are you doing?"

"Following the trail." Mary answers, but her voice is muffled, and the last Martha sees of her, Mary's legs are kicking frantically as she bellies into the blackness beneath the stone.

Martha doesn't want to go that way. She looks around. A few steps back down the way they had come, she spies an easy way to cross the stream. The water is deep and cold, but Martha hops across and follows what appears to be an open stretch of sand along the other side of the ravine. She glances back to the giant stone, and sees Mary emerging. "I'm over here!" Martha calls.

"Oh," Mary calls back, "well...if you run into trouble, just yell for me."

Martha, however, is indignant; what an arrogant thing for Mary to say! She resolves not to call for help, but to find her way on her own.

After a mile or so, Martha is lagging far behind her sister. It seems that every time she crosses the stream to follow what looks like an easier way up, some cliff or rock or big gnarly bush in her path makes her backtrack and start again on the other side. She is trying to be careful, trying to look as far ahead as she can, but she always ends up expending many times the effort she thought it would require just to go a little bit further. She catches a glimpse of Mary ahead of her, looking back with a perplexed frown. Mary waves, and then takes off her pack and sits down by the stream. Martha tries to hurry, and by doing so stubs her toes and bruises her legs repeatedly as she stumbles over the rocks. Finally, out of breath and beside herself with embarrassment, Martha reaches the place where her sister is sitting.

"Would you like a sandwich?" Mary asks.

Martha looks at her. There isn't any triumph in Mary's expression – not even a hint of *I told you* so in her tone – and Martha relaxes and plops down beside her. "Sure. Let's eat," Martha says; then she asks, "Mary...how can you do this so easily? How can you find your way?"

Mary looks puzzled, then replies, "I'm just following the trail."

Martha is incredulous: "*What* trail?! I think you're just making it up as you go along!"

But Mary shrugs and hands Martha a sandwich, saying, "I don't think so. In fact, I think a lot of other people have used this trail before. Whenever I think I might be on the wrong track, I see a reminder that I'm still following the path."

"A reminder?" Martha asks.

"Sure. Like a hiker's cairn, a footprint, or a spot of rock worn smooth by other travelers."

Martha thinks about that, and sits silently eating her sandwich.

When they are done eating, Martha decides to stick with Mary for a while, and try to understand what her sister is doing. As they walk, she asks, "Why are we crossing the stream now?"

Mary considers, and replies, "See that bush up ahead? The big one with yellowy leaves on one side?" Martha nods. "Well, I think the reason it's yellowing on that side is because the footpath crosses right over it's roots – I don't *know* that that is true, but I have a hunch it is. Since it's on the other side of the stream, I'm thinking we should cross now, since it looks easier to cross here."

Martha is stunned. "That's all? That's how you have been choosing your way?"

Mary shakes her head. "No, there are some other things. Once I saw the bush, I looked further upstream on this side, and I could see that all of the rocks ahead are covered with lichen. The lichen would be worn off at least a little, if people ever went this way. It doesn't prove anything...but it confirms my hunch."

Martha looks back, now noticing the rocks and lichen. So, there was a combination of subtle factors that were leading Mary forward.

Martha keeps asking questions, and Mary keeps explaining. Sometimes Mary just has another "hunch," but other times there are clearer evidences, though Martha doesn't see them until Mary points them out. Even then, sometimes it's hard for Martha to understand why Mary sees certain things as significant. Why is that broken branch different from this broken branch? Why is this part of the stream safer to cross than that one? And the higher they go, the sparser these evidences seem to be, and the longer it takes Mary to decide which way the path is leading. Eventually, sweaty and hot with the climb, they reach a magnificent waterfall. At the base of the waterfall is a wide pool of cool, clear water. The two sisters take off their shoes and soak their feet, lying back in the afternoon sun. "On the way back down," Martha says quietly, "I want to lead the way...I'd like to try and follow the path myself."

"I'm sure you'll find it," Mary says quietly.

Martha is surprised, and asks, "Oh...you mean because we've been up it once already?"

"No," Mary replies, "because now you believe that you can."

This is one example of what it means to herd wind across stones. Over time, we can learn to access the limitless mystery of our own wisdom, the subtle perceptions that will guide our way, and the indescribable joy of being that simmers just below the surface of everything around us, inviting us ever onward.

> "Let all these things go, and do not look. Shut your eyes and wake another way of seeing, which everyone has but few use."
> Plotinus, 3rd Century Mystic

Correspondence with Spiritual Evolution

There have many excellent surveys of mystical literature and studies of the mystic's way over the past few decades, and adding to this prolific and authoritative canon might at first appear to be a daunting task. But where many authors have focused on differentiating one school from another, lauding the benefits of one approach or tradition above its siblings, or attempting to aggregate or unify diverse spiritual systems, our purpose here is to distill the central principles of a mystical quest into something easily transmitted and duplicated by anyone and everyone. To distill and make accessible, without oversimplifying. Certainly, one convenient explanation for the existence of so many varieties of mystical experience – or of the many seemingly divergent religions in the world, for that matter – is the infinite diversity of humanity itself. Different methodologies are bound to appeal to individual temperaments and disparate cultures. Yet at the center of every unique mystical journey is a unifying understanding of self in relation to others and the Universe as a whole, and the same spiritual and experiential milestones inevitably appear along each of the many different paths.

What are some important objectives shared by nearly all schools of mysticism? One is to achieve what I have called a harmonized existence. What elements are being "harmonized?" You could say every facet of our self with every other, the soul with the Divine, our conscious identity with the inexpressible Source of Life and Light, our entire being with the entire Universe, non-existence or "emptiness" with existence, or our individual consciousness with the Absolute. Instead of some part of us inadvertently rejecting or working against any of the others, all work in concert to achieve and maintain this state. Beyond this, there is a further consummation in the complete dissolution of our learned identity through an inhabiting of the True Self, the Most Sacred and calm center – what I call a *consummate acquiescence*. At this stage, the harmony of our being and our action simply ceases to be a conscious effort, and all that we are is no longer differentiated from all that we – and everything around us – are becoming.

Though these pinnacles of perception, cognition and actualization have many names, I believe all mystical paths lead to them. To help clarify what is occurring over the course of our mystical quest, here is a brief revisiting of stages of being in the context of progressive mysticism. Once again, and perhaps of spiritual necessity, there will be variations from person to person, and the ordering and distinctiveness of events and experiences listed are only a loose suggestion. At one point or another, however, each of these phases is bound to occur in some sequence or combination.

Table 5: Stages of Being and the Mystic's Way

Pyramid of Self	Stages of Being	Correlating Phases of a Mystical Journey
Physiological Animal, Emotional & Rational	Stages 1-2	Initial suspicion of there being "more than meets the eye" about our existence. Curiosity, often characterized as spiritual thirst, leading to the first exploration and insight into transcendent experience.
Experiential Instinctive, Sagacious & Intuitive	Stages 3-4	First momentous encounter with spiritual forces, other realms of existence, or the wisdom of our own soul, and a resulting "awakening" to – or confirmation of – an awe-inspiring vastness beyond comprehension. For some the Divine, for others the Eternal, the Infinite or the Void. After some initial doubt and resistance, our "thirst" deepens.
	Stages 5-7	An adoption of personal discipline to further develop sensitivity to, and application of, spiritual cognizance in day-to-day life. This almost always manifests as improved management of emotions (relinquishing fears and compulsions, for example), freeing ourselves from attachments, desires and expectations, and expanding and sharpening our watchfulness – our "contemplative attention." Like any birthing process, however, there can be considerable emotional and existential distress involved as we leave our "pre-integrated self" behind.
Spiritual Shared Under-standing, Moments of Epiphany & Mystical Awareness	Stages 8-9	The first fruits of disciplined effort: a noticeable improvement in self-awareness; greatly clarified thought; a better understanding of spiritually healthy objectives and processes; overall humility; and increasing ease and congruity to all choices. A more transparent access to intuition and the shared understanding of the Universe, and progressively deepening epiphanies or "moments of awakening."
	Stages 10-11	An unconditional commitment to love: that is, compassion without boundaries or expectations; a true blossoming of love-consciousness from the soul. Perfection of the golden intention and freedom from ego. A resulting fluidity of action and positive outcomes, and continued strengthening of wisdom. This is often the natural segue to exploring more advanced mystical practices (see Mystic Activators).

	Stage 12	A surprisingly easy letting-go of selfhood. Ongoing exploration of an ever-changing mystical horizon. The first taste of true spiritual freedom (from confining concepts, attachments and desires). A profound understanding that surpasses words or ideas; a spiritual knowledge dwarfing intellectual apprehension. A gnosis of the Absolute, resulting in a complete reorganization of reality and a whole new orientation of consciousness. A glimpse of the harmonized existence that results from persistent mystical practice.
	Stage 13	The continually expanding consequences of living in harmonized existence with our Divine nature, gnosis of the Absolute, and the Source of Life at all times. Among these are a more spacious comprehension and actuation of *agape* from moment to moment, reinforced clarity of purpose, a profound sense of tranquility that subordinates all concerns, and a greatly simplified life-approach.
⚜ Divine Spark or "True Self"	Stage 14	Dissolving into the Divine Spark, the Sacred Center of our soul, where we no longer sense, or feel, or know, but are forever *being and becoming*. This is truly beyond words, but could be described as: "entering into the ultimate reality behind all that is," or "letting go of all concepts and differentiation to inhabit the essence of what remains."

You may also notice that the phases of the mystic's way roughly correspond to certain chapters of this book. For instance:

> Chapters 1 & 2 speak mainly to Phase 1 of the Mystic's Way
> Chapters 3, 4 & 5 speak mainly to Phases 2, 3, 4 & 5
> Chapters 6 through 15 expand on Phase 5, and lead into Phase 6

Of course, there are aspects of every phase of our progression addressed throughout nearly all chapters. This is why, at the beginning of the book, I encouraged readers to begin where their hearts led them, rather than be restricted to a linear exploration.

Intuitive Promptings & Mystic Activators

> Even muddy water, when it is still
> eventually becomes clear.
> A heavy burden, when you set it down
> will eventually move on its own.
>
> *Tao te Ching*, 15

So how do we access the shared understanding of the Universe – that is, the deepest wisdom of our own soul? When do we know we have had an epiphany? How do we brave the inexpressible awe of mystical experience? When should we remain passive, and when should we act on our insights? Each person will have a different beginning, and our experiences and approaches will inevitably change over time. However, I think it is safe to say that anyone can begin the process of mystical awareness simply by listening to their intuition, and learning when to act on it. Yet intuition itself can be described in many ways – a physical sensation, an inarguable emotional conviction, an expansive vision or insight that ignites our imagination, or a combination of these events – and some people might think they have no intuitive capacity at all. In addition, separating what is truly intuitive from the many other voices, sensations and influences that crowd our consciousness can seem a discouraging challenge. Let's break it down into a manageable sequence.

First, there is a subtle distinction between simple intuition and mystical awareness. However intuition expresses itself, it is an *internally developed sensitivity to the dynamics of an immediate situation*, drawing on our life experience in concert with our soul's wisdom. Mystical awareness, on the other hand, expands this sensitivity into the broader context of our life's purpose and the interdependencies in everything around us, trusting a deepening connection with the shared understanding of the Universe almost exclusively. Another way of saying this is that intuition helps us assess the nature of the moment, and mystical awareness reaches toward the nature of eternity in the moment. They utilize similar mental and emotional disciplines, and I believe they are both forms of spiritual perception-cognition, but they have vastly different scope. Mystical awareness also requires a different kind of effort; that is, it prolongs and broadens the intuitive reflex into a non-referential and persistent condition. With intuition, we are generally navigating the choices of our own actions, oriented to ourselves and specific concerns or outcomes. With mystical awareness, we completely let go of our ego, our concerns and the relevancy of our actions, and enter into a realm of being and inter-being which reveals a *totality* of sacred wisdom, a *gnosis of the Absolute*, rather than context-specific knowledge. It's a lot like the difference between information and understanding: information is what we use to make decisions, understanding is the backdrop for that information which contextualizes its significance for us.

To begin, then, we can examine ways to activate our intuition, and begin shifting our orientation for immediate responses and decision-making from external rules or primitive impulses to a developing internal sense. After that, the floodgates of mystical awareness and a broader, more spiritualized context for our existence will be opened.

Figure 6: The Mystical Learning Process

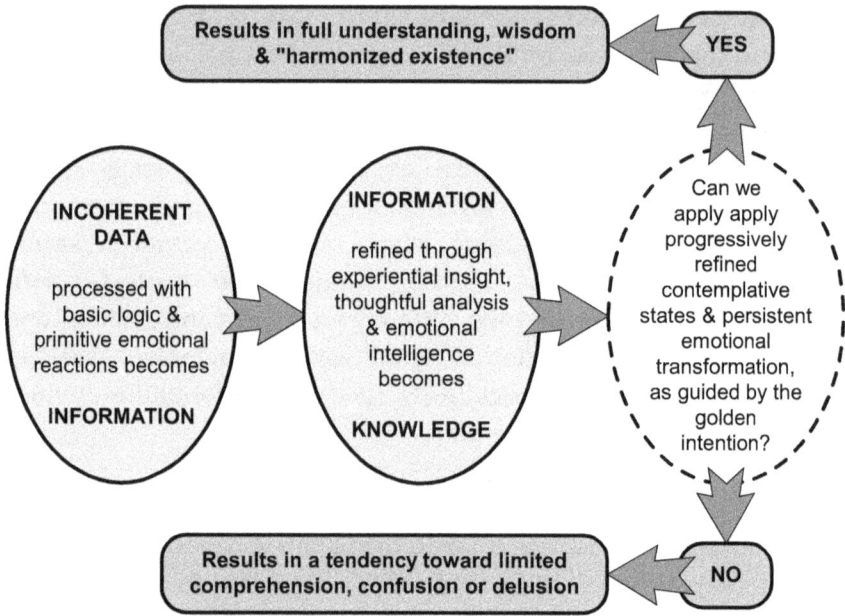

Results in full understanding, wisdom & "harmonized existence" ← **YES**

INCOHERENT DATA

processed with basic logic & primitive emotional reactions becomes

INFORMATION

→

INFORMATION

refined through experiential insight, thoughtful analysis & emotional intelligence becomes

KNOWLEDGE

→

Can we apply apply progressively refined contemplative states & persistent emotional transformation, as guided by the golden intention?

Results in a tendency toward limited comprehension, confusion or delusion ← **NO**

The Art of Letting Things Happen

In his commentary to Richard Wilhelm's *Secret Of The Golden Flower*, Carl Jung suggests that our resistance to letting go of critical, rational thought processes is natural, and that our conscious mind "raises prolific objections" to anything smacking of free, unguided imagination. With certain exercises, however, we can relax the "cramp in the conscious mind," and by experiencing the seemingly fantastic, irrational and unbelievable directly, slowly come to accept it as a valid part of our experience, and just *let things happen*. Intuition, and the gradual inception of mystical awareness which follows, require exactly this approach, for in the beginning they inhabit the realm of unconscious, non-critical perception almost exclusively. Eventually, the rational mind can add value to information gleaned from the non-rational, but for those of us raised in the orderly confines of Western culture, it is particularly important to release the impulse to analyze and dissect intuitive responses before we attempt to reapply our rational faculties at a later time. In fact, it is nearly impossible to benefit from the full fruits of mystical awareness unless we can unhinge our psyche at will. Here, then, are some exercises that encourage a habit of letting go. If one approach doesn't work for you, try another...and be patient. A minimum of thirty minutes is recommended for each exercise, and in all cases recording your experiences in a journal afterwards greatly augments the process.

- In a quiet place, visualize someone in your mind...not someone you know, an imaginary person. Imagine them talking to you. Notice the emotions you feel. Notice how the person looks at you and interacts with you. Can you hear them, or are they speaking silently? Do you understand their words, or at least the meaning they seem to be conveying? Ask this imaginary person a question, and listen to their answer. If something specific is on your mind, ask for their advice. Then thank them for their time, and reflect on your experience.

- Go for a walk in a place unfamiliar to you, without a clear destination or time-limit. Begin by deciding which way to go – left, right or straight – without a logical or a deliberate objective. Instead, try to feel your way through each change in direction, noting the sensations in your solar plexus as you consider which way to go. Do you feel a lifting, freeing sensation for one option? Try going in that direction. Do you feel a clenching sensation? Try avoiding that direction. See what happens. At some point you may lose your sense of place and time altogether – that's great! If this happens, you can try to follow your internal promptings back to where you began.

- Journaling connects us with our thoughts and emotions in a way that can be both fun and intense. To spend a half hour each day writing about our life, the reactions and reflections of our day-to-day existence, or just the random thoughts and

images that appear in our mind, peels the onion of our
experience down to its core, so that with each new sentence
we come closer to our personal truths. I am always surprised
by what springs forth when I write, as if I'm having a
conversation with someone I thought I knew very well, but
find they are saying something I never would have expected.
This is true of any form of creative self-expression.

- Opening yourself to the messages of the Tarot can be a great
  way to practice letting go. By this, I don't mean memorizing
  a structured interpretation of the cards, as much as letting the
  images, names (in the case of Major Arcana), and patterns
  speak to your intuitive sense. Perhaps the colors will evoke
  an emotion, or the images inspire a memory, connection, or
  gut reaction. Think about what your responses might mean;
  this is the intuitive voice making itself known, and by
  noticing it, we nurture it. One further step is to draw one of
  the Major Arcana from the deck and gaze deeply into the
  card, memorizing every detail of the picture. Once
  memorized, think about the image with your eyes closed,
  giving dimension to the landscape, perhaps even stepping
  into it with your mind's eye. Stay in this place for a while
  and observe what happens around you, then withdraw. In
  Michele Morgan's book *A Magical Course in Tarot*, she
  encourages us to: "Move lightly, as you would move near a
  wild creature glimpsed in its natural habitat." This is a great
  description of how to encourage our innate intuitive abilities
  without frightening them away.

- If you live near trees, find a comfortable place to sit among
  them and listen to the wind whisper through the branches.
  Close your eyes and let the sound of the wind fill your mind,
  letting all other sounds fade away. Now imagine the wind
  itself, as a sound and a sensation, coursing through your
  body. As the breeze moves around and through you, does it
  have a texture or pattern? Do these characteristics change? If
  you listen very carefully, is there perhaps a message there in
  the changing pitch, in the breathing of the sky? If you live

near a beach, try the same exercise with the surging rhythms of ocean waves. Near a river or stream, try it with the sound of flowing water. It is best if there are few other people around, but even if there are, see if you can listen so intently to wind or water that only these can speak to you.

- There are countless ways to practice intense awareness of our physicality, from various Yoga to the Buddhist practice of mindfully contemplating the body. Try something along these lines, and pay attention to all the nearly limitless sensations of your physical self. One approach already mentioned is to simply ask yourself where you physically experience your emotions. What parts of your body react to different thoughts and intentions? Where do you feel hunger, or sleepiness, or fatigue? What are the characteristics of these sensations? As we become more attuned to our physical self, we are more ready to notice subtle promptings or reactions that may express as a tightening of muscles, a sharp intake of breath, a rush of heat through our chest, or a tingling at the back of our neck. Paying attention to these is yet another avenue to intuitive sensitivity.

"Intuition, like all meditative disciplines, can be enormously effective if, and only if, one has the courage and personal power to follow through on the guidance it provides. Guidance requires action, but it does not guarantee safety. While we measure our own success in terms of our personal comfort and security, the universe measures our success by how much we have learned."

Caroline Myss, *Anatomy of the Spirit*

There are so many other ways to approach intuition, I am sure you will find something helpful to you once you start down that road. Whether you are calmly listening to silence, interpreting your dreams, staring at a waterfall, or making random squiggles on a blank sheet of paper, it's all about paying closer attention to what is going on inside you and freeing yourself from analytical deduction, external expectations, and impulsive reactions. Once the intuitive bridge is crossed, the mystical will begin unfolding before you, and one powerful experience after another will reinforce the value of your newly developing skill. Remember what you learn, and act on your new knowledge. Perhaps you will feel a deepening sense of connection and joy; or more readily observe the changes required for continued growth; or subtle promptings will guide you through improving your relationships or handling difficult situations. Eventually, as we learn to trust ourselves and act on this new flavor of information, our practice isn't just an occasional effort to initiate and align with the spiritual, but a continuous stream of awakening, discernment and effective decision-making which electrifies our existence. As we embrace this developing faculty, we will firmly establish a wise and capable way of being.

The Mystical Eye

The next phase in our mystical journey connects us with something both far vaster, though still inherently immediate. However, the methods, milestones and characteristics of this awakening are markedly varied among the different traditions of the world, and although I have attempted to find a common thread of experience, a distillation of practice, and a reasonable synthesis of these traditions, I believe each exists specifically because human beings are not identical; our variety requires different approaches. This is true in terms of cultural context, temperament, and upbringing, as well as our current beliefs and stage of being. As with intuition, different exercises and techniques will resonate and facilitate more effectively than others for each of us. With this said, is there still perhaps a way to generalize the mystical experience or reasonably group its traditions and approaches? A means of consolidating our understanding, and finding a way through the maze of endless variations? I believe there is.

To begin, there is one component of mysticism which is common to all practices, and that is the practice of detachment, of letting go: to cease differentiation in our relationship with the Universe, to abandon of our ideas of selfhood, to free our identity from its attachment to primitive desires and selfish ego, and to experience that freedom in an entirely new type of consciousness. Yet the approach to, and culmination of, this mystical milestone can be distinctively described from seemingly divergent perspectives. In the Sufi *Tariqa* we have an annihilation of self in Allah (*fana*) and a persisting union with Allah (*baqa*) as our goal; this is achieved through a gradual deepening of faith, self-discipline and single-minded devotion. In the Buddhist *Vipassana,* our culmination is an expanded consciousness without an object (*nirvana*), and ultimately a complete cessation of consciousness (*nirodh*), through progressive degrees of mindfulness, expanded awareness, and insight into the nature of our existence. In Hindu *Tantra Yoga* we have the attainment of a consciousness that underlies all other forms of consciousness (*turiya*), and the utter tranquility of cosmic consciousness, an experience of the Self-in-All (*turiyatita*), through the raising of *kundalini* energy into the higher *chakras*.

Further descriptions of peak mystical experiences are virtually endless. Agehananda Bharati expressed the zenith of his own mystical efforts as a "zero-experience."[17] St. Catherine of Sienna describes a state where "the seeing eye sees not, and the hearing ear hears not, and the tongue does not speak."[18] Robert Forman describes a "pure consciousness event" and an "empty plenitude."[19] A 14th century Christian monk finds himself in "the cloud of unknowing." And, quite poetically, Mahendranath Sircar offers us "the supreme silence of Peace which reigns unnoticed in the heart of things."[20] Add to these "divine quiet," "transcendent reality," "unutterable truth" and "nonduality," and we begin to see wonderful distinctions – and perhaps limitations – in human perception and language...but not necessarily entirely disparate events. I find

---

[17] From *The Light at the Center: Context and Pretext of Modern Mysticism*

[18] From *Mysticism, A Study in the Nature and Development of Spiritual Consciousness* by Evelyn Underhill

[19] From *Mysticism, Mind, Consciousness*

[20] From *Hindu Mysticism According to the Upanisads*

myself wondering if these experiences are that unlike how our emotions and consciousness are oriented in the womb, which we likewise have difficulty recalling or articulating...but that is another discussion altogether. However, all of these descriptions reinforce a central theme: a relinquishing of ordinary perception-cognition, and of previous definitions of self. For the moment, I would like to call this commonly shared mystical encounter a *gnosis of the Absolute.*

Regardless of our specific approach or conceptualization, as our intuition transitions into deepening mystical awareness, we will experience a sea change in how we view ourselves, process our environment, and interact with the world. Sometimes this comes abruptly and unbidden, as in the case of epiphanies, and sometimes the awakening happens gradually during the course of deliberate and focused effort. Sometimes our emotional perception will provide the primary view of our experience, and sometimes our intellect will interpret it for us. This reliance on certain of our faculties, colored by our current stage of spiritual development, creates a "perceptual orientation of the moment" for us. This, in turn, generates different interpretations of similar events, which then must be translated into the language of appearances – a symbolic representation far removed from the core subjectivity of our awakening. Unfortunately, all of this tends to muddy the waters of definition and communication even further.

And although these experiences may be similar, or described in similar ways, they are certainly not identical, for using as our reference the seven contemplative states, seven stages of the emotional transformation cycle, the unique perspective each stage of being provides, and the *transitions through gnosis* to be discussed in a moment, there are likely dozens of interactive gradients in our dynamic progression of consciousness; a whole matrix of possibilities! But all of this needn't concern us, for once we have been infused with mystical contact for the first time, we will immediately recognize it, and emerging from the crucible of its intensity, our clarity of purpose and directedness of will can undergo continual refinement. It is true that we may not always be able to rationally interpret convey our experiences, but this does not detract from their reality, or their value.

> "By your persistent commerce with mystic visions, leave behind both physical perceptions and intellectual efforts, and every aspect of sense and intelligence, and all things which exist and don't exist, and be raised aloft unknowingly to the union, as far as attainable, with One Who is above every essence and knowledge."
>
> Pseudo-Dionysius, 5th century Christian mystic

One way to depict the initial onset of mystical awareness is "everything suddenly being out of context." Have you ever encountered a common word or phrase that abruptly loses its ordinary meaning for you? Something like "ripe melon," or "all tuckered out," or "a lost cause;" a wording that you have never really pondered in detail before? Or perhaps you have regarded a person, place or thing you thought you knew very well with new appreciation or insight, saying to yourself, "I never noticed those qualities!" The leap of consciousness during spiritual awakening is much the same, bending our mind away from a flat and mundane organization of experience into broader, multidimensional landscapes.

A widely recurring sequence of these sudden shifts – these transitions through gnosis – is outlined below. All of these share three distinct traits, which are perhaps the primary features of all mystical awareness: a riveting absorption in – and appreciation of – the present moment; increasing clarity about personal purpose and universal truth; and a radical departure from previous understanding. Once again, these differ from intuition not only in scope, but also in the force of impact they have on our lives. They are listed here in fairly a predictable – though by no means rigid – order of occurrence, an order that suggests a peeling away of abstractions, a gradual freeing of the mind from its attachment to "aesthetic and reasonable appearances" of what initially seems incredible or incomprehensible information. The end result is a direct experience of truth which reforms – or removes altogether – all of our previous constructions. This is not necessarily a progression in the quality, substance or import of our mystical experience, on the contrary: the deeper we go, the less meaning all such concepts and comparisons will hold for us.

Transitions Through Gnosis

Transporting Perceptions

- Journeying outside of the body in the physical realm or to other planes of existence

- Communicating directly with other spiritual intelligences

- Prophetic visions, inspirational voices, automatic writing, or other forms of revelatory knowledge

Merging of Self with Divine

- Complete openness and seamless union with a Sacred Presence or Vital Continuum, often coinciding with a fathomless embrace of transcendent love

- Pervasive joy beyond comprehension; a bliss exceeding our capacity to contain it; an awakening of love-consciousness, where unconditional adoration and compassion for All Things consumes our being and directs our will

- Direct, unmitigated contact with the Divine Spark within us – our transcendent nature, our True Self

Dissolution of Self

- Infinite awareness, expanding inward and outward, incomprehensibly encompassing all time and space, transfixed by a unity of existence that has no discrete components or differentiating characteristics

- An awe-inspiring – and sometimes terrifying – submersion in emptiness, nothingness, or a state of unknowing free of all concepts, emotions, or sensations, and ultimately devoid of any self-conscious awareness

- A complete, unconditional surrender of self to these unitive states

Such moments are both a uniting experience for all mystics, and uniquely personal. Once again, there is probably more universality in how they influence our consciousness than in how they appear at any given time for different people, are defined or actuated in different traditions, or in how individual personalities respond emotionally to them. Much like intuition, mystic awakenings arrive in varying degrees, and are induced through many kinds of activity. Most of these activities focus on some combination of emotional, mental and/or physical discipline to achieve a supersensory or transpersonal state of consciousness, a state that is nearly always preceded by a detached and contemplative stillness of mind and heart. That is, in fact, a pattern that has already been established so far: the constant balance and interplay of the feeling self and the thinking self. In levels of the Pyramid of Self, in describing different emotional and contemplative progressions, in self-awareness and self-esteem, and even with praying without ceasing and the art of suspension, the necessity of parallel development between contemplative states and cycles of emotional transformation is revealed.

In the next chapter, we will examine some specific techniques that both prepare for and culminate in mystical awareness. Should you pursue this, the wisdom, humility and letting go that are encouraged through intuitive exercises and self-nourishing practices will help you navigate deeper spiritual waters – so it isn't advisable to skip those preliminaries or rush through them. Take your time, and tap into the full benefit of each phase of exploration. Once you have established a strong contemplative and emotional foundation, the following table describes three common categories of "mystic activators" intended to induce supersensory perception and, ultimately, a gnosis of the Absolute. Many of the practices overlap or blur into each other, and I have indicated only what I believe to be their primary distinguishing characteristics. Also, this is merely a sampling of practices I am somewhat familiar with, and is by no means a comprehensive list of approaches. Hopefully, I have not abbreviated the depth, quality, intended emphasis, or wonderful diversity of spiritual adventure by organizing them in this way.

First, here some definitions for the four main categories of mystic activators. Upon careful examination, the most striking commonality among them all is a single theme already alluded to: *a means of detachment and letting go of our habitual patterns and responses.*

Subtractive Meditation

Detaching from emotions, thoughts, and sensory experience in order to restructure consciousness and make room for mystical awareness. Often this is achieved through a systematic disassociation of subject and object – self from other, mind from body, unconscious process from conscious process, being from doing, *this* from *that* – which sets our consciousness free. Sometimes, detachment is merely a byproduct of singular focus or a merging of subject and object (such as self with the Divine). Expanded perception-cognition tends to be more incremental as the subtractive practice deepens, though epiphanies can also be surprisingly sudden.

Ecstatic Induction

Seeking to arouse a highly energized or blissful state that actuates mystical insight. This is frequently devotional in nature and often employs physiological means of accelerating the letting go of habituated consciousness. Ecstatic induction can also result in what the ancient Greeks called *mania*, "possession by deity," a form of trance where self-awareness is greatly or entirely attenuated. Supersensory experiences tend to be more sudden and extreme than with other techniques.

Symbolic and Synchronistic Ritual

Procedures that are esoteric or symbolically abstracted, sometimes associated with devotional worship and sometimes not, which purposely invoke natural, energetic and/or spiritual forces. Mystical awareness can be an unintentional byproduct of these practices, or the goal. A key difference between this and other activators is that such rituals usually invite external agents or forces – rather than a particular quality of internal effort – to help generate transpersonal experience.

The Perfection of Love

A refinement and intensity of love that reforms our awareness. Once again, mystical perception-cognition is sometimes an intended goal, and sometimes a side effect of the central journey. The object and expression of love may vary: a deep compassion for the suffering of others; or fervent devotion to a transcendent presence; or intimate worship of deity. But the nearly universal outcomes are a surrendering of personal ego, new certainties and convictions (often imbued with a sense of holiness or awe), an aligning of personal will with the object of love, and a passionate desire to translate conviction into action. A transformative union with the Sacred, however that is defined by the tradition, is often the primary objective of this path.

Table 6: Mystic Activators [21]

√ Primary Emphasis • Secondary Emphasis ∇ Incidental	The Perfection of Love	Ecstatic Induction	Symbolic & Synchronistic Ritual	Subtractive Meditation
Sufi muraqaba ("watchfulness")	•			√
Buddhist zazen (sitting meditation), vipassana (insight meditation/bare attention), and jhana (concentration meditation)	•	∇		√
Bhakti Yoga	√	√	•	•
Kabbalist kavannah (holy intention/concentration)	•	∇	√	√
Christian theoria/contemplatio (contemplative prayer)	√	∇	√	
Buddhist metta bhavana (loving kindness cultivation)	√	∇		•
Gyana (jnana) Yoga	∇		•	√
Hermetic visualization and meditation		∇	√	√
Transcendental Meditation	∇	•	•	√
Other mantra or mandala meditation/Yoga	∇	•	•	√
Sufi dhikr ("remembering God")	√	•	√	•
Hasidic prayer – hislahavus (bursting into flame) and devekus (clinging to God)	√	•	√	∇
Invoking certain "spiritual gifts" in Christianity (tongues, prophecy)	∇	•	√	
Kundalani, kriya, or other tantra Yoga	•	√	√	•
Taoist Hsiao Chou Tien (circulation of Chi meditation)	∇	•	•	√
Chanting, breathing and imagery techniques of ecstatic Kabbalah	∇	√	√	•
Shamanic trance	∇	√	√	•
Trance-inducement via controlled breathing, psychedelic drugs or extended fasting	∇	√		•
Sufi "turning" (ecstatic dancing)	√	√	•	•
Hermetic initiations and symbolic rituals		∇	√	∇
Earth-centered ceremonies such as Wiccan rites of power or polarity	•	•	√	∇
Angelic incantations and use of gematria (numerology of the Hebrew alphabet) in the magical Kabbalah		∇	√	

---

[21] With most of these descriptions, the many subtle differentiations, subsets and schools for a given category of practice are not separately addressed.

Divination (Tarot, I Ching, Runes, Bibliomancy, etc.)			√	∇
Christian rituals, such as adult baptism, "laying on of hands" by elders, and the Eucharist	•	∇	√	
Energetic healing arts such as Reiki	•		√	∇
Spontaneous Communion (an unintentional state inspired by nature, during sex, through music, during extreme crisis or pain, in a dream, etc.)	∇	∇		∇

For a survey of personal encounters with different modes of mystical awakening, from many different traditions, I recommend *Moments of Enlightenment* by Robert Ullman and Judyth Reichenberg-Ullman

In every individual's spiritual walk, there will be certain benefits and drawbacks to each of these activators. Once again, our own history, culture, religion, temperament and current stage of being would greatly influence both our choice and how we interpret our experience. Clearly, each of these practices is entirely unique, and some who have committed to specific systems might disagree that they should be categorized as "mystical" at all – or intended to induce mystical awareness as I have described it. For example, the mainstream Christian tradition avoids suggesting that adult baptism "transforms consciousness." And yet, when I emerged from my own baptism, I experienced a life-altering redefinition of self: my physical body became like a distant object, fleeting and insubstantial and irrelevant to my identity; as a result, my previous attachment to the desires and appearances of that body were vanquished for a time. This happened so suddenly and unexpectedly I began to weep and laugh at once, and I certainly felt at the time that the Holy Spirit was laughing and weeping right along with me. So I would contend that even if the mystical eye is not a deliberate objective, it is often a natural byproduct of many spiritual practices to varying degrees. Does it occur more readily in some practices than others, or for some people more easily than others? Some would argue this is entirely subjective. Nevertheless, the following are some guiding principles I have found helpful in evaluating the benefits and drawbacks of different approaches.

As discussed in Artifacts of Will, we can correlate some propensity for "imposition," "annihilation" or "neutrality" of personal will within all actions, and this applies to each of these disciplines as well. That is, while some practices unfetter the human will through subjugation to external influences (annihilation), and others try to focus it (imposition), a third approach consciously relaxes the will (neutrality). Having sampled different activators over time, what has bubbled to the surface throughout my experimentation and observation are three principles:

1. All approaches have mystical potential, but some are more resonant or effective for a particular person, or during a particular phase of spiritual development.

2. The disposition of will (annihilation/imposition/neutrality) implicit to a specific practice tends to influence our quality of intentions – though the extent of this influence depends on our current stage of being.

3. No matter how rapid or potent our access to the mystical becomes, our preceding and subsequent intentions determine the spiritual value of the results.

Therefore, what is appropriate for us *right now* will probably change as we change and grow, and the application of our will must of necessity shift even as it inhabits the same spiritual discipline. Developing a "neutral" will is usually the most profitable at the onset of mystical practice; but the one constant, regardless of our tradition, disposition of will, or stage of being, is the quality of motivation that initiates and sustains our efforts. If we are holding on to ideas of power or influence, the gratification of worldly desires, or the bolstering of our ego, we will cloud our mystical course. Ergo: the "I-me-mine" orientation must be relinquished. In all of these instances, mature self-awareness is therefore critical. When we attempt to enslave the mystical eye, permitting greedy fascination or wanton self-gratification to infect moments of clarified sight, we are much more likely to grab onto whatever convenient but shallow conclusions we encounter, asserting that we fully comprehend transitions through gnosis that have been crippled by unhealthy intentions. Unfortunately, such confidence is a sure sign that we comprehend very little, for the only reliable metric I have found to evaluate deepening gnosis is to ask "what is this?" and be incapable of any satisfactory explanation within the bounds of conventional language. Rather, it is "that from which all words turn back."[22]

In essence, if the golden intention – and the self-nourishing practices that support it – are absent from our quest, our access to spiritual realms can become distracted and perplexed, and the richest benefits lost to us – regardless of the path we choose. We simply won't grow. Thus a requisite companion to every process culminating strong, enduring and spiritually profitable mystical awareness is the perfection of *agape*. As reflected in the activators chart, an emphasis on maturing unconditional compassion or devotional love is in itself an avenue to spiritual awakening – kindling unconditional love-consciousness and transcendent insight. But even where selflessness or worship are not directly prescribed, our heart, mind and spirit will not be sufficiently elastic and receptive if we are holding on to primitive compulsions, selfish motivations, or purely intellectual curiosity. I repeat this sentiment frequently because it is profoundly important and often overlooked in contemporary discussions of mysticism, and this is precisely why developing the habits of praying without ceasing and the art of suspension can be so useful in any mystical practice. So begin and end by asking a lot of "whys;" interrogate your heart before presuming you are ready to greet the Infinite, or before you rush to any conclusions about your experience.

Insight and Action

Which comes first, mystical insight or spiritual discipline? Which leads to the most spiritually productive decisions, careful meditation

---

[22] *Taittiriya Upanishad II: 4.1*

or mind-blowing epiphany? Is there ever a point where we become a "master" of mystical practice? And once we comprehend a personal truth with unavoidable clarity, how should we act on it? Over the course of our encounters with the Absolute, we will revisit these questions again and again. It is, in fact, the process of constantly revisiting them that helps us refine our practice, deepen our sense of purpose, simplify our decision-making and enter into that indescribable state of harmonized existence. As a starting point, however, I offer these observations, which have greatly assisted my own attempts to translate numinous knowledge into practical choices.

No matter where we are in our journey, knowing when to act, and when not to overreact, is indispensable to the mystic's way of being. Justifying an extremely impetuous action by asserting it was "an intuitive prompting" is akin to saying "the Devil made me do it" – which is clearly irresponsible and counterproductive. There is also the danger of becoming so sensitized to the importance of every event in our life that we miss the threads of truth woven between them; there can be meaning everywhere, when we decide to look, but it is that which converges into the greater good that guides and empowers us. As an example, the majority – perhaps two thirds – of my own spiritual insights have exhorted me to be silent or refrain from acting at all. I will pause, reflect on the situation, feel my way through it, and often discern that the wisest and most loving thing I can do in the moment is...nothing. Perhaps just be present, observe what is going on around me, welcome new understanding, and amplify my compassion. Is this just my own lesson? Maybe so, but far too often I have witnessed an intuitive observation to be more damaging than helpful when it is recklessly translated into action.

> "It is a trap for someone to say rashly, 'It is holy!'
> And after the vows to then make inquiry."
>
> *Proverbs 20:25*

Let me offer some real life examples. When I administer Reiki or facilitate a Tarot reading, I often come across insights into someone's life that are intimate and raw. When I first began these practices, I would blurt out every image, sensation, or idea that popped into my head, often asking my subjects they thought each insight meant. This wasn't all so helpful, however. For example, what if I become aware that someone was horribly abused as a child? Or that their marriage is oppressing their spirit, or is about to disintegrate? Or that they will not be happy or well until they quit the profession in which their ego is currently so invested? Is it my place to tell someone about some denial deeply rooted in their psyche? Is it my place to reveal *any* specific observations? What if such insight is meant to inform my own best course of compassionate understanding, instead of theirs? What if spiritual perception aims to instruct us how best to love ourselves and others through deepening relationship, instead of justifying our counsel, opinions, or hurried attempts to "fix" the situation?

In a similar vein, I once believed I was responsible for immediate and drastic action regarding all the ills I encountered in the world. I was always quick to rectify a wrong, reconcile a conflict, and offer help or advice. Now I live by another standard: that everyone must come to their own conclusions, and I am but a resource should they seek me out. The active choice I make each day is to put myself at the disposal of the Universe, and to remain ready, willing and open. When I administer Reiki, I am content to let the Reiki help a person come to terms with the root causes of their illness, rather than to impose my understanding of their illness on them. It doesn't matter if my intuition is "right," if its revelation is not spiritually beneficial in the moment. In Tarot readings, I find the querant often rejects (or conveniently forgets) what they don't wish to hear. So rather than blurt out my rendition of reality, I now encourage querants to explore some readily apparent facet of their situation, or reflect on a theme of the reading that might open their eyes to their own intuitive truths. Using a Socratic approach, I don't need to hear the answers myself – it is enough to plant the seeds for thought. Although a crisis may create an exception, it is seldom necessary to be callously blunt or corrective in a reading or healing; instead I try to place greater trust in a person's own ability to learn and grow from the wisdom within them.

In my own walk of late, I have noticed that both intuitive promptings and mystical awareness have become increasingly...subtle. The strong emotions and colorful flashes of comprehension have faded, replaced with very simple and understated intimations – sometimes reminders of past lessons, sometimes something new. Although I may still be left reeling from many of these insights, the spiritual information seems to be presenting itself in less convoluted ways. It is hard to describe, but my point is that more vibrant or elaborate perceptions are now triggered by primitive (i.e. less spiritually evolved) impulses, desires or thought patterns. In the same way, how I express my will in the world has also become more subtle, and the challenge becomes less about what to externally accomplish, and more about an internal restructuring of thoughts and feelings. For all that I am will flow where my mind and heart takes it, and thus we return to artifacts of will, and the importance of praying without ceasing, the art of suspension, and wishing without wanting.

This, therefore, is a critical distinction: that there is a difference between imagination, sensation, and synchronicity of action which are still oriented to our previous stage of being, and the quiet voice of mystical certitude which leads us toward the next major event on our spiritual horizon, concurrently bringing us ever-closer to the essence of "action-without-action." From personal experience and studying the accounts of other mystics, I have suggested that this shift in emphasis from the intense, vibrant symbolism to subtler and more intimate communication with the Absolute is, in fact, evidence of ongoing transitions through gnosis. Likewise, the externalization of our mystical experience, its evidence-in-action, becomes increasingly understated until it seems to disappear altogether. Detachment from "results" is that much easier because our faith is not dependant on them. The miraculous may still occur, but we no longer so fascinated by it, and eventually tend to stop noticing it entirely. That is not to say that earlier stages of our transition are inferior in import, substance or impact, but that our continued progression will of necessity strip away a more concrete perception, ideation and actuation of the mystical, and arrive at both a more transparent encounter with the Absolute and a more unconscious mode of being. The center does not change, we are only moving closer to it: as within, so without.

> "Intuition without reasoning is blind, but ideas without intuition are empty."
> Francisco Varela [23]

What if, after a concerted effort to put the mystical into practice – either through engaging one of the established traditions or implementing the disciplines in the following chapter – we simply don't have any results to speak of? That is, we experience no intuitions, promptings, or insights, no spirit guides appear in our mind's eye, and communion with our soul remains purely theoretical. What if we have no "sudden awakenings?" I believe that a great majority of the time this indicates some part of us lacks nourishment, that we are out of balance in some way, and that healing on an intermediate level must occur first. Caroline Myss explains that healthy self-esteem is essential in developing our intuition,[24] and everything I have experienced and observed bears this out for mystical awareness as well. Yet if, after a sincere and conscientious application of effort, we have still achieved little in the way of heightened supersensory perception, it is probably time to let go. Just forget about spiritual cognizance for now, concentrating on other areas of your well-being, and remain present to each moment.

Years ago, when I managed a school district's computer network, one of my technicians came to me upset and stressed that it was taking her too long to fix problems in the field. I suggested the next time she felt frustrated, with no idea of what to try next, that she walk outside and watch kids on the playground for ten minutes with complete attention. She tried this, and found it very difficult to let go of her

---

[23] *Neurophenomenology : A Methodological Remedy for the Hard Problem*
[24] In *The Four Stages of Personal Power* from *Anatomy of the Spirit*

task and stop pushing herself to find a solution. It took all of her energy to go outside and watch children play on the playground. Even then, her mind kept drifting back to the problem she had been working on. Abruptly, in the midst of her struggle to force her mind away from her work, she burst out laughing. "I laughed until I cried," she said, "because I realized how silly it was for me to be so stuck. Why not just let go of it? The job really wasn't that important!" After watching kids playing for a few more minutes, she returned to her task. Without even trying, she knew exactly how to fix the problem. This illustrates a simple principle: at some point, usually when we least expect it, we will experience a sudden insight that takes us out of ourselves – as obvious and arresting as a bell ringing clearly in the stillness of the night. This is the principal quality of an epiphany, and of all spiritual discernment. If we trust this eventuality with an open mind and a patient heart, relinquishing any fixation on possible outcomes, it will arrive.

Spirit Guides

> "An uninstructed person will lay the fault of their own bad condition on others. Someone just starting instruction will lay the fault on themselves. Someone who is perfectly instructed will not place blame on themselves, or others."

> From *Enchiridion*, the Manual Of Epictetus, 1st Century Stoic, by Arrian

I would like to touch on the topic of spirit guides – that is, other intelligences that influence our spiritual advancement. Do I believe in them? Absolutely: they have been with me all of my life, and I feel great love and gratitude for their presence. Whether we view them as Angels, Spirits of Nature, Saints, Deities, Buddhas, Spiritual Gifts, or Aspects of the Cosmos, such intelligences are accessible in nearly every spiritual tradition. But do I entrust my every decision to them? No, and I do not think it is wise to do so. Coming to rely on something we perceive as an external influence to direct the currents of our existence tends to trivialize our soul's wisdom, mutes the effectiveness of our own insights, and distracts us from developing a reliable spiritual compass. As often as we might ignore the advice of friendly spirits when we should be listening to them, we could also become enamored of their influence and overly dependant on them. This is equally true of divination, the advice of mentors and soul friends, or mystical dreams and visions. Like any good friend or counselor, a truly wise presence will withdraw on its own to allow us the space to grow confidence and discernment in ourselves. If you find this is not happening in your relationship with spirit guides, it may be time to take a break from them and wean yourself from potential habituation. Also like good friends, loving spirits do not take offense at who we are, or what we choose to do, but are full of compassionate patience for us if we choose additional paths to understanding.

Lastly, but perhaps most essential of all, it is our task to filter all insight and spiritual guidance, as well as every desire to act, through the golden intention. In the Bhagavad-Gita it says: "Once we have achieved the consciousness where the soul perceives its essence, we are content, firmly rooted in a perpetual happiness transcending the senses, and do not deviate from the truth we have found, for we can think of nothing better."[25] To focus my own spiritual course and remind myself of the truth I have tasted in deep meditation, I often reflect on the following passage to examine the character of my decisions, and to distill every intuition and mystical insight. For me, this conveys the epitome of unconditional love-consciousness.

> "Love is patient, love is kind, love is not jealous. Love does not brag and is not arrogant. It always acts appropriately, and does not pursue things for selfish advantage. Love is not easily provoked, nor does it dwell on any wrongs it has suffered. It does not take pleasure in the wickedness of others, but rejoices in a life of truth. Love endures all things, is continually trusting, never ceases to hope, and endures anything. Love never fails."

New Testament, *1 Corinthians 13:10*

---

[25] *Bhagavad-Gita 6.21-22*

The Physical-Spiritual Balance

There will come a time when we mystically perceive more than we
can accept or incorporate into our consciousness or practical decision-
making. As eager as we may be to understand the vast mysteries of
existence, the parts of us that engage the world must of necessity
manage our time and energy, and choose pragmatically. In Stages of
Being, the idea was introduced that we arrive at a phase of spiritual
development where we choose to remain in the world to serve it. In
order to do this, and retain our sanity and connection with other
people, we will find a balance between expanding our spiritual
comprehension and applying this ever-increasing wisdom in our
day-to-day life. A friend of mine once described this as the tension
between living *physically* and living *spiritually*, recognizing that
spiritual life can, by its nature, remove us so far from the physical
world that we have trouble interfacing with it, while at the other
extreme reveling in our own physicality will retard our spiritual
growth. Jesus once described this balancing act as *being in the world
without being of the world.*[26]

Is some of what we encounter in our spiritual perception simply too
powerful or overwhelming for us at present? There will be times,
especially early on in our journey, when this is especially true. Part
of this has to do with the differences between *Head Time, Heart Time*
and *Spirit Time* – the progressively slower pace of deepening mystical
processes. In my own walk, there has been a tendency for spiritual
exploration to minimize the physical world. That is, once I taste
manna from heaven, worldly food seems bland and insubstantial.
And yet here we remain: the phone still rings, the bills still require
payment, a friend still desires our companionship, and all the
material dynamics of life still knock at the borders of our being. So in
response, as I have attempted to balance the world's demands with
the spiritual yearnings of my soul, I have sometimes closed the door
on eternal questions for a time. And yet, those few instances where I
remain receptive to the Universe – where I am able to pray without

[26] New Testament, *John 17:11-16*

ceasing – the incorporation of my new understanding into daily life has helped manage my physical existence. Yes, the world may view some of our spiritually motivated choices as folly – certainly as contrary to the status quo – but such moments, if they authentically stem from our deepening alignment with the Source of Life and Light, are inevitably attended by a sense of freedom and empowerment rather than sacrifice.

On the other hand, I have also experienced that instead of being edified and encouraged to do good by new knowledge, my ego has sometimes been inflated, and confidence in my own wisdom or abilities exaggerated. To return to humility, I must forget what I have learned for a while, or at the least resist applying my new understanding, and instead concentrate my efforts on simpler, less ego-inflating tasks. Service to others, for example, is always a good standard. There may come a day when I am ready, with purified intentions, to explore the intricacies of what I at first believed to be esoteric knowledge, or to wrangle with the more far-reaching manifestations of my will, but if I cannot subject my every wish and whim to the good of All, the preparation of my heart is inadequate to these tasks. Thankfully, one of the inherent benefits of progressive mystical practice is the constant reminder that prideful self-conceptions are but flimsy illusions, easily erased by union with the Absolute.

> Jesus, with the full knowledge that the Father had put everything into his hands – and that he had come from God and was going to God – rose from the supper-table, took off his clothes, picked up a towel and fastened it around his waist. Then he poured water into a basin and began to wash the disciple's feet and to dry them with the towel around his waist. And so he came to Simon Peter, who said to him, "Lord, are you going to wash my feet?" And Jesus replied, "You do not realize now what I am doing, but later on you will understand."
>
> New Testament, *John 13:3-7*

For many of us, there remains the question of how to be in a stressful workplace that constantly challenges our spiritual nature or overwhelms our gentler sensibilities. An enduring analogy of this tension is the worker who gets yelled at by their boss all day, witnesses conflicts and hostility among fellow employees, and is constantly reprimanded or warned by everyone that they are wasting too much time "being nice to people." The company's goals must be fulfilled! In varying degrees, this is an unfortunate reality for much of North America. At one time, my answer was to escape by starting my own business. In a superficial way, this worked quite well, as I could filter my exposure to unpleasant demands through managing my own schedule, spreading out new projects and client contact, and "firing" especially difficult customers. Even though I closed that first business years ago, I still keep in touch with a few of my favorite, long-term customers, because they are the kind of high-quality relationships cultivated in mutual respect and trust.

Of course, even though I believe the U.S. would be better off with many more such small businesses – and many fewer impersonal mega-conglomerates – clearly not everyone wants to be an entrepreneur, and the question remains as to whether such "escape" is really the wisest course in healing ourselves and our society. So how do we cope? How do we deal with government bureaucracy, nosy neighbors, a workplace that seeks to demean or antagonize us, traffic congestion, increasing crime, or any of the dozens of other seemingly permanent fixtures in modern human society?   This question brings us back to three fundamentals of mystical practice:

1. Evaluating our own stage of being,
2. Asking a lot of "whys" about our life, and
3. Continuing undaunted through our emotional transformation cycles and progressive contemplative states.

If we are in a phase of spiritual evolution where we believe we should exit a hostile, competitive, and materialistic world, hoping to cloister ourselves away or go on a lengthy journey in order to pursue our inner light, *then that is what we should do.* If, on the other hand, we are in a phase where we decide to remain immersed in the world in order to serve it, and from that place want to reshape every interaction – no matter where we find ourselves – into something loving and compassionate, *then that is what we should do.* And so on. The question is no longer "How can I cope with an unpleasant situation?" but rather, "I wonder what will happen around me when I begin doing what is honest, kind and patient, and live in integrity with who I truly am?" And that is when our underlying assumptions inevitably rise to the surface: Why do we want this job? What lifestyle choices have we made which led us to feeling "trapped" in our career? What expectations, values or societal pressures led to the personal choices that created our current lifestyle?

This is discussed further in the Lifestyle Choices chapter, so I won't go into more detail here; but suffice it to say that to live in productive spiritual-physical balance does require passion, faith, and courage – and we are never without options. Most critically, our focus as a mystic shifts away from consciously trying to alter our immediate environment, relinquishing that desire in favor of the inner transformation that inherently presents compassionate empowerment to the world. Because of who we are, things will change around us for the good of All. But we are not concerned with that external impact, only with being true to our convictions, and expressing the light of our own soul.

Dry Spells, Misreads and Forgetfulness

Mistakes are inevitable. Sometimes our interpretation of signs and patterns in our lives will miss the mark. Sometimes our assumptions or convictions, earnestly derived from mystical experience, will turn out to be sheer silliness. And sometimes we will simply forget to pay attention to obvious synchronicity or sound advice, and miss a turn in our path of spiritual progress. All of these come from the same place, and ultimately have the same remedy: they are the product of being human.

Some of the most commonly misinterpreted or overemphasized signs have to do with intimate relationships. Regardless of age or experience, falling into romantic love overwhelms our senses with the piercing realities of vulnerability and desire, and we are often easily convinced that we know what is best for ourselves and our lover – no matter how loudly anyone or anything testifies to the contrary. Even the most cynical curmudgeon seldom escapes such romantic rationalizations.

TRANIO

> I pray, sir, tell me, is it possible
> That love should of a sudden take such hold?

LUCENTIO

> O Tranio, till I found it to be true,
> I never thought it possible or likely;
> But see, while idly I stood looking on,
> I found the effect of love in idleness:
> And now in plainness do confess to thee,
> That art to me as secret and as dear
> As Anna to the queen of Carthage was,
> Tranio, I burn, I pine, I perish, Tranio,
> If I achieve not this young modest girl.

> William Shakespeare, *Taming of the Shrew*

Of course, our capacity for rationalization is not restricted to romance. Wanting anything too much – even the most transcendent, spiritually healthy thing – becomes a breeding ground for creative justification and imaginative distortion. A fulfilling vocation, peace and quiet, a close friend, words and actions which edify or heal, a like-minded community, definitive insight...all of these are worthwhile pursuits, but when we become invested to the point of rejecting any boundaries for our abilities and knowledge, and in our eagerness deny all fallibility and ignorance, we enter the realm of prideful deceit. It seems as though careful attention to our intentions would protect us from such missteps, but even if we begin with noble motives, a good idea can still be crippled by a lack of watchfulness, overconfidence, or willful disregard of new information. These situations are intrinsic to our humanity, and provide some of the most meaningful lessons for us when we pause to take note of them. Usually, however, we end up benefiting only after we have been tumbled and bruised by a fall.

Outside of misreading a situation because we desire a certain outcome, there are also times when spiritual perception is inaccessible. I call this "seer's block," and it can be disorienting and unnerving for those who come to rely on their mystical abilities. Our individual response to such a spiritual dry spell is telling. If we are frightened by our loss of sight, *why* are we frightened? If we are frustrated or angry because we cannot break through a veil of ignorance, *why* do we react this way? Have we become too attached to our mystical awareness? Are we out-of-balance, investing all of our well-being in our intimacy with the Divine, to the neglect of our worldly existence? As discussed in Warning Signs, sometimes we are so overwhelmed by a new stage of being that we reflexively shut down parts of ourselves – including spiritual perception – and disorientation, fear and frustration can be part of this plateau. Also mentioned earlier, friendly spirits may withdraw deliberately to help us grow in confidence and self-sufficiency. Yet even in these circumstances, being deprived of spiritual connection should be met with patience, humility, and renewed diligence to balancing our self-nourishing practices. For the more attached we become to anything, the less value it will have for our well-being and the good of those around us.

"There is nothing new except what is forgotten."
Mademoiselle Bertin, Hat-Maker of Marie Antoinette

I would like to say that my own forgetfulness is a natural consequence of aging, or the stresses I have chosen to endure, or perhaps a result of my diet. Unfortunately, there is an observable pattern in my life that belies such excuses. It does not matter how important a lesson, how profound a certainty, or how elated a discovery, there will be periods where my ability to recall such moments slips into the abyss – usually when I most desire to recall them. This is, in fact, so prevalent in my life, that without my journals close-at-hand I would have had tremendous difficulty completing this book. I recall Einstein's observation that it isn't necessary to know everything, just to know where to look it up. So I keep countless tomes of reference material nearby. But there have been moments of epiphany which, had I not had a voice recorder or pen and paper handy, would likely have been lost to me thereafter. Although friends and acquaintances frequently demonstrate they possess a recall more agile than my own, all of us can expect to forget the important spiritual lessons of our past. Even the heights of blissful mystical union tend to fade with time. The good news is that we will revisit everything we *need* to know. In the area of memory, we can be grateful that the Universe does not forget, but will persist in reminding us who we are and what we have to learn, until we finally integrate that understanding into how we live, feel, think and are.

There are many examples of misreads, forgetfulness and dry spells in my life. I have relied on intuition, vivid dreams, prayer, divination and other forms of spiritual commerce to inform many important – and unimportant – decisions. Over time, applying spiritual discernment and thoughtful consideration to each of them, I have increasingly found these practices to be unerring, and not at all ambiguous in their communications. But it is still easy to recall a once loyal and honest friend whose betrayal of trust completely blindsided me; or the job I was initially sure was a perfect match for me, but which alienated and debilitated my spirit; or the illness I was confident I understood, which then took an unexpected turn for the worse. And although such surprises have admittedly become less frequent with time, I am still grateful when they happen, for they remind me that mistakes are excellent teachers, and that I still have much to learn.

Accepting that these hiccups in discernment are bound to happen, what are some mature responses to apparent spiritual failure? One is to surround ourselves with wise and honest people, who know us well and are willing to remind us of our strengths and weaknesses. Another is to maintain self-nourishing disciplines, enhancing the clarity of our perception and purpose. Certainly, we will also improve our discernment through continued practice of what we already know. But perhaps the most important response is the same for any kind of mistake: to forgive ourselves, recognize our limitations, and welcome those humble, often humorous moments when we throw up our arms, relinquish all control, and begin again.

Apophenia

> "This deception of false feeling, and of the false sense of knowing which follows, has diverse and wonderful variations, stemming from the diversity of states and dispositions in those who are deceived."
>
> From *The Cloud of Unknowing*, by a 15th Century Christian Mystic

There is one last area to consider, and that is mental illness. Some people are subject to inspiring visions, lengthy dialogues with people others can't see, and powerful emotional and spiritual convictions – not because they have achieved mystical supersensory perception, but because their brain chemistry is impaired. I have interacted with schizophrenics who can't differentiate between real voices and imaginary ones, and bipolar disorder sufferers who believe they can do anything – no matter how incredible or irresponsible – when they are in a manic upswing. When I first reached out to alcohol and drug abusers who lived on the street, I was fooled many times by the paranoid certainty, delusions, and deceptive manipulation of which every addict is capable. Could some of these mental illnesses be an unfortunate gateway into mystical experience? Perhaps, but rarely. More commonly, such events, which are similar to spiritual cognizance only in their sense of subjective reality, do nothing more than reinforce the fears and delusions of the mentally ill. Freud described such events as "omnipotence of thought," where the mind imposes imaginary control over reality out of neurotic or narcissistic compulsion. A more recent term offered by Klaus Conrad is *apophenia*.

Apophenia describes a condition where the mind perceives patterns and meaning where none actually exist. An example most of us can relate to is the toddler who hides beneath their blankets at night, absolutely sure the shadows in the corner of their bedroom are a malevolent monster. In the same vein, skeptics of mystical experience are quick to conclude that changes in brain activity through mystic activators may only be generating apophenic illusions in receptive minds. Will science ever resolve this dispute? Emerging approaches such as neurotheology and neurophenomenology offer promising potential, but as yet have not focused on differentiating spiritually healthy cognitive processes from unhealthy ones. For instance, we can now say that "suspending parietal lobe function" may induce a sense of timeless oneness with the Universe, but we cannot evaluate the quality of that experience, or its impact on human development, without the context of dynamic and comprehensive wisdom such as that provided by our spiritual traditions.

For now, the lesson for a mentally healthy spiritual seeker is that the lines between imaginative constructs, mental disorders, and helpful mystical awareness are not always definite. However, the outcome of authentic mysticism is enhanced self-awareness, a greatly enriched personal life and humane contribution to society; whereas the outcome of untreated mental illness is continued suffering, a paucity of self-awareness, spiritual stagnation, and a socially unproductive existence. That is one way we can ultimately test the validity of our mystical experience: does it bear positive spiritual fruit, or does it only antagonize our growth, stifle our wisdom, and impede our compassion?

Throwing Out the Bathwater

> "Just as you can't make love if you think too much about it, so you can't *be* love if you think too much about it."
>
> Ram Dass, from his Foreword to *The Varieties of Meditative Experience*

There are those who would say of everything written here and elsewhere about mysticism: "Just forget what you have learned. Throw it out and start over. None of this is true. There are no teachers, no valid methods, no profound precepts, and no meaningful exercises. All such pursuits are futile. If you grasp at the truth this way, you will lose it." While certain advocates of this response might indeed be anti-spiritual, others have been spiritual teachers themselves. Consider the lives and teachings of Moses, Mahavira, Jesus, Buddha, Muhammad, Martin Luther or Baha'u'llah: all of them railed against the conventions of their time. In fact, the message of freeing ourselves from preconceptions and expectations of what something is – truth, power, spirit, soul, love, Deity, consciousness, Self, Universe, existence – is the central message of nearly every notable revolutionary throughout history. The great thinkers of religion, philosophy, art, science, and social activism have slapped the status quo in the face to enable change, only to be revered as models and the basis for whole systems in later times. And there is another decisive commonality among these agents of change: before they emerged into their own versions of brilliant, radical innovation, they most often first immersed themselves existing beliefs, customs, and teachings. Those would-be agitators who did not first ground themselves in an understanding of history and tradition were usually destined to become, as Voltaire once wrote, "rebellious without a cause, factious without design," soon to be swept under the carpet of a forgotten, misspent life. From this we can speculate on a general principle: that in order to "let go," we must first fully comprehend and even embrace whatever we wish to be free of.

> "I maintain the Truth is a pathless land, and you cannot approach it by any path whatsoever…The moment you follow someone you cease to follow Truth."
>
> Jiddu Krishnamurti [27]

---

[27] From *Moments of Enlightenment* by Robert Ullman & Judyth Reichenberg-Ullman

At the other extreme, there is also a strong Western tradition of trying to understand a thing's usefulness through theoretical discourse and logical constructions. If you want to make the most use of a powerful telescope, so the argument goes, you had better learn the basic principles of astrophysics – or at least have an operating manual handy. After all, pointing such a finely crafted instrument randomly around the heavens won't help you understand the visible Universe, but only provide a smattering of blurry images and empty space. In order to coalesce any observation into knowledge, the Western mind desires structure, process, and at least a hypothetical context within which to appreciate new information: a logical operating manual. If only mysticism conformed to this way of thinking! But it doesn't, for mysticism posits that we can't rely *exclusively* on the logical, the sequential, or the analytical, and that we won't reap the full benefits of mystical experience by imposing such systems on it. We can approach, examine and hypothesize over a gnosis of the Absolute from without using purely rational means, carefully constructing an interpretation of our experience, but arriving at that gnosis is another matter altogether.

This is not to say that mysticism intends to "subvert a belief in the power of reason, science, and technology to render society and the human experience rational and free," [28] but rather that, regardless of whatever aspect of our reality we are trying to decipher, reliance on linear reasoning can only get us so far. For there is always a gap between what we perceive and how we interpret that perception, and that gap must be filled by trust in something. In the natural and applied sciences, the gap of trust is mainly occupied by a system of evolving assumptions, empirical tests of those assumptions, and a metric of fixed, often dualistic analysis. Although a level of indeterminacy and non-linear dynamics has been tolerated and even incorporated into these fields – systems theory and quantum physics are rife with examples – logic still reigns supreme. But in the gnosis of the Absolute, where we will consistently encounter fundamental paradoxes and subtle gradients of Truth, the gap of trust is occupied

---

[28] From *Re-Enchanting Humanity* by Murray Bookchin

by faith, or love, or stillness, or detachment, or disciplined concentration, or other letting go of fixed relationships and expectations, permitting spiritual cognizance to blossom. These evaluation and actuation mechanisms are different from logic, but they are an equally innate capacity, extraordinarily beneficial in their own right, and no less deserving of our trust.

Einstein described many theoretical possibilities for our Universe, many of which could not be empirically verified until long after he proposed them [29] – some are still debated today. And yet his ideas gained broad acceptance because he spoke the language of mathematics, a language shared and accepted by many others. But the language of mystical experience, though appreciated and understood across disparate cultures and throughout centuries of spiritual practice, is spoken by very few in the West. For those who are more comfortable filling the gap of trust with logic, *lingua mystica* lacks the glamorous evidentiary precision and rational transparency so highly honored and respected in Western culture. In the end, if the light of reason is the only recourse for doubt, then that light must be introduced into the mystical process itself, and that can only happen through direct experience. We must simply sit down at the telescope and take a look. For anyone willing to travel a while down the mystic's way, a compelling confirmation of an alternative and viable perception-cognition is waiting to be had.

> "This is the source from which so many controversies arise – that people either do not properly explain their own thoughts, or do not properly interpret those of other people; for, in truth, when they most contradict one another, they either think the same things or something different, so that those things which they suppose to be errors and absurdities in another person are not so."
>
> Spinoza, *The Nature and Extent of Knowledge*

---

[29] For example, an expanding universe under General Relativity, later observed by Edwin Hubble.

North American culture, as a fast-paced and highly commercialized subset of Western civilization, has historically demonstrated a strong predilection for easily-packaged conclusions, black-and-white reasoning, and oversimplified discourse. Until such habits are softened by wisdom, or the next phase of our socioeconomic evolution relaxes popular fear of complexity, there will always be critics of mysticism in the U.S. At the same time, our societal disposition adds tremendous value to the mystical process: in its diversity of viewpoints, its reflexive skepticism, its curiosity for all things new – these are all wonderful additions to our spiritual toolkit, and as ever are helpful agitators of the imperfect status quo. But mysticism does not meet the skeptic half-way: the search for immediate gratification and external validation must end before the mystic's journey can begin.

Today, I will try to maintain the joyful, loving and accepting equilibrium of my heart; the quiet, detached and reflective state of my mind; and the peaceful, expansive and all-embracing disposition of my spirit. To me, these are the essential qualities of an integrated, harmonized existence, the full fruits of mystical effort and careful intention, and the only meaningful evidence of an "unutterable importance that vouches for itself."[30] Everything else is secondary. All knowledge, all abilities, all achievement, everything past and everything to come…these things are interesting, to be sure, but utterly without significance. For all such phenomena are simply an outpouring of what Divinely is, and who I inherently am, and I have every confidence that they are no more than the moment which has just occurred, and no less than the preparation required to meet whatever arrives next.

For an astute and detailed examination and comparison of scientific and metaphysical thought, please read Franklin Merrell-Wolff's *Transformations in Consciousness*.

For ongoing exploration of mystical consciousness and the cognitive sciences, I recommend the *Journal of Consciousness Studies*; see www.imprint.co.uk/jcs.html.

---

[30] William James

Chapter Questions

1. If mystical awareness is available to everyone and anyone, why has it been so assiduously resisted as a natural skill in Western culture?
2. If you have a highly developed sense of intuition, but the consequences of your actions seem equally divided between positive and negative results, what might that indicate about your intentions, self-awareness, or self-esteem?
3. How should we decide when to act on our spiritual perceptions, and when to remain still?
4. What is the difference between "common sense" and "discernment?"
5. What do "holiness," "worship" or "spiritual union" mean to you?
6. Why is it important for us to pay attention to our own mystical awareness, without expecting others to think of it as consequential?
7. What is the single most important characteristic of all insight?

Part Three: Practical Applications

8. "JUST for TODAY:" a MEDITATIVE PRACTICE

Why have I waited until so late in the book to introduce a specific meditative practice? Because I believe all that has gone before is critical to your success in applying this discipline. To have an internal compass of the golden intention; an understanding of how we assemble meaning for our lives; an appreciation of self-esteem and self-awareness and their importance in spiritual growth; insight into the miraculous power of your own soul; the relevance of meditation for self-nourishing practice and mystical awareness; the importance of self-sufficiency; and at long last the real point of it all: your potential to live a rich, fulfilling and purposeful life as you progress through new stages of being. Without this foundation and framework for your efforts, meditation and all its permutations will not be as productive; in fact, it has the potential to become nothing more than "consecrated narcissism." [31] I only hope that the process outlined here will serve you as well as it has served me.

There are two types of meditative practice covered in this chapter: a walking meditation, called "Just for Today," which is a fairly straightforward and sequential series of conceptual reflection meditations, and a sitting meditation that integrates some of the more advanced mystic activators. Here is how these practices fit into our current categorization of approaches:

---

[31] Thomas Merton

	Meditation Technique	Potential Mystic Activators
"Just for Today" walking meditations (combined)	• Conceptual Reflection • Self-Inquiry • Watchfulness	• Perfection of Love • Synchronistic/Symbolic Ritual • Subtractive Meditation
"Source of Life and Light" sitting meditation	• Single-Focus Concentration • Conceptual Reflection	• Perfection of Love • Synchronistic/Symbolic Ritual • Subtractive Meditation
"Controlled Breathing" sitting meditation	• Watchfulness • Direct Activation	• Subtractive Meditation • Ecstatic Induction
"Fountain of Light" sitting meditation	• Direct Activation • Watchfulness • Single-Focus Concentration	• Synchronistic/Symbolic Ritual • Subtractive Meditation • Ecstatic Induction

The "Just for Today" meditative model is inspired by Mikao Usui's principles for Reiki practitioners, which in turn is said to have been derived from "The Five Meiji Principles." Though by no means intended to augment or replace Usui Sensei's instruction, I utilize Just for Today as a central part of my own spiritual habits, to prepare and align myself each morning and to maintain integrity and purpose throughout the day. These meditations reinforce the values and attitudes I feel are important, and coincide with the core teachings of many ancient belief systems – both mystical and non-mystical. They are also meant to be a useful tool for any seeker of spiritual evolution, regardless of their religious affiliation, as they can provide a wealth of self-awareness and spiritual fortitude by helping encourage progressive contemplative states, as well as reinforcing the golden intention.

These "walking meditations" are divided into three groups. The initial twenty-seven Meditations of Preparation are intended to prepare the heart and mind for mystical gnosis. Whether this will be effective for everyone is not a claim I wish to make; even for me, the effectiveness of each meditation has changed over time, and may continue to do so. The next section, the seven Meditations of Initiation, are an immediate departure point for transitions through gnosis – potential mystic activators – and are best reserved for a quiet, ego-free moment when the preparatory meditations have been comfortably practiced and deeply understood for some time. The last group, the Meditations of Culmination & Continuation, are the beginning of a new journey, easily fathomed in the context of a deepening gnosis of the Absolute.

Just for Today

Meditations of Preparation

Just for today, patience and acceptance in all things
Just for today, nothing has to be wrong
Just for today, acknowledgment without prejudice in every situation
Just for today, courage to be compassionate and kind to all
Just for today, embracing the Natural Realm as part of self, with honor and respect for all
Just for today, remembering the well-being of others, nourishing them through being well
Just for today, transforming all things into the good of All
Just for today, faith which far exceeds all hopes, desires and fears
Just for today, insight and understanding into fruitful conduct
Just for today, listening from stillness, and seeing what is
Just for today, confidence without arrogance, and humility without passivity
Just for today, clarity and sincerity in purpose and intentions
Just for today, balance in caring for the house of Self and all the selves within
Just for today, tranquility in relinquishing ego, and flowing with the Source of Life and Light
Just for today, a generous spirit, free from attachment and expectation
Just for today, being in the now, without illusions
Just for today, honesty and integrity in all situations
Just for today, thoughts and words that edify, encourage and inspire
Just for today, with each breath, breathing in wholeness and vitality

Just for today, diligence and mindfulness in every moment
Just for today, persisting gratitude from the heart, and celebration in every
    action and interaction
Just for today, filled with Divine laughter, the heart sings
Just for today, ease and simplicity in every choice
Just for today, a living example with conviction and contentment
Just for today, creating something, destroying nothing
Just for today, great care with whims and wishes
Just for today, the soul is never compromised

Meditations of Initiation

Just for this moment, love, devotion, completion
Just for this moment, mind touching the INFINITE beyond the Infinite
Just for this moment, welcoming the LIGHT behind the Light [32]
Just for this moment, body warmed by a single illuminating flame
Just for this moment, spirit lost in union with the Beloved
Just for this moment, soul resting in the depths of never having known
Just for this moment, ... [33]

Meditations of Culmination & Continuation

Just for today, there is no difference, and no concept of difference
Just for today, there is only now, brimming with eternity
Just for today, surrender; pierced by the Absolute, ceasing to exist

What is the Intended Meaning of Each Meditation of Preparation?

In general, each meditation can be directed toward ourselves, toward
others, toward all that we understand to exist, toward a Deity we
worship, or toward the unknown. There are therefore many
implications for each meditation. Repeating the meditations, each

---

[32] I often add: "through which all things come into being."
[33] The ever-diminishing silence, or the silence behind the silence.

time with a unique audience or objective in mind (or none at all), can thereby achieve multiple meanings.

Although I want to avoid nailing down the aspects of each and every meditation, and won't discuss the Initiation and Continuation groups at all as of yet, here are some suggested approaches to interpretation for Meditations of Preparation:

> *Just for today, nothing has to be wrong*

There is no reason to expect failure today, in one's self, in others, in the world around us, or in the Universe itself. There can be harmony everywhere, and we can be both an agent of positive change and a recipient of blessing. As with many of the meditations, this can be a request, an assertion, a personal commitment, or all three at once.

> *Just for today, acknowledgment without prejudice in every situation*

This is the attitude of perceiving without judging. We can acknowledge what we experience, what we feel and what we observe around us without prejudicing those perceptions, that is, without pre-judging them by associating them with our past or with negative or positive assumptions. Instead, we can rely on compassion and intuition to guide our responses. At the same time, the idea is to actively acknowledge, and not ignore, what is happening around us.

> *Just for today, remembering the well-being of others, nourishing them through being well*

More than just intentions, this is an act of love. To remember and act upon what is nourishing to another's well-being…through a conscious focus on what is *best for all*, including ourselves. "Being well" means nourishing ourselves, and through it nourishing others. This could be helping someone move furniture, or praying with them for healing, or a more indirect artifact of will. At its center, this practice shifts the focus from ourselves to others for the good of the

Whole, and also acknowledges the influence on distant events acting in agape – in full and unconditional love-consciousness – can achieve.

Just for today, transforming all things into the good of All

This is both an orientation and an invocation. Here we demonstrate our confidence in good, align our will with all that is healing, constructive, illuminating and enriching. Anything that happens in our lives is transformed by the forces we summon, and to which our will contributes, to effect positive change both in us and through us into the world. How we individually conceive of these forces originating and manifesting is important...for that *is* our belief system. But by inviting them to work with us and through us to the good of All, we align ourselves with the Source of Life and Light. When I first began, I phrased this: "Just for today, welcoming goodness and light into the world."

Just for today, faith which far exceeds all hopes, desires and fears

A faith in what, exactly? The practitioner's own beliefs and the context of the moment guide them here: faith in our own discernment, in benevolent Deity, in Love or Fate, in the Tao or The Way Things Are....For me, this is a faith which trusts the Source of Life and Light to guide all of existence into its most spiritually productive course. The meditation helps me let go of outcomes, and focus on how I am being – right now.

Just for today, clarity and sincerity in purpose and intentions

Having clarity in our purpose and intentions is a wonderful beginning down the road to satisfaction and peace. If my purpose is unclear to me, this meditation becomes a question – a question that *expects* an answer in my mind and heart. Sometimes the answer comes immediately, if I am ready. Sometimes it may be months, or even years, as I consciously (or less-than-consciously) learn and change, before I begin to feel a certainty about why I am on this planet. The treasure is not in the knowing, but in the seeking. I have often added to this meditation to make it more specific, though that risks closing myself to other possibilities that are more intimately suited to who I am or am becoming – however, this is what I frequently append: "...as a healing, loving and creative presence in the world."

Just for today, listening from stillness, and seeing what is

This denotes listening to one's own whisperings of Self, to the subtle signs and evidences in the world around us, to the emotional and intentioned content of another's speech and actions, and to the mysterious promptings in our spiritual perception. To hear properly, I believe we must be still, both in terms of our physical nervousness, our emotional demeanor and our mental noise. Stillness is, then, a state of complete calm that both precedes and results from a meditative state. It is also, fundamentally, a spiritual openness guarded only by good intentions, strong faith and sound practices. From that space we can *perceive what is* – the form of reality beyond what blind habit conditions us to accept.

Just for today, balance in caring for the house of Self, and all the selves within

To accept the meaning of this meditation as it is intended is to embrace a certain approach to self-awareness. This asserts that although we are one person we are made up of many selves, each with its own agenda, wants and unique personality. There are different ways to view this. For instance, each aspect of self might be created by me to cope with, and adapt to, various events in my life in the form of an internalized persona or "social mask;" or they may represent something inherent to my psyche, such as the shadow (i.e. alter ego, id), the anima (the soul), the unconscious will, or the ego. In any case, using active imagination I have since consciously developed them into characters and creatures that live in my "house." It is my responsibility to love them, care for them, heal them and – ultimately – integrate them. Through entering into dialogue with these characters, I come to know my "selves" better: what each of them expects from me for nourishment, contentment and reassurance. With this understanding, I am more fully able to transform any dysfunctional personas through self-nourishing practices and evolving values and beliefs, and allow my most authentic and individuated "self" to emerge with confidence.

My house of Self represents both my physical body and my framework of constructs, ideals and values. This framework is a physical representation in my mind, with rooms and levels, walls and towers, each with specific purpose and significance. My house contains the whole of me as I grow in understanding and realization. It is where my personas and underlying identity live in safety and warmth. This meditation therefore implies a continued practice of engaging and nourishing my inner selves, and reinforcing, reinventing and rebuilding my beliefs. I am very grateful for the counseling that introduced this approach to me.

> *Just for today, tranquility in relinquishing ego, and flowing with the Source of Life and Light*

This is about giving up control. Letting go without fear. By ego, I mean stubborn willfulness, pride and arrogance. As to what the "Source of Life and Light" is, one's own beliefs can guide them here. In this way, I align my will with the universal forces of creation I believe in, accepting that the Universe doesn't need me to fix it.

> *Just for today, a generous spirit, free from attachment and expectation*

On one level this simply repeats the sentiment of letting go. On another, it describes a basic approach to the act of letting go: the belief that holding onto things (an immutable idea of self, a strong desire for something, an expectation of the world, a powerful emotional response) is what enslaves a human soul to suffering, and ultimately to harmful thoughts and actions that are provoked by that suffering. This meditation is meant to disengage us from the desires and intentions that distort our love and compassion into things like selfishness, possessiveness and greed.

Just for today, with each breath, breathing in wholeness and vitality

I will often accompany this meditation with several deep, slow breaths. I also practice Reiki on myself throughout this and other meditations, inviting wholeness and vitality to well up inside me. Like the house of Self meditation, this represents the principle that I must consciously nourish and care for myself, and actualizes that principle. Directed towards someone else who has asked for healing, this becomes an *artifact of will* to that end.

Just for today, diligence and mindfulness in every moment

In one way, this refers to the Buddhist concept of mindfulness – of paying careful attention to the present. It also invokes the Christian ideas of self-restraint and self-discipline. There is also an element of Sufi watchfulness involved, which is both similar to, and subtly different than either of these. Through diligence and mindfulness I remember who I am, what I am, and what I am doing here. In this meditation, I also commit to remembering and practicing all the other meditations throughout the day, being as conscious and deliberate as I can in every moment.

Just for today, filled with Divine laughter, the heart sings

I must thank Hafiz for this meditation. To read his poems is to feel the fulfillment of these words and realize the totality of their meaning. One important measure of my own well-being is whether I have been laughing aloud – as in carefree knee-slapping guffaws – over the course of my day.

Creating a Daily "Walking Meditation" Habit

There are undoubtedly as many approaches to learning as there are people in the world. However, here are some things you may find useful in refining your practice:

1. Pick a meditation from the list that appeals to you.

2. Spend a day or two memorizing it.

3. Begin to think about it each morning as you go about your regular routine. Ponder its meaning. Repeat it to yourself with varying emphasis on words and phrasing.

4. Throughout the day, speak it aloud as a question, as an affirmation, as a declaration. Apply it thoughtfully to your interactions and your responses in each new situation.

5. Speak it silently, and feel it in your heart as a hope, as a desire, as a belief, and as an acceptance of what is.

6. Literally and symbolically, try breathing *in* the words, meaning, and potency. Now try breathing them *out*.

7. In a moment of uninterrupted quiet, make the meditation an all-encompassing presence: let it fill you up as a sound, as a color of light, as a sensation of warmth. Flood your body, mind and spirit with its possibilities.

8. Once you feel the depth and breadth of one meditation, let it go. Forget it for now and move on to another. Continue this process over weeks and months – at a pace that does not feel forced or rushed – until you have danced through the entire list.

9. Begin the process again, only this time in the order they are written. It may go faster this time, it may not. Try grouping two or more Just for Todays together into one continuous meditation. Try connecting some of the groupings you have memorized into one uninterrupted stream of thought...a prayer without ceasing which you feel in your heart.

10. Break things up again into individual ideas. Now that you know the words, avoid going too quickly through the list as you recite it. Take time to reconsider each idea, weigh each word, understand each principle on an emotional, spiritual and practical level before continuing your meditation.

11. Reduce through practice the gap between comprehension and self-expression. Let these meditations become part of you, and let yourself become part of them.

12. At the end of your day, repeat the meditations again and consider the impact they have had on your thoughts, feelings and choices.

Through such an approach, we enable a rich tapestry of meaning in our meditation, and a powerful manifestation of good in our lives. When we live our lives as a continuous meditation-in-action, without division between thinking, feeling and doing, a harmony begins, an interplay of comprehension, conviction and sensation that gain momentum, and something deeper like a force of nature wells up through our practice to strengthen the very fiber of what every moment means to us.

Dilution Through Repetition

Dilution through repetition is a challenge for any practice. Sometimes, I will take a day off, or let the concepts course through my mind unattended, without structure. Sometimes I will let myself forget whole ideas, entire meditations, and revisit and rediscover them in the following weeks. It is a game with myself, really, to keep from being bored with rote or inadvertently allow meditation to become empty habit. On the other hand, repeating words without thought to meaning has a strong tradition in meditative practice as well, so that may be yet another approach to fresh understanding.

How Can this Practice be Deepened?

Through living the words. Through being surprised by their
newness after years of repetition. Through suspending certainty in
what they truly mean, and being open to new potentials. By holding
all of these meditations at once within the art of suspension. The key
is not the mind's grasp of truth, but the heart's practice of it, lifted in
the worshipful ascension of spirit. Return to emptiness and revisit
them there. Renew perspective for each meditation by applying
them within the many different artifacts of will. I enjoy reciting my
Just for Todays each morning when I go for a walk – a walking
meditation of perhaps thirty minutes. After I think each phrase or
utter it aloud, I listen to the silence afterwards, noticing the reactions
of my heart, mind, body and spirit. When I am finished, I open
myself to whatever is around me and revel in the present. In the
evenings, I will repeat this process as a reflection on my day.

Adding Your Own Personal Meditations

Sometimes I'll try out a new meditative idea for a while, to see what
impact it has on my life. The fertile ones tend to stay in the list, while
the empty ones fall away on their own. This is a process of
distillation, and may also happen for you with what I have already
written or what you decide to add yourself. Success lies in reflecting
on why something has suddenly become important to you, while
other things have become less critical: is this evidence of your
deepening self-awareness, a weakness you wish to avoid addressing,
or an expansion of your spiritual perception?

Is the Order Important?

For me, the order is...a matter of interdependent meaning. I have
changed it and will likely continue rearranging it for this reason.
Perhaps that has been part of keeping it new for me. However, some
combinations have proven more resilient than others, and those have

resulted in the order you see here. In particular, it is important to understand how Initiation follows Preparation, and Continuation follows Initiation. I practiced the Preparation meditations for several years before encountering the underlying Initiation meditations, and have only begun to explore those fully. Occasionally, I will brush against the Meditations of Culmination & Continuation, which I believe are the very heart of mystical orientation, but I admittedly do not have a persistent grasp of these, only a passing, partial and very humble glimpse every now and then. However, even as I haltingly proceed into a broader sense of unknowing and divestment of selfhood, I still return to the "preparatory" meditations as a helpful part of my ongoing practice. This revisiting of fundamental practice helps to both perpetuate degrees of harmonized existence, and reflectively assess progress. Like "returning to emptiness," moving forward often requires distillation and simplification. So take your time, enjoy the process, and send me a note via *www.searchforclarity.com* when you reach the Center – the essence of your own personal mystical understanding – for I would love to hear what that place looks like to you.

And that is what I have discovered so far about these walking meditations. I trust there is more to come, and have left few of them without clarification to encourage your own exploration of meaning and purpose.

Integrated Sitting Meditation

Assuming we have developed a strong self-awareness, healthy self-esteem, are well-practiced in the continuous refinement of our intentions, and are ready for departure into more advanced meditative techniques, is there an "ideal" mystic activator? A one-size-fits-all methodology for seekers of Truth? To answer this, let's return to a discussion of the perceptive faculties of emotion and intellect and examine two contrasting statements.

> "[Mysticism] is essentially a movement of the heart, seeking to transcend the limitations of the individual standpoint and surrender itself to ultimate Reality; for no personal gain, to satisfy no transcendental curiosity, to obtain no other-worldly joy, but purely from an instinct of love."
>
> Evelyn Underhill, *Mysticism, A Study in the Nature and Development of Spiritual Consciousness*

> "Religious mysticism is a delight of the God-consciousness in some form of fellowship, and is a delight that can be felt. Mysticism in the Upanisads has not this import. It denies the ripple in love. It denies the joy in beauty. It denies the concrete, it denies the common. It denies the vivid feeling and joyous consciousness."
>
> Mahendranath Sircar, *Hindu Mysticism According to the Upanisads*

At first, these approaches seem to contradict: one emphasizing an experience anchored in love, and the other denying all emotions as it pursues reductive concentration. But from this contrast of focus a synergy is created. Both of these writers conclude elsewhere in their work that mystical consciousness transcends both heart and mind, and that any attempt to encapsulate a gnosis of the Absolute in emotional, intellectual or sensual terms falls short of the truth. It is natural, however, to want to emphasize one path over another or to define the spiritual in empirical or scientific terms. In response to this, I have proposed not only that our Pyramid of Self contains a spiritual cognizance which is a separate faculty from ordinary senses, emotions and intellect, but also that the process of mystic realization most readily occurs when competing viewpoints and emphases are equally embraced and integrated. For where opposing dispositions meet, a unifying fabric from which both have been constructed is revealed.

Not that the mystical can't be felt with the heart alone, or perceived by the intellect alone, or even induced through physiological means alone, but it is a synergy of these avenues with direct spiritual cognizance which incepts our most fertile experience of gnosis. Discovering this requires mental discipline, patience, and faith in the ultimate guidance of our Divine Spark in concert with the Source of Life and Light. We may explore different methods, following the path of the heart for a time, or an ascetic discipline, or a particular mental process, perhaps vacillating between extremes until we discover a profitable synergy. And in pursuing our mystical course, something miraculous occurs: we arrive in a sensual, emotional and intellectual absorption of the Now; an absorption moderated by detachment from – and sometimes even a complete negation of – those very faculties. It is an inexpressible state, where we will of necessity revisit the principle of dialectic synthesis through the art of suspension, and where complete understanding can only be achieved through *being*. So to answer the question of whether an "ideal" mystical activator exists, I can only conclude that there are various systems of meditation which combine different activators, but there is probably no single, ideal practice suitable for everyone. However, one fruitful approach for me has been to assimilate the essence of different disciplines, combining them into one seamless event, nudged into its most rewarding orientation through the golden intention.

> "Every statement about the transcendental is to be avoided because it is invariably only a laughable presumption on the part of the human mind, which is unconscious of its limitations."
>
> Carl Jung, from his commentary in *The Secret of the Golden Flower*

Tracking Your Progress with Contemplative and Emotional States

Contemplative States	Cycle of Emotional Transformation
1. **Simple Reflection:** We become consciously aware of all phenomena and begin reflecting on them.	1. **Recognition:** We recognize and acknowledge our current emotional state.
2. **Contemplative Self-Awareness:** We become consciously aware of the process of *simple reflection* as it occurs in us from moment-to-moment, observing and evaluating the qualities of this process.	2. **Examination:** Without judgment or overreaction, we examine and accept our emotions.
3. **Suspended Valuation:** We consciously suspend valuation altogether, and just observe our experiences, thoughts, feelings and physical sensations without placing them in the context of our values, beliefs or assumptions.	3. **Admission:** We admit to ourselves that change would be beneficial – that having a different emotional state would be more healthy and productive.
4. **Non-Thought Awareness:** We let go of both valuations and any thought process, entering into a state of mental, emotional and sensory quiet – even though we may still be consciously observing this state in ourselves, we do not reflect on it.	4. **Detachment:** We let go of the counterproductive feelings – that is, relax our emotional state until is greatly diminished, or dissipates completely. We may also choose to relinquish some of the underlying beliefs or assumptions that brought this state about.
5. **Non-Thought Non-Awareness:** We stop acknowledging even the supersensory, just as we did the sensory, and directly experience the bedrock of our own existence – the foundations of our sense of self and our relationship to the Universe.	5. **Equilibrium:** We achieve a state of neutral and objective calm where we can decide in which emotional direction we wish to go next.
6. **Non-Being Awareness:** We cease to discriminate between the state of non-thought non-awareness and any independently constructed sense of self – we come to identify ourselves with this state and thus develop a subjective submersion in "non-being."	6. **Commitment:** We choose a specific new emotional direction and begin to actuate that state.
7. **Non-Being Non-Awareness:** Where self-awareness and other-awareness – and any acknowledgement of subject and object – completely evaporate.	7. **Action:** We facilitate and support the newly chosen state with reinforcing actions, thoughts, beliefs, experiences, etc.

Although each spiritual tradition has different numbers of states, stations or stages, and uses different names and subsets of characteristics – emphasizing heart over mind, mind over heart, or transcendent sense over both heart and mind – I believe the contemplative-emotive process occurs intuitively throughout all of them, even where it is not specifically identified. If this is indeed true, then the contemplative-emotive model can be used to design an integrated meditative practice. It can also be used gauge the aftereffects of our experiences and measure our progress. Without being distracted from a tranquil, compassionate and empowered existence, you can consider these states as you move forward, evaluating the impact they have on your life. But remember the most important caveat in mystical experience: if we are forever trying to interpret, define and compartmentalize our moments of enlightenment, we are preventing the enrichment of our being by holding on to our ideas. Instead, continually refresh the habit of letting go, and simply enjoy the indescribable light that flourishes within and without.

> "Just as catching a fish takes as long as it takes for the fish to
> bite, so it is with meditation. There is no guarantee the fish will
> bite today. We must simply work and accept the results when
> they come."
>
> Tsung Hwa Jou, *Tao of Meditation*

Synergy in Practice

The following are experimental exercises that sample each of the different categories of mystic activator – drawing from many different traditions – with the objective of combining them into one meditative practice. The combined meditation is meant to be sequential – the first two being comfortably and independently mastered before attempting to integrate them into the third. For each, find a quiet, undisturbed place of solitude to practice. Expect to set aside thirty minutes for each of the first two exercises – even if you only meditate for fifteen minutes, having the quiet, unhurried space surrounding these fifteen minutes is essential.   Afterwards, you may want to just sit for a while, and it is also helpful to have a bottle of water handy to rehydrate without having to get up. Remember also that such exercises will be of little benefit, and may in fact be harmful to you, if you have not sufficiently conditioned your mind and heart to the art of letting things happen, matured your contemplative awareness through the Just for Today meditations and the intuitive practices outlined in the Mystic's Way, and developed a strong love-consciousness through continually refined intentions.   In addition, lethargy, sleepiness, restlessness and distracting thoughts during meditation can best be addressed by maintaining a healthy and balanced routine of self-nourishing practices…and by persisting in daily meditation.   As with any mystic activators, these may be difficult to master, demanding commitment, patience and a solid understanding of previous   chapters.   A suggested process of integration will follow the meditation descriptions.

Inviting the Source of Life and Light.   This meditation invokes a similar orientation of mind and heart to praying without ceasing, and is in essence a form of contemplative prayer. Before you begin this exercise, you will want to decide how you view the Source according to your own belief system – whether Deity, spiritual force, the energies of Nature, the substrate of reality, or an entirety of the Cosmos. Begin with a sincere commitment and invocation of "May this be for the good of All."   With eyes closed, consider your idea of the Source, opening your imagination to the Divine Presence. For some traditions, this may of necessity be a compassionate intermediary for the Source, but the ideas is to get *as intimately close as you can.* When you begin, you may want to repeat the name you have for the Source, first aloud, then silently, and then only as a memory in your heart. Remain receptive and unguarded, accepting and appreciative. This is your conscious connection to the Source, the force that creates and sustains you, animating your body, thoughts, emotions and spirit. Without the Source, you would not exist.   However your faith inspires you, express your gratitude. Expand your heart to receive this infinitely loving Presence. Express your longing for greater closeness, and your unconditional devotion – in words, in song, in the motion of your body, or however you are moved. Don't hold back or constrain your feelings, thoughts, word or actions. Release from the depths of your being a swelling wave of passionate adoration, and keep your awareness wide open to an intimate rejoinder from the Source itself. If joy or pain or laughter or tears overwhelm you, let them come. Feel as deeply and as honestly as you can, for as long as you can, and flow into a complete transparency of vulnerable being, embracing the depths of your communion.

Controlled Breathing. Begin with a sincere commitment and invocation of "May this be for the good of All." Consciously relax your body, starting with your hands and feet, then working your way towards your torso: legs, then arms, then shoulders, and neck. Place your hands in your lap as you sit comfortably, breathing easily and deeply through your nose and down into your stomach – that is, breath deeply without lifting or moving your shoulders, but by "inflating" your stomach with each breath. Do this for several minutes. Now begin to slow your breathing, still keeping it deep and even. At the crest of your inhaled breath, hold your breath for a moment – not long, just a second or so – and then slowly exhale. At the end of your exhale, pause for another few seconds, and breathe in again. Continue breathing deep into your abdomen – that is, without moving your shoulders or chest. Continue pausing at the end of each inhale and exhale until you are comfortable doing so. Now lengthen these pauses – not so much that you become light-headed or short of breath, but as long as possible. You may find you begin to breathe even more slowly and deeply. Try to fall into a consistent rhythm, so that you are no longer conscious of the breathing itself. Release your thoughts, your emotions, your concerns, and any images in your mind, until there is only a soft, velvety emptiness within you. *Listen to your breathing with your heart,* from the center of your emotional self, until your hearing and physical senses fade away. Now listen to the silent emptiness you have created within yourself, and relax into that space. If an idea or image keeps returning to your thoughts, or an emotion keeps distracting you, hold them with gentle consideration until they dissipate, and all of your faculties are completely at rest. Maintain this state.

Fountain of Light. Plan to spend at least forty-five minutes in meditation, and provide an hour total as a "buffer" for the practice. Once again, seat yourself comfortably in a quiet, solitary place. Consciously relax your body: hands, feet, arms, legs, shoulders, and neck. This time, sit in such a way that your hands and feet are gently touching, and breathe easily and deeply. Begin with a sincere commitment and invocation of "May this be for the good of All." The following stages are described in sequence, but you may progress to the end of only one stage over a series of sitting meditations. Take your time, moving on only when you honestly discern and intuit you are ready, and be comfortable with the process. If you become distracted or interrupted at any point, you can sometimes pick up where you left off, but more often you may need to start that stage over again.

i.   *Stage One – Light to Cauldron.* As you breath in, imagine that you are breathing in a gentle, airy light. Direct that light down through your lungs as you inhale, all the way down through your abdomen, to the Cauldron indicated in Figure 7. As with all of the other focal points, the Cauldron is horizontally centered in the body. Allow the light to build there until you have a sense of steadiness or permanence to its presence. Maintain this state until it is comfortable and reliable. You will experience some representation of the Cauldron. This may be a sense of warmth, or a molten substance filling a curving shape, or a dim glowing, or even sexual arousal. Note these things without trying to change them, perpetuate them, or interpret their meaning. Just relax into the moment, let them be, and maintain your focus. Now move to Stage Two.

ii.   *Stage Two – Light to Heart Gate.* Still directing the light you inhale first to your Cauldron with your inhale, now let it rush up from your Cauldron into your Heart Gate with your exhale. As this energy gathers in the Heart, encourage it to form into a spherical concentration of light that rests within your chest. If you have difficulty visualizing a sphere, begin with a point of radiating light. Allow the light to build there until you have a sense of steadiness and permanence. Maintain this state until it is comfortable and reliable. There is often a progression of sensations: a growing heat in your chest, a pleasant scent, a mild vibration, strong emotions, a sense of expansion – or of warm light expanding within you – perhaps even unexpected sounds or images. Within all of these fluctuations, maintain your breathing rhythm. Note these things without trying to disrupt them, perpetuate them, or interpret their meaning. Just relax into the moment, let them be, and remain focused. Now move to Stage Three.

iii.   *Stage Three – Light to Mind Eye.* Still directing the light you inhale first to your Cauldron, and then up through your Heart Gate, now also let it rise up into your Mind Eye. As light gathers in the space of your mind, encourage it to form into a sphere or radiant point as you did for your heart. Allow the light to build there until you have a sense of steadiness and permanence. Maintain this state until it is comfortable and reliable. At some point, you may sense a non-substantive, non-colored, non-light shape beginning to replace or "shadow" the gathered light. This is like an absence, or a nothingness, and is normal, and you should shift your attention to it when if forms, spending some time within that new presence. This often causes the nothingness to expand, to dampen your physical senses, or to disorient your awareness; allow this to happen, and relax into it, as this will lead to one type of mystic activator. If, however, this shadow doesn't appear, maintain the sphere or point of warm light, and it will begin to take on substance and solidity. Spend time paying attention to all the properties of this light. You may drift into new emotions, visions, and sensations, and should hold them for a time without reaction. This can be especially difficult the first few attempts, because you may feel either too removed from your immediate experience to pay attention to it, or, at the other extreme, utterly swept up in it. Note all phenomena that happen without trying to disrupt them, perpetuate them, or interpret their meaning. Just relax into the moment, and let them be. Now move to Stage Four.

iv.   ***Stage Four – Fountain of Light.*** Maintaining the process of breathing light in, down, and up, let the focus of substantive light in your Mind Eye expand until it touches the crown of your head (if you are maintaining a steady point of light, move the point itself to the crown). Maintain this state until it is comfortable and reliable. Now, very gently, as if it were a flower opening to the sun, encourage the sphere or point of light to drift upwards. In terms of sense-space, this is very much like passing through the top of your physical head. But the destination of your focus is not the space immediately above your head, but to that *elsewhere* place which the mystic somehow perceives is both within, without, and neither. You will likely have visited this place in the earlier meditations. Maintain the "projection" of your focus in this *elsewhere* place for as long as possible.

At some point, you will encounter the "Fountain of Light" aspect of this meditation, losing yourself in a rapid intermingling of something Other and your own essence. Some may experience this as entering an infinite realm of Light; for others, a sense of Divine omnipresence, or perhaps shifting into an entirely new form of consciousness. You may sense a rushing in or out of the same substantive energy from which your Mind Eye focus was formed, or something else: a kind of intense vibration, or even a loud roar of sound. There may be intense colors, or distant sounds, or transportive visions, or a combination of powerful emotions that extends beyond the normal peak of feeling. Frequently, you will sense that your whole being is entirely permeated by brightness, warmth, energy or Presence. If you have thoroughly prepared yourself to let go, allow the climax of this experience to progress on its own, and do not try to control the results.

v. ***Stage Five – Rest.*** The Fountain of Light will subside naturally, without conscious effort (you may, in fact, not be conscious of the transition at all). When it does subside, release deliberate focus altogether – that is, do not concentrate on anything. If you notice any uncomfortable or intense physical sensations – you may not register them until you return from Stage Four – allow them to gradually subside from your awareness. As with the Controlled Breathing meditation, you are completely letting go of your thoughts, emotions and physical senses. A sort of "non-meditation." If any awareness at all remains, it will be a *listening from the heart* to the silent center of your being. Maintain this state for as long as possible.

When you emerge from Rest, you may feel disassociated from your body, so allow your consciousness to slowly drift back into place. You will emerge from this last stage refreshed, calm and centered, and now may wish to sit a while longer and reflect on your meditative journey. Consider with sincere gratitude the many facets of your experience, but don't expect to understand all that has happened right away. Give yourself space and time to unravel the meaning of your own personal gnosis...or better yet, don't attach any meaning to it at all.

Figure 7: Path of Light

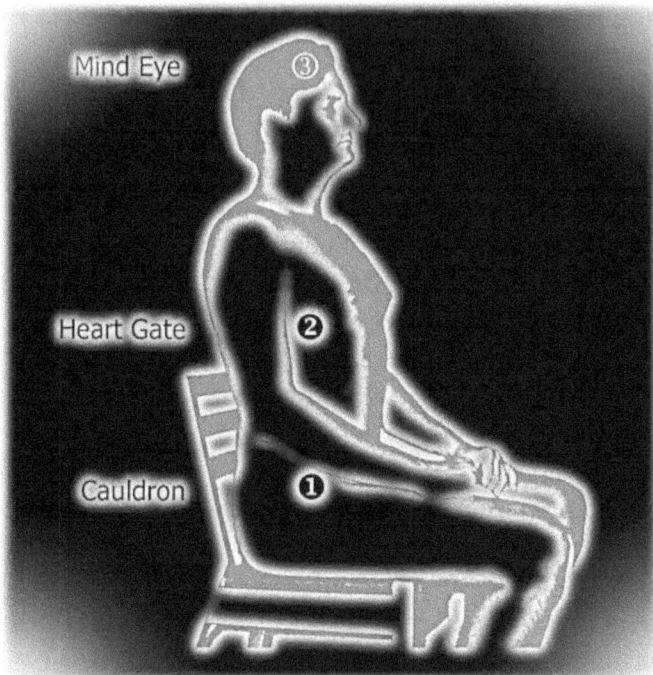

After practicing the Source and Breathing meditations separately every day for a number of weeks, you will become aware how they interact with each other, each stimulating a mystical awareness similar in character, but differing in quality – or vice versa. You may even find yourself gravitating towards one, while finding another quite difficult to effectively practice. This is natural, but try them both nonetheless. When you feel a certain confidence that you have plumbed the depths of each experience…reach deeper. Repeat them again for the same duration of days or weeks, until you discover what is behind superficial appearances, and can achieve a pervasive influence over the focus and spacious quietude of your mind and heart.

Once you have been surprised – and perhaps humbled – by the new depth of your awareness, try to combine the first two exercises into one. It is usually easiest to start with Inviting the Source, and then to add Controlled Breathing, but there isn't a right or wrong order. You will need to find the binding commonality below the surface of each practice in order to unite them comfortably. For instance, how could you express profound devotion and neutrality (i.e. equilibrium) of emotion at the same time, or even in close proximity? Trust yourself to find a way. There will be new vistas, new plateaus, and ever more stripping away of initial appearances. There is likely be new false confidence, new humility and renewed exploration. There may be awe and bewilderment, and peace that surpasses understanding. And there are always difficult truths.

> "There is but one universal mode of thought, that of interior consciousness freed from schools and systems…With all our systems and conventions the secret essence of the mind can no more be forced into fixed grooves now than in the olden times."
>
> Francis Grierson, from his essay "Modern Mysticism"

One final exhortation on discipline in mystical practice: there are risks inherent to some levels of consciousness or energetic actuation that suggest additional caution; without adequate preparation and conditioning, certain mystic activators can result in injury or illness to the mind and body. I am not being dramatic, the danger is real. You wouldn't try running a marathon without any physical training, would you? So I will again exhort you to thoroughly familiarize yourself with the whole of this book before attempting the integrated meditation.

Many traditions detail other instructions; for example, that women should avoid direct activation meditations like the Fountain of Light during menstruation, and that abstinence from sexual activity for a period prior to such activators assists with their success for both men and women. In addition, approaching and achieving mystical consciousness can sometimes result in a subsequent, though temporary, state of distress, anxiety or depression. Initially, there can

also be some physical side-effects to certain practices,   such as
jitteriness, numbness, hot or cold sensations, etc. If any of these cause
concern, or you find it difficult to relax your way through them, stop
meditating for a time, or at a minimum reduce the length and
frequency of your meditation. When in doubt, take a break. We may
intermittently find ourselves both spiritually fortified and
emotionally depleted by our mystical journey, and having the
support of friends, fellowship and routine spiritual practice during
these times is also indispensable. So however you choose to deepen
your gnosis, thoroughly consider why you are doing so, approaching
your awakenings with the informed intent, respect and forbearance
they deserve.

As with the walking meditation, there is ample reason to revisit the
earlier, separate components of the integrated meditation even after
successful integration. As a natural extension of praying without
ceasing, the Source of Life and Light meditation ignites the fire of
spiritual passion in our hearts – and love-consciousness in our minds
– which we can then carry with us throughout the day. The
Controlled Breathing meditation is a great stress-reducer, is healing
to the mind and body, and is a helpful baseline practice when
emotional space, physical time or mental energy are in short supply.
In addition, transitions through gnosis are equally accessible via any
of these methods, and integration is really only an experimental idea
that may or may not enhance the meditative experience for you. As
with any form of meditation, however, our goal should not be
mystical awareness alone, but the nourishment to mind, body and
spirit a routine spiritual practice provides, and a sincere desire to
fortify the good of All.

My Own Meditative Experience

To illustrate my own experience may or may not be instructive for
others, and is only a reflection of my personal "best practices" for
meaningful meditation. It works for me; perhaps it will assist you as

well. Here, then, is a brief distillation of my sitting meditative practice:

Sitting Meditation

Prior to the sitting meditation, I most often take care of other routine daily efforts first, seeking balance, perhaps, or a lessoning of distractions. This isn't always necessary, but I find it facilitates a deeper focus if some of the other segments of my day are already accomplished – my morning walking meditation, work projects, some errands or activities I've committed to, and so on. I once received instruction to meditate early in the morning (before sunrise), and I understand this is helpful to many people – but it simply isn't for me. So I will sit comfortably – this could be anywhere – with the souls of my feet pressed together, and the palms of my hands gently touching. I find that having my hands and feet touch helps still my mind and focus my energy. For the same reason, I will rest my tongue gently on the roof of my mouth. To start, I refine my intentions with the commitment and invocation: "May this be for the good of All." Then I begin by "just sitting;" that is, doing nothing more than sitting with neutral but observant attention, gradually releasing the orientation of my consciousness from the influences of my will, thoughts, emotions, and physical sensations. This is an effortless emptying, a great sighing of self which I find readies me for the journey. Then come elements of the integrated practice just described.

I will sit with my eyes barely opened or completely closed – it depends on my mood and immediate environment. I will focus my mind on my own conception of the Source – not as a symbolic representation, but as a living connection. I then open my heart to the Source of Life and Light so that a worshipful, thankful and intimate love springs forth. Sometimes this is so intense, it feels like my heart was breaking, and I must spend a few moments accepting this. Other times, this will be a more delicate and fleeting sense. My breathing is regular and deep, and I slowly (and sometimes without conscious effort) begin lengthening the "holding" pause at the end of each inhale and exhale. Once I am comfortably maintaining this breathing rhythm and worship-from-the-heart, I begin the Fountain of Light meditation. This can be an awkward transition, and sometimes interrupts the earlier processes; if this happens, I begin again. Sometimes I may become self-conscious of the exercise – or an overwhelming sense of disorientation will jolt me out of my meditation entirely – and I must start over. But most often I am able to relax into shifting perceptions, become adjusted to them, and progress into other states of contemplative awareness.

Sometimes these states include visions, sometimes clear ideas or strong emotions, sometimes an emptiness far removed from thoughts and sensations, sometimes a thrilling sense of the Infinite, and sometimes nothing at all. There is no set or guaranteed progression. On rare occasions, after a prolonged period of meditation (either leading up to Stage Four of the Fountain of Light, or during the "Rest" period) my breathing pauses for a long while. I haven't measured how long, or what leads up to this event, and the duration probably varies (it is likely no more than a few minutes). During this time, all perception-cognition is suspended entirely, or I enter a dreamlike state of rapidly changing images, though neither condition is recognized in the moment for what it is – only afterwards do I realize what has happened. These events may occur at other times, but most often here. From the deep breath I take upon emerging, I deduce that this extended pause comes at the end of an exhalation, and does not seem to have an impact on my ongoing stages of meditation until I surface completely; that is, I am able to continue until the meditation ends naturally.

Should the "Fountain of Light" event occur, I will sometimes feel a cresting wave of overwhelming emotion, and on other occasions am very calm or free of emotion, but nearly always I will experience a rapid intermingling – and often a sort of translucent union – with the torrent of light, which seems to welcome me even as I welcome it. The effect is that I "become" the light, and the light becomes me, and my physical self fades into the background, most often remaining incredibly distant, and sometimes dissipating entirely – as if it is part of another continuum than the one I have newly entered. Ideally, any lingering "I-me-mine" orientation also dissolves.

Other aspects of my experience are difficult to describe, and even after all the mystical concepts and metaphors utilized so far no words seem to fit particularly well. There is, in the Christian tradition, an expression of the heart crying out to the Creator as a child cries out for its parent; in the Sufi tradition, a similar idea is found in the lover yearning for the Beloved. Such adoring conviction surfaces in peak experiences whenever emotion is present. And then there is the more conceptual experience of "Oh...I see now." How can I explain this? It is like finally getting a joke you remember someone telling you a long time ago, and laughing in appreciation, humility and satisfaction. But here, the appreciation is awe, and satisfaction is a profound peacefulness. These intellectual and emotional elements are also subordinated by something else, and *that* is the thing which so resists description. It isn't knowledge, or conviction, nor is it pure bliss or a far-reaching intuitive insight...and yet, somehow it includes, reshapes and transcends all of these at once. In the post-experience analysis, I might call it Truth, but when immersed in the experience itself, even "Truth" is an inferior construct, like a small object in a great hall, or a childhood toy set aside for the *real thing*: pure gnosis. Such encounters understandably inspire "despairing efforts to interpret the contents of this experience, to count up, as it were, the inestimable riches poured out...all at once." [37]

Beyond this hyperextension of consciousness and intimate mingling with *elsewhere*, there is a sustained state where suspended perception-cognition is no longer an event, but becomes an identity. More than awareness, this is *being*, or a state of being, which also rejects categorization. What is it? A gnosis of the Absolute? I don't know. It just is. Zen Master Gutei responded to his own peak mystical encounters with a lifetime of silence, more able to convey its meaning by raising a single finger than through any attempt at words. And

---

[37] From *Prayer* by Hons Urs von Balthasar, Sheed & Ward, 1961

indeed I find more benefit in acceptance and gratitude, and the quiescent and effortless application of this new kind of *essential being* from moment to moment, than from any subsequent intellectual interpretation.

The aftereffects of sitting meditation are fairly consistent. When achieving any state of contemplation including or beyond a suspension of valuation, I emerge refreshed, relaxed and highly energized. The deeper (that is, the "higher" or more progressed) the contemplative-emotive experience, the more pronounced the effects. One of the more lasting impacts is a deep-felt confidence that very few things really matter in the great scheme of life. However, what few things *do* still matter have a more obvious significance than they did previously – and how to approach them becomes clearer. A sense of being still, centered and grounded persists for hours after meditation. Sometimes, this can be accompanied by feelings of vulnerability, or even irritability and a desire for isolation from others, but more often there is an all-encompassing sense of equanimity. Perceptions are also frequently sharpened: objects are more crisply defined and distinctly individual, yet concurrently more unified in substance. Sounds are also more acute; and there is more pliancy in my thinking. Although entirely subjective, I would say there is an overall stripping away of confusion and illusion, a "perceiving things as they are" in every area of life. As a natural response to this perception, things like humility, patience, compassion – and even creative invention – arise more freely and spontaneously.

The Cliff

With all of my being I scrambled and trembled and strove
   climbing ever higher
but the most detailed maps, the most disciplined techniques
   and the careful advice of sages widely revered
     did not avail me – for I could not reach my goal, or even
      comprehend it
until, one day, with unexpected insight
I just let go

and began an endless falling into God

After even a brief survey of mystical writings, it will become evident to anyone that each person's transitions through gnosis are uniquely their own, and that the subjective consequences of restructuring heart and mind through mystical practice are equally diverse. Thus we return once again to the beginning: to the quality of our intentions moving forward. For me, that is all that matters in the end, for it is all that differentiates self-absorbed mental gymnastics from sincere openness to the Divine. But there remains the question of how to apply mysticism to everyday life: how does our burgeoning understanding of self and the Universe alter our interaction with others? How does it alter our course in the world? That is what we will discuss in the following chapters.

Chapter Questions

1. What is the purpose of mysticism?
2. How do the Just For Today meditations contribute to training the heart and mind?
3. How is meditation that induces ecstatic states or contemplative stillness enhanced through a devotional attitude?
4. What is a good guideline for personal goals and expectations in mystical practice?
5. How can we measure our progress without becoming attached to that progress?

9. RELATIONSHIPS

Solitude and Self-Sufficiency

> A little while alone in your room
> will prove more valuable than anything else
> that could ever be given to you.
>
> Rumi [38]

Are you easily bored when you are alone? Is solitude threatening to you? Is it important to always have something occupying your mind, always stimulating you? Keeping busy is really not the same as being productive, although certain cultural values – certainly the work ethic of the West – reinforce this mistaken belief. At the other end of the spectrum, do you find yourself dropping into a mild depression every time you intend to relax? Do your feelings grow numb and your thoughts turn lazy and incoherent? Both of these extremes are symptoms of the same malady: many people find it challenging to be alone with themselves. As a prerequisite for deep meditation and the finer forms of mystical awareness, it is important to remedy any such resistance to solitude. I have observed that a

---

[38] From *The Essential Rumi* by Coleman Barks, Harper San Francisco, 1997

discomfort with being alone is often the result of some or all of the
following conditions:

1. Internal dilemmas or old hurts that haven't been resolved.

2. Having no clear purpose in this life.

3. Never having learned how to nourish ourselves without
    external help.

4. An inability to resolve the guilt or angst over our lack of
    integrity in some area.

5. A tendency to abandon ourselves to primitive impulses,
    because it's just...easier.

There are many ways of addressing these impedances to our well-
being – for that is what they are, and leaving them unattended will
not assist us in our spiritual voyage, or benefit the people we love.
For when we have not worked through the land mines and
quicksand of our own inner worlds, not only are we incapable of
seeing beyond the superficial appearances of life to the core realities
beneath, but we tend to pull others into our struggle, hoping they
will either help us with our process, or provide us a new horizon we
can run towards – anything to keep us from focusing on ourselves,
by ourselves. In fact, those with whom we choose to be close
generally mirror the state of our inner life, and the lessons we learn
from each relationship will probably be the same ones, over and over
again, until we apply that knowledge to healing our most primary
relationship – our relationship with Self. When the same, seemingly
unfair and antagonistic events keep occurring in our closest
friendships and partnerships, it is almost certainly due to our own
unfinished internal business.

When we engage the mystic within, the paths of inner contemplation
and transformation of the heart will bring these issues to the fore. To
look inside ourselves with increasing honesty and intensity, we
cannot avoid discovering our fears and inadequacies. And so
preparation for a meditative life has the same characteristics as

ongoing practice does: introspection, reflection, and intuitive sensitivity. I have already mentioned that I am a big believer in cognitive-behavioral therapy, and feel that CBT is an excellent beginning for our contemplative process. This can be approached through workbooks and exercises, but may also require professional guidance. Of course, visiting a "therapist" might be challenging for our ego, and our upbringing, peers or surrounding culture may have programmed us to reject formalized assistance. Yet choosing this course despite our fearful resistance demonstrates genuine humility – a key component in the transformation of the heart, and a loving and powerful investment in wellness. Eventually, we will have a fully developed toolkit to consciously explore and process our internal world, but initially we may need guidance to start us down the path.

Continuous self-examination has led me to discover that my own recurring challenges were tied to a lack of emotional self-sufficiency. That pattern, in turn, originated in how I related to my own parents and peers as a child. The greatest leap of emotional health I have ever made was realizing that I could be *whole* without anyone loving me – not my parents, or siblings, friends, or romantic partners, or even a Deity of my belief system. I am awed by and grateful for the support and encouragement the Universe has offered me, but the only person from whom I really require compassion and caring is myself, and I believe this is true for each of us. Unfortunately, the search for *external* love and acceptance is deeply embedded in Western society. We are bombarded with this theme in mass media and entertainment, and even many popular self-improvement books focus on how to change our interactions to get what we want from others, rather than helping us realize how we can better nourish ourselves. Chasing after an Unholy Grail of external support, I made myself miserable for many years of my adult life, until I learned some important contemplative skills. Here are the top three of these meditative and therapeutic practices:

- **To create some solitude, without external stimulation or internal cacophony**. This is time for meditation, reflection, and a careful inventory of my emotions. I try to fully

experience everything I am feeling, paying careful attention
to where emotions become physically apparent in my body.
For instance, I might feel anxiety in my stomach, or loneliness
in my chest. With the flat of one hand, I will then touch the
areas where these emotions are localized, and project
acceptance, calm, and caring into them. If this exercise
evokes imagery, I pay close attention to that as well,
projecting the same touch of kindness and acceptance into
those images. What an amazing effect this has! I have also
added Reiki to this healing touch of my inner Self, greatly
enhancing the results. Finally, I reflect on what in my
thinking or behavior has led to each of my strong feelings,
and decide whether I would like to change those patterns of
thought and action in order to feel differently. The principles
behind this approach are discussed further in the Dealing
with Fear and Avoidance section.

- **To dialogue with every part of my emotional self that has
strong wants.** I dig beneath the surface of the obvious desires
to what lies beneath them. I create a personality for the want
– a character with whom I can interact in my imagination.
Through this I discover the musings of my personalities, and
what might be engendering certain types of behavior or
thinking. Sometimes I might feel an all-consuming panic at
being so close to a chaos of desires and longings, or angst at
realizing I will never be able to fully satisfy them all. This is
where compassion once again comes into play: to be a good
listener is not to promise immediate satisfaction, but to
empathize and understand. Sometimes, through these
dialogues, I am able to completely let go of unreasonable
demands I have placed on myself. I do not, after all, really
need very much at all. Sometimes I discern what lies beneath
a strong yearning for worldly joy, and can translate it into a
softer wish for something that enriches my spiritual life
instead, once again modifying my thoughts or behaviors for a
different outcome. For instance, an impatient desire for

intimacy is transformed into a joyful creation of music or poetry. Whatever the solution, I move gently toward it, once again herding wind across stones. By listening to my wants and acknowledging them, I gain a relief from both impulsiveness and denial. By working peacefully through what underlies my desires, I achieve a deeper satisfaction and empowerment. By letting go and reconsidering what goals I can choose, I am truly free to discover all that nurtures me and those I love. This is really a form of "self-inquiry" meditation using active imagination, and is a common therapeutic practice.

- **To dialogue with my family of origin, the place where I gleaned my first impressions of personal identity.** This has entailed long, non-judgmental talks with my parents about how they feel regarding events in my childhood. I then expressed my own feelings about those events, with forgiveness and gentleness. The greatest surprises came when I asked my parents what was important to them now, and what the happiest moments of their life have been. Understanding them as people, instead of just as "my parents," was essential. Through such conversations, I have created a new kind of relationship with my mom and dad, one with greater mutual appreciation and understanding, and I believe this process has been healing for everyone involved. Even for those relatives who have passed on, or with whom I was never able to have such discussions, the mantle of forgiveness and acceptance that I place over them is really the forgiveness and acceptance I offer myself. It's a powerful thing.

As suggested in earlier descriptions of the stages of our spiritual journey, there may come a time when stillness and solitude become not only necessary, but our preferred environment. Some people have this penchant early on, and for them the thought of integrating with the world is troublesome. But whether a natural inclination or a stage of being, the lure of seclusion, isolation and emotional detachment can be strong. In the context of acknowledging a necessity to withdraw from the world, I think it is also good to seek out community and fellowship during these times. Although being self-sufficient is a worthwhile goal in itself – with quality solitude both leading to, and resulting from, a prosperity of mind, body and spirit – it is not meant to exclude social interdependency or investments in friendships and community. People nourish and are nourished by people, and our fellowships and alliances are very important. Whether a worship assembly or monthly activities group, an artist's colony or a volleyball league, attempting to integrate with other people who share our values becomes a litmus test – and a validation – for the new patterns of self we have discovered in the rarified atmosphere of spiritual quietude.   All of this provides important grounding for us as we manifest a new self in the world.

> "There is an appointed time for everything, and a time for every delight under heaven."
>
> *Ecclesiastes*, 3:1

When Self Intersects with Other

Once we peer beneath the surface of things, the seamless interconnectedness of all life becomes increasingly clear. Well then, why don't we just relinquish everything that makes us an individual and merge with the Source of Life and Light, becoming indistinguishable from all its inestimable manifestations? There are certainly degrees of consciousness that allow us to do exactly this, but the moment we take a self-conscious breath or have an egoistic thought, we distinguish ourselves as unique and resurface from our submersion in the All. Consider the harmonies of music, where each part has its distinct voice, but combines with all the other voices to become a cohesive whole.   The choice to be alive and contribute our voice to the symphony of existence makes us unique, even as we celebrate those harmonies.   To let go of ego, or feel a deep and empathetic connection, or expand our awareness into the

Infinite...these do not detract from that uniqueness and individuality, and thus selflessness – and even complete abandonment of self – is but a facet of our distinctly contributive identity. To share that identity with others, to create mutual support for a spiritual journey that all of us share, and to synergize compassionate solutions for a suffering world are all part of a fully harmonized existence.

Fellowship

After a superficial overview of my life, some might consider me fairly unqualified to discuss relationships of any kind. I am divorced, live far away from my family, have no children, have a very small group of friends, and spend a lot of time in solitary pursuits like writing, hiking in the wilderness, reading books, meditating, and otherwise being very selective about my contact with people. That being said, there are a smattering of observations about relationships which I feel are universally true – having experienced them myself as well as witnessing others go through them – and which I hope would be beneficial to anyone. As a result of shaping my own interactions around these observations and the insight gained from a contemplative life, I believe I am perpetually becoming a healthier person, both emotionally and spiritually. After many years of struggling with self-esteem and self-inhibiting patterns, I eventually emerged from the chrysalis of shattered pretenses to characterize all of my lasting relationships as honest, genuine, intimate, trusting and delightfully spiced with joy.

Fellowship is a chosen association, and our most important associations are high-quality friendships. Even where there is a romantic bond, if the elements of strong friendship aren't there, no amount of passion can compensate for what is missing – at least not over the long run. Our closest and most trusted friends become those who enhance our spiritual growth, and who create an easy camaraderie for our faith. So, too, our life partners will compliment – and not compete with, or compensate for – who we are. Ideally, we should be able to get along with anyone simply by finding something in them we can appreciate. I do enjoy listening to people with views that contrast my own – it can often be intellectually stimulating. But in order to nourish and be nourished on many levels, we will cultivate friendships that have more than superficial interests in common, and which by their nature mutually encourage us to improve, while simultaneously embracing who we are right now.

Yet finding those relationships is not always easy, and despite the abundance of traditional activities that attempt to synthesize new friendships and communities in this highly transitive world, success is elusive. So I will suggest an alternative to personal checklists, social conformance and manufactured commonality: let the Universe take care of it. Make yourself available to others with similar values by choosing a lifestyle that invites them into your life – create space for them in terms of time and energy, and remain open. Engaging in a workplace, hobbies and organizations that place you around like-minded people will undoubtedly help, but don't *expect* these to supply all of your relationships. Instead, be conscious of your intuitive promptings about people, and trust them. At the bus stop, in a café, while you are out walking, and when you interact with anyone at any time, pay attention to synchronistic events without being attached to the outcome. For when we are overly concerned with finding our own niche community, we once again risk shifting what sustains us from self-sufficiency to external support, and tend to suppress our intuitive insights. As a result, we will likely be frustrated by what we find. For example, at one time or another, all of us have experienced meeting people who met all of our criteria for friendship, only to be sadly disappointed in the resulting relationship. Perhaps we don't find them reliable, or feel they misrepresented their true disposition with external personas, or had completely different expectations than we did about friendship. But when we rely on our spiritual cognizance, wisdom and discernment to navigate interactions with people, the most unexpected and delightful surprises arise in the most unusual places.

> "Indeed, it is illuminating to the point of astonishment to talk to a Zen Buddhist from Japan and to find that you have much more in common with him than with those of your own compatriots

who are little concerned with religion, or interested only in its external practice."

Thomas Merton, *Mystics and Zen Masters*

Some further thoughts on self-sufficient relationships. If we love our friends without attachment – without holding on to them or our ideas of relationship too tightly – the question of over-investment never comes up. Honesty never makes us feel vulnerable, and careful listening is never fraught with judgment or impatience. When we celebrate the present moment of companionship – as opposed to an anticipated outcome of that moment, or some distant expectation of what our friendship might provide – it is our willingness to invest *right now* which reaps the most precious rewards. We never become codependent, because we are clear about what healthy, mutual compassion and nourishment look and feel like. We don't fall into emotionally rescuing others, because we know that every person's well-being is their own responsibility. And we don't inadvertently overtax, abuse or misuse our friends, because we have compassion for them and our well-being is not dependant on their responses to us.

Most importantly, we recognize and accept that we won't receive the nourishment we most deeply crave from other people. This is like relying on any other external for our happiness. At one extreme, we may find ourselves surrounded by spiritually primitive people, where the most we can do is expect the best, and patiently forgive the worst. At the other end of the spectrum we may find ourselves among those more enlightened than we are, and experience discomfort or frustration with our own shortcomings. In reality, all of us are completely equal, but rarely in the same spiritual place at the same physical time. If we remove a linear perception of spiritual evolution, we are all assured to arrive at the exact same destination: a highly evolved and spiritually successful stage of being, whether in this life or some distant future. And what a party that will be! In the meantime, we may sometimes feel very alone. This is why developing self-awareness and compassion for ourselves is so critical, because the relationship we have with that self is the model for every other relationship we try to create.

The underlying principle of fellowship is simple: those around whom we spend the most time have the most influence on us, regardless of how self-sufficient we may feel. This proximity effect can have a positive or negative impact on our spiritual development, so it behooves us to consciously choose environments and relationships that align with our goals and values. The strength we derive from each other can be an enormous benefit during this shared journey, and having a supportive community within which to trade ideas and experiences generates surprising synergies. So, while it is never spiritually healthy to yearn intensely for either isolation or community, it is always beneficial to have a balance of solitude and a supportive social environment.

As for assessing the quality of our relationships, it is really an extension of contemplative self-awareness. Take a moment to reflect on the nature of the friendships in your life right now. Would you say they are predominantly:

1. Uplifting, inspiring, and nurturing?
2. Provide an opportunity for personal growth, or fulfillment of a greater purpose?
3. Antagonistic to your well-being, or draining to your energies?
4. Seemingly stagnant, neutral in their net effect, or empty of meaning?
5. In some closer relationships, there are undoubtedly many components of interaction, but what has the balance been over time? What do those friendships mean to you right now?

Now turn these questions back on yourself. How are you with your friends? What impact do you have on others? Uplifting? Draining? Seemingly very little at all? What value does your presence have to those close to you? Answering these questions is a window into self and our impact on the world. How we interact with people is, after all, who we really are – at least as far as people around us are concerned: "A good tree cannot produce bad fruit, nor a bad tree produce good fruit."[39] That is, the value that I contribute to the Universe is wholly expressed in *my current interaction* with my immediate environment. What greater gift could I offer those I love than the quality of my intentions in the present moment? But here is an important caveat: sometimes we will be ignored, misunderstood or forgotten. Sometimes the gifts we offer will seem to be undervalued. This is where patience, faith and detachment come in – for we may not fully know what impact we have on others for a very long time, if ever, and our motivation is not to gain external approval anyway, but to evidence compassion without attachment to outcomes. Thus we live in the tension of trying to understand how effective our relationships are in furthering this end, while trusting that our intentions will get us there without any obvious or persistent confirmation.

But what if, after observing one painful failure after another, we find the quality and depth of our relationships is not what we envisioned for ourselves, or what we think of as healthy? Since we have constructed the meaning of every friendship, we have the power to transform them. The choice is ours, based on our level of commitment – not to others, but to ourselves. I remember a woman who was going through a divorce saying of her soon-to-be ex-husband: "After all our years of marriage, we have such great communication, and we know each other so well...I can't imagine starting over with someone else." She realized what her investment in a long-term relationship had created, and valued what she had. But what ultimately drew her out of the marriage was her inability to use the very tools and qualities she appreciated to transform aspects of the relationship she didn't like. And that is the heart of all such transformation: to find common values, beneficial qualities and mutual appreciation in the present, and build on them. In this way, we can consciously decide what that relationship will mean for us in the next moment, regardless of what it has meant to us in the past.

---

[39] New Testament: *Matthew 7:18*

"I merely point out to you that, as a matter of fact, certain persons do exist with an enormous capacity for friendship and for taking delight in other people's lives; and that such persons know more of truth than if their hearts were not so big."

William James, *Essays on Faith and Morals*

Healing What Is Broken

The following chart provides ways to evaluate and mend broken relationships, as well as understand the dynamics of new relationships as they are formed. The premise is simple: there are many different types of love, and unless we understand what specific combination applies to any given relationship, we are liable to either be disappointed and frustrated with our fellowship experience, or to disappoint and frustrate others. Consider the many flavors of emotion and intention represented here, and reflect on your past relationships that have in some way broken down; is there a correlation between the type of love you anticipated from each other and what you actually experienced? Would you still be friends if either of you had been willing to accept what the other had to offer, without confining it to preconceived notions of "what it *should* be?" In seeking out new friendships, have you been clear in your communication of the types of love you are willing to offer and receive? With this matrix in mind, what dynamics exist in your current relationships, and how might you navigate them differently?

Table 7: Love Matrix

Level of Commitment	Type of Affinity or Attraction
A. **Profound** (there has never been a question about this being a lifelong and mutually committed relationship) B. **Pronounced** (one of our closest and most important relationships) C. **Moderate** (social bonds like work relationships, those between doctors and patients, family members who aren't emotionally close to us, etc.) D. **Mild** (general commitment to social expectations, such as conforming to laws or traditions) E. **Dysfunctional** (obsessed, addicted, or compulsive)	1. **Spirit** (a inexpressible but deep attraction that shares a common understanding of events in the context of spiritual priorities) 2. **Heart** (sharing mutually important values, goals and attitudes – including spiritual ones) 3. **Mind** (intellectual affinity – thinking alike or understanding each other's thought process with surprising ease) 4. **Physical** (enjoying how someone looks or moves, the sound of their voice, their smell, etc.) 5. **Sexual** (sexual attraction)
Level of Intimacy	**Level of Social Acknowledgement**
I. **Devotional** (wide open passionate worship that knows no bounds) II. **Soul Friends** (deep spiritual trust, openness and honesty) III. **Companionship** (a comfortable closeness, frankness and mutual trust) IV. **Compassionate** (an unconditional acceptance and desire to relieve suffering – often initially one-sided) V. **Convenience** (sharing common, cooperative goals for a limited duration)	a. **Public** (everyone knows) b. **Immediate Community** (only our closest friends know) c. **Private** (i.e. "just us" – we only acknowledge it between ourselves) d. **Self** (we know, but we haven't shared with anyone else – even the other person with whom we feel a connection) e. **Unknown** (a relationship already exists, but we don't consciously acknowledge it to ourselves)

Clearly, these definitions apply to all types of interpersonal relationship, and there are thousands of different combinations. For instance, one or more levels of Affinity may apply (i.e. we might share both a "Mind" and "Heart" Affinity with the same person). It then becomes that much more complex when one person feels multiple levels of Affinity or Attraction, while the object of their affection reciprocates on different levels. When two people have completely dissimilar understandings of what attracts them, what level of social acknowledgement exists, or the kind of intimacy is expected...well, the potential for disappointment, frustration or conflict is obvious. Try this exercise: make two copies of the Love Matrix, and invite a close friend to "rate" each area of your relationship while you do the same on the second copy. Be honest and considerate in your assessment – perhaps spending a day or two contemplating it – then compare your ratings...and be prepared for surprises.

If relationship expectations between two people are not "in sync," how do we go about redefining them, especially if such dissonance becomes antagonistic? Admittedly, the historic patterns of certain relationships may be so ingrained that we find it difficult to do this – it may be especially challenging with marriage partners, family members, friends we have known since we were very young, or with a coworker who really gets under our skin. Yet, if we want to evolve spiritually, is it possible we will be leaving some of these people behind if we fail to resolve these dynamics? Here again there is a choice. When we decide to break a negative cycle, we may take time away from old influences, but I believe it is incumbent on us to explain who we really are, our expectations, and what we intend to do – clearly, patiently, and with real emotional honesty. Authentic love is not exclusive, but inclusive: if we are growing in wisdom and compassion, then we will be able to tolerate and eventually transform any and all spiritually unhealthy relationships in our lives into spiritually healthy ones. There will always be antagonisms we find particularly daunting, and we may set new boundaries and avoid certain activities or insulate ourselves; but the transformation of our most difficult relationships is the clearest evidence of our own evolution. Like anything else, it's simply a matter of accepting our own limitations and abilities, and recognizing that redefining any relationship begins in our mind and heart, not in changing someone else's behavior. That is why we will eventually be able to offer ourselves anew, with clearly communicated expectations, without invalidating others. If we do this humbly, without accusation or blame, we open a door of choice for our friends, family and loved ones through which they will venture – in their own good time – if and when they desire to remain in our lives.

> "No mind was so good that it did not need another mind to counter and equal it, and to save it from conceit and blindness and bigotry and folly. Only in such a balance could humility be found…."
>
> Charles Williams, *The Place of the Lion*

Soul Friends

There is a special category of relationship that, like fellowship, creates mutual support for our deepening spirituality. But unlike most fellowship, there is often an openly stated commitment and level of accountability that makes this our most significant spiritual companionship. These are the people with whom feel comfortable sharing our most intimate vulnerabilities and recurring challenges. Likewise, we would turn to them first with our greatest joys and achievements. Our soul friend will be a spiritual teacher and mentor to us, and we will be the same for them. There is no set hierarchy in this relationship, and though there may be times when we place each other on pedestals of admiration – or pull each other out of dark holes we have carelessly dug for ourselves – soul friends remain equals.

Clearly, a soul friend is a rare thing. We may open ourselves up to such a relationship only to find out our current life-lesson is about self-sufficiency. Someone may offer this close friendship to us only to learn we already have sufficient spiritual intimacy in our lives. The process can, in fact, be a lot like searching for a compatible life partner, and there is no guarantee we will find either. In the Sufi tradition, the *awliya' allah*, the "friends of God," who have advanced farthest in their spiritual intimacy with the Divine, are not necessarily recognizable to each other, or to anyone else. Perhaps this is a cogent lesson for us as we consider soul friendship. But when we are ready, neither closed to such a relationship nor despondent over a lack of support, but evenly balanced in the contentment of our spiritual practice, our soul friends are most likely to appear. When this happens, be ready for challenges! Be ready for growth. One of the chief characteristics of this type of relationship is a raw vulnerability as we share our spiritual progress, leaving every social mask behind and exploring shortcomings and victories with humble honesty. In this deep and trusting exchange, we mirror the love that surpasses understanding and amplify the Light that illuminates all souls.

> "Not counting the unmarked paths of misdirection
> My compass, faith in love's perfection
> I missed ten million miles of road I should have seen...."
>
> Emily Saliers, from her song *Love's Recovery* [40]

The term "enmeshment" has been used to describe the merging of identities – or completion of self – in an intimate romance. There is a strong cultural legacy in Western society that lauds and magnifies this idealistic notion – i.e. "you make me *whole*," or "I *can't live* without you." But enmeshment is an extremely injurious condition for our spirit and for the health and future of any relationship. This is not meant to trivialize real moments of intimacy, for that intertwining of essences is one of our richest experiences. But I would describe the aim of our closest bonds to be interdependency rather than enmeshing. The difference is the same as that between trusting someone to be mutually nourishing (a good thing), and relying solely on them for our happiness. It is also the difference between having a deep sense of connection and joy with another

---

[40] *Indigo Girls* album, 1989

person (also a good thing), and allowing their emotional state to completely control our own well-being. I am not suggesting we maintain a safe emotional distance from each other, or avoid investing ourselves in intensely personal relationships, but rather that we commit fully, and trust completely, without vanquishing our own ability to nourish ourselves or direct our own spiritual course.

For an inspiring exploration of this topic, I recommend Gay and Kathlyn Hendricks' book *Conscious Loving*, where the concept of "co-commitment" is introduced, and additional tools to cultivate healthy relationships are amply provided.

This balanced approach to partnership is what it means to love deeply without attachment. Interdependency permits lovers and life partners to share connection, while creating an environment where everyone feels free to continue their own inner journey. A loving commitment is one which provides space for each person to breathe and thrive, and is not a smothering and all-consuming flame. We all know how easy it is to fall into a maelstrom of ardent emotion when we desire companionship, and part of the joy of sexual union is abandoning control and giving our bodies over to one another. But sharing one's body, energy, space and time is not the same as giving over one's soul. This is why agreeing clearly about emotional boundaries, personal values and life goals is so important when entering into an intimate relationship – especially before a strong physical connection is established.

Absense

> I awoke in the night
> and you were there, next to me
> I pulled you closer
> pressing my heart to yours
> and smiled all through
> big and warm.
> In the morning

you were with me still
though it had only
been a dream
and you are with me now
moving all that I am.

Recently, I have been wrestling with the question of whether each of us has a destined "soul-mate." Among the Kabbalist writings are assertions that each of us enters the world with only half of our whole...that the other half is wandering around looking to reunite with us, just as we long to reunite with them. I don't know if this is true, but I do know that fixating on such a reunion is counterproductive to our spiritual well-being. When we become attached to the idea that some specific person is the perfect fit for us, or that they will somehow will make us feel complete, and expend tremendous emotional energies casting around the Universe for our "other half," we can't help but stunt or delay our own spiritual evolution. After all, are we here on this earth only to pair up and reproduce? This may be part of why many of us are here – though we can't presume it for everyone – but if marriage, partnership or parenthood becomes an all-consuming obsession, our only meaningful identity, and the sole validation for our existence...we will almost certainly be distracted from discerning or actuating a greater purpose for our lives.

"Now that I am free to be myself, who am I?"

Mary Oliver, from her poem *Blue Iris* [41]

There is a reason why many spiritual traditions encourage celibacy in their most devout practitioners. Although it is clearly not for everybody, anyone can give freedom from coupledom, as well as not feeding their sexual gratification impulses, a disciplined try. Such restraint differs from neurotic denial or meticulous asceticism in that it transforms the focus of our efforts from self-gratification to compassionate service. Sex and partnership are still an option, and

---

[41] *What Do We Know*, Da Capo Press, 2002

there is no moral imperative attached to our choice, but we observe the constructiveness of our redirected energies almost immediately. The Apostle Paul put it this way: "One who remains unmarried is concerned about pleasing God, but one who is married is concerned about the world, and how to please their spouse."[42] So although this isn't a matter of right or wrong, shouldn't the spiritual profitability of *any* relationship be carefully weighed in the context of our life's work? If we don't know what our life's work is, pleasure and companionship are intoxicating default behaviors. But when we are embroiled in an intimate relationship, it becomes our priority, just as anyone with a family is often more concerned about the welfare of their own children than someone else's. If we are not in an intimate relationship, our devotion can be directed toward nourishing friends and community, filling the gaps of ministry and support in our immediate environment, and utilizing the gifts we have been given to nurture this Earth and all who live on it – all of which might otherwise be neglected.

> "Chastity is one of the greatest disciplines, without which the mind cannot attain requisite firmness."
>
> Mahatma Gandhi

Communication

Stephen Covey, in his book *The Seven Habits of Highly Effective People*, says it well: "Seek first to understand, then to be understood." Seeking to understand is not just hearing the words, but feeling them too. Empathy is crucial in all communication, for without it there is little sense of connection or opportunity to trust. As Stephen Covey writes: "The essence of empathic listening is not that you agree with someone; it's that you fully, deeply understand that person, emotionally as well as intellectually." Developing this reflexive *other-awareness* requires the same skills as perfecting self-awareness, and is supported and enhanced in the same way by self-esteem. In fact,

---

[42] New Testament: *1 Corinthians 7:31-32*

self-esteem has an immense impact on the quality of our interactions simply because we tend to project, habitually and helplessly, every insecurity and apprehension we have about ourselves onto those around us.

The harmony or dissonance in our adult relationships is, of course, always a fifty-fifty proposition: each party contributes equally to the outcome by choosing to communicate and interact a certain way, by expecting certain unexpressed outcomes, or by having different standards of openness or integrity. Consider this example:

Sue: "Mark, I thought you said you could help me move this weekend!"

Mark: "I still will. I just can't bring my pickup truck."

Sue: "But that was the whole point."

Mark: "You didn't say anything about the truck when you asked me, Sue."

Sue: "Well, I'm glad you can help carry furniture, but I need a pickup, too."

Mark: "Why not just rent a pickup? The day-rates are pretty cheap."

Sue: "I'm trying to save money."

Mark: "Well, you could tell everyone they'll have to buy their own dinner, instead of you paying for them."

Sue: "Dinner? What are you talking about?"

Mark: "You weren't going to buy us all dinner for helping you move? I can't believe it!"

Sue: "And I can't believe you would expect that!"

Both Mark and Sue were surprised and upset because they each projected assumptions onto each other, believing their own expectations were justified while the other's were ridiculous. In addition, their defensive reactions were likely further fueled by insecurity about being judged – for attitudes or values the other clearly didn't appreciate. This illustrates the confusion that differing expectations can create in any type of relationship, when communication lacks empathy, clear expectations, or shared values. For some – as with children, a person who is emotionally immature, or the very ill – a mature adult clearly has more responsibility to define all of these parameters for both parties, and meets the less able wherever that person is. In various work environments, I have been a manager and mediator in the midst of seemingly impossible conflicts, and observed exactly the same disconnects in communication as those of intimate and family relationships – it's all the same dynamic. So for any level of interaction, I have found that all effective communication has eight requirements:

1. First and foremost, **maintaining our own healthy self-esteem**.
2. **Clarifying and agreeing on roles and expectations** (i.e. what is the result of this interaction intended to be? A specific action? Understanding and compassion? A revision of previous assumptions?).
3. **Practicing emotional honesty, openness and integrity** by stating our own wants and feelings without attaching blame or passing judgment on someone else's behavior – which of course requires a high level of self-awareness and self-control.
4. **Listening patiently, from the heart**, to whatever someone is trying to tell us...without interrupting them.
5. **Verifying that we understand what we hear,** either through restating it back to the person in our own words, or by asking clarifying questions.
6. Empathizing with their perspective or experience **without invalidating or exonerating it** (i.e. without imposing our own meaning on what they are saying – even when we have an invitation to do so).
7. **Providing an appropriate response** – within the agreed-upon expectations and roles, and with honest, non-judgmental expression of the emotions we are feeling.
8. **Following up** – determining at a later time if the communication was successful for everyone involved, and if the conclusions and responses are still valid.

This really isn't as exhausting as it sounds, and these steps quickly become habit once we begin to practice them consciously. And when it comes time to ask for what *we* want for ourselves from a relationship – including what we hope for in our communication – the formula is even simpler: we clearly express what we think will be nourishing to us, tactfully confirm that we have been heard and understood, and then let it go. If we feel we have done this, but still aren't getting what we want, there is no reason to feel resentment. Why? Because we have either:

1. become too demanding;
2. are not communicating clearly; or
3. have asked for something that our friend or partner can't – or won't – provide.

And in all of these cases, the responsibility of remedying the unsatisfying situation is ours, not anyone else's. We simply have to change our own expectations, redefine the relationship, and let everyone know that this is what we have decided to do – leaving room for negotiation if that is appropriate. In the same vein, when we begin new relationships we often ask: "Is this person well-suited to my wants?" When really we should be asking: "Am I well-suited to be this person's friend or partner? Am I willing to unconditionally accept them for who they are?" If we are thinking along these lines, we will have tremendous influence on the success of our relationships, based on the discernment and wisdom we exercise in initially choosing them, the quality and character of our ongoing communication, and our freedom from attachment to preferred outcomes. Every person is, after all, exactly themselves – not what we want them to be. It is our privilege to know them and encounter the lessons they bring, a precious discovery to witness the many facets of their being, and our abounding joy to love them in whatever way we are able and they are willing to accept.

Lastly, one final comment from Stephen Covey that I think summarizes the nature of integrity in communication: *that we should never make a promise we will not keep.* I would expand this idea to include even a casual comment that we will accomplish something for someone – if we mean it, we will not forget to do what we have said we will do. A high standard, but if this is not our sincere intention, with a real dedication to following through, how can we build trust? Without trust, there is no authentic intimacy; without real intimacy, there is no sense of connection; without a sense of connection, what is the point of communicating at all?

Chapter Questions

1. Do you tend to act impulsively in relationships, or consciously?

2. What criteria have you used to decide whether or not to maintain a friendship, romantic relationship, or family tie?

3. Have you recently been frustrated enough with someone that you wanted to lash out at them? Were there unspoken expectations you consciously or unconsciously imposed on them which caused you to react this way?

4. What are three important things you can do when you think a fellowship or partnership may be failing?

5. Because you are able to choose what your friendships mean to you, is it also important for you to communicate that meaning to each of your friends and loved ones? If so, with what frequency? If not, why not?

6. Do your most important relationships support and contribute to the purpose you have chosen for your life?

7. What can you do over the next few weeks to reshape interdependencies with other people into what is most spiritually healthy for both them and you?

8. What is the difference between isolation, loneliness, and constructive solitude?

9. What are the likely consequences of leaving difficulties in our relationships with our parents unresolved?

10. What is should the underlying reason be for creating a healthy relationship with Self?

11. Why is it important to have a purpose in life?

12. Would you be willing to try cognitive-behavioral therapy? Why or why not?

10. LIFESTYLE CHOICES

The Perfect Vocation

> "May we all find salvation in professions that heal."
>
> From Shawn Colvin's song, *Cry Like An Angel*

Not having a clear purpose or structured goals and boundaries for our life will dilute and distract our efforts to be self-sufficient, and frustrate our attempts to succeed – that is, at anything other than what almost certainly will be someone else's goal for us. Existence without a thoughtful, self-generated purpose is likely to be a depressing one, and though I would not try to persuade you that we each have some preordained worldly objective (though neither would I exclude that possibility), it is certain there is opportunity and capacity for us to create our own purpose, and to look deeply into ourselves for the patterns of self expression and natural inclinations which inform a worthwhile direction for our lives. In this arena, the mystic has tools that not only reveal that innermost Self, but also access a shared understanding – the wisdom of the Universe – which offers surprising avenues of fulfillment and lifelong aspiration.

Learning about ourselves – through ever-improving self-awareness, meditative practice, and exploration of different vocations and avocations – helps us identify our strengths, talents and limitations. Understanding our stage of being provides a spiritual context for our efforts. It is also extremely beneficial that we remain curious, and expose ourselves to new ideas and new ways of thinking, as well as the many different paths available to us. Yet, at the end of the day, when we have collected all this information and insight and experience and have a quiet moment to reflect upon the direction of our efforts, it is ultimately our own free choice what we will do right now, and what we will become tomorrow. It is a choice we can exercise with great joy and anticipation.

While for some people choosing a vocation is relatively easy, for others the process seems intimidating. One person has always known they will be a professional athlete. Another discovers in college that they are gifted at physics. I have always been a creative person and a healer, though I did not fully commit to my life's work for my first thirty years or so. Some people are completely unaware of what they could or should pursue, while others have so many skills and talents they find it hard to settle on any single discipline. But that is the key: discipline, focus, application. To decide to do something and stick to it is the only way we can ever test our capacity, and all of us have capabilities far greater than we imagine.

> "A person knows when they have found their vocation when they stop thinking about how to live, and begin to live."
>
> Thomas Merton, *Thoughts in Solitude* [43]

Like anything else, our search will expose us to many different approaches. The questions and exercises in *What Color Is Your Parachute*, by Richard Bolles, or those found in Steven Covey's *7 Habits* series, are two popular approaches I have sampled. One technique I have found especially helpful is imagining myself at the end of my life, looking back over the years and asking what four or five major accomplishments and experiences will have defined my life as a success. What do I truly care about? What are the values and beliefs about life I hold in my very core? But although these logical approaches may inspire us to act, they do not always provide us with a strong foundation of confidence and courage. Like most

---

[43] Paraphrased with permission of the Trustees of the Merton Legacy Trust

people, I began my search by looking outside myself. When I was seventeen, I relied on a random roll of dice to decide where to go to college. In my twenties, I was heavily dependent on prayerful petitions and the advice of close friends and mentors. In my thirties, financial security played an increasingly important role in my decisions. At long last, after many false starts and dead ends, I have learned to trust spiritual perception as my guide through this world. For the mystic, all the clutter and distraction of material concerns and dependence on externals falls away, leaving an ease of being in which every decision and action is a manifestation of our ever-broadening spiritual understanding. Vocations and other lifestyle choices are thereby transformed from an uncomfortable striving to a natural extension of our compassionately and authentically being.

Without some sort of vision for our lives, some sort of dream, we will have a tough time being committed to any course. In this bustling, goal-driven world, it is easy to be swept away by external priorities or primitive impulses. At the same time, if we obsess over our own self-absorbed wants, we will obstruct or constrict the flow of life's most powerful energies and thrash against the Source of Life and Light. Where is the balance? That is a large part of what this book tries to convey: that our equilibrium lies in working toward emotional strength and spiritual enrichment while aligning with the good of All, and at the same time letting go of all the "must-dos" our ego demands of us. While in the depths of mystical awareness, we trust ourselves to dream the dream of our own life, resisting the pulls of obsession and fixation on the one hand, and dependence and procrastination on the other. Equally important, the *yin* of our creative and spiritual vision is activated in the *yang* of the real world – a world of commitments, compromises, and consequences. Only when we invest in ourselves – and rely on ourselves by following through on intuition and mystical insight – can we fully appreciate our individual purpose. Finally, we will let go of whatever we discover and achieve so that the creative authority of our Divine Spark can continue to flourish. If we avoid this internal exploration and affirmation and fumble from one externally-guided path to the next, seeking support or approval in the material world, we will never be satisfied and never truly succeed.

> "That which rules within, when it is true to its nature, always easily adapts itself to whatever comes. It requires no definite material, but moves towards its purpose and makes material for itself out of anything which opposes it, just as fire lays hold of whatever falls into it. A small light may be extinguished, but when the fire is strong, it soon appropriates for itself whatever is heaped on it, and consumes it, and rises higher."

From Marcus Aurelius' *Meditations*

In the broader context of our soul's journey, does it matter what we choose as our life's work, as long as we can apply ourselves with compassion, kindness and continuing spiritual growth? Well, if we choose a path which conflicts with our core beliefs and values, we will likely undermine our own progress and the impact we wish to have on the world – which brings us full-circle back to maturing self-awareness, and acting from spiritual discernment. Otherwise, though, the freedom and myriad choices before us can themselves be frightening and sometimes hard to accept, but that is what the Universe offers us. People do wax ecstatic at finding their "true calling," and sometimes there is regret at not discovering this intense connection with Self – for I think that is what a true calling is – earlier in life. But we would not be who we are if not for the many side trips we took along the way. Like anything else, it isn't the arrival that matters, it is the state of our mind, heart and spirit during the journey of self-discovery, and the space we continually create in and around us for new possibilities.

> "Certain professions are more or less completely incompatible with the achievement of [humanity's] final end; and there are certain ways of making a living which do so much physical and, above all, so much moral, intellectual and spiritual harm that, even if they could be practiced in a non-attached spirit (which is generally impossible), they would still have to be eschewed by anyone dedicated to the task of liberating, not only [themselves] but others."

Aldous Huxley, as quoted in the book *Chop Wood,
Carry Water, A Guide to Finding Spiritual Fulfillment
in Everyday Life*

What About Materialism?

"Whoever loves money will not be satisfied with money, and
whoever loves abundance will not be satisfied with their income.
This too is futility. For when good things increase, those who
consume them increase. So what is the advantage to their
owners, except to observe this?"

King Solomon, *Ecclesiastes 5:11*

In my few first jobs out of High School, I was a salesman. I sold paint
and hardware, I sold cameras, I sold TVs and VCRs, I sold
computers, copiers, water heaters and sewing machines. And in the
process, I sold my self-esteem. One day in my early twenties, coming
home from one of these sales jobs, I remember staring down at my
feet and thinking, "Why is it that my feet seem to be all I look at
anymore...?" I suddenly realized that whatever was left of my
connection with Self was melting away under the constant pressure
of sales quotas, incentives and greed. A gloomy haze abruptly lifted
from my mind, and for the first time I clearly saw avarice, jealousy,
possessiveness, competitiveness and striving for what they were: the
primitive responses of a fearful animal that won't let go of material
security. I realized there wasn't enough room in my life for both
spirituality and exceeding my sales target for the month; I could not
serve two masters. So I quit, and hired on with a non-profit agency
for missing children.

Clearly, the addiction to a materialist way of being is prevalent in
U.S. culture because that is the system of economics we have chosen
for ourselves. In the most archaic, worldly set of assumptions, this
system dominates and thrives. But at its root, money is an
abstraction of trust, and wherever authentic trust between people is
supplanted with the artificial trust of riches, the quality of human
relationships suffers. But like nearly all of the cooperative constructs

societies have employed throughout history, this will of necessity evolve. Someday, the ideas of money, ownership, and competitiveness will pass away completely. In the meantime, to be a member of such a culture is to constantly confront the lure of materialist reinforcement. Work, earn, acquire, collect, buy, own, provide...these are the building blocks of "success" in a greed-based society, and if we choose to live in that society we cannot escape a temptation to conform. But financial security is only a child-construct of dependence on external power, and such dependency will arrest our spiritual growth and cloud our understanding until we let it go.

Just as with a search for truth, a focus on achieving some intermediate but absolute assurance, some specific evidentiary outcome, effectively shackles the Universe's creative capacity to fulfill our hopes and dreams. I believe that the Universe offers a matching funds program for our faith: if we are willing to trust, with an attitude of equal parts humility, positive expectation, and deference to the good of All, the Universe *will* meet us half-way – though frequently much more inventively than we ever imagined. This type of faith has not failed me yet. I won't claim to know with certainty the instruments of fulfillment, and once again I contend that it doesn't matter what the mechanisms are. What matter are our intentions, our capacity for compassion, our freedom from the prison of material lusts, and our ability to experience the present with ineffable gratitude and joy regardless of what the Universe sends our way.

> Don't be tempted by the shiny apple
> Don't you eat of a bitter fruit
> Hunger only for a taste of justice
> Hunger only for a world of truth
> 'Cause all that you have is your soul.
>
>> Tracy Chapman, from her song *All That You Have Is Your Soul* [44]

---

[44] *Crossroads album*, 1989

Measuring True Success

> Before enlightenment, chop wood, carry water.
> After enlightenment, chop wood, carry water.
>
> From a Zen *Koan*

There is a way to measure our spiritual success, and that is in the quality of our interactions with others. Here is how the Apostle Paul puts it: "The fruit of the Spirit is love, joy, peace, patience, kindness, goodness, faithfulness, gentleness, and self-control."[45] Are the fruits of your spiritual growth evident in your life? Do you feel love, joy, peace, patience and kindness towards yourself and others a majority of the time? Would you ascribe goodness, faithfulness, gentleness and self-control to most of your thoughts, feelings and actions? When we are truly living these things, instead of conforming to an idea of what they are supposed to look like, we can know their inherent power and value to the Universe. If we are struggling to maintain equilibrium, or feel like an empty shell of conformance, then we must reexamine the suppositions of our life: our core values, our purpose, our limitations, and our strengths. As everyone finds their own way to Self, the outward evidences of our well-being are but an echo of the potent and thriving Divine Spark which inhabits us.

A spiritual awakening or epiphany can change the appreciation of our existence without necessarily changing the structure of our lives. The challenges come when our environment is antagonistic to our new way of being, and we can't see a way to reconcile the two. Should we change careers? Should we exit an unhealthy relationship? Should we move to a new city and start over? In my own experience, it is often prudent to try changing what, how, who, and why we are without any radical "relocation therapy." Otherwise, how do we know we have really changed the patterns of our life instead of just placed ourselves in a less challenging environment? As difficult as it may sometimes seem, it is often best

---

[45] New Testament: *Galatians 5:22*

to start with some of the smaller aspects of our routine, the ones that don't disrupt everyone else in our life, and conform those facets to our newly evolving Self.   After a predetermined amount of time – recently, I committed to do this for one year – if we find that even after incremental but substantial changes to our way of being the old environment is still dragging us down...well, it may be time to move on. For some, such as an adult child who is still living at home, or a partner who is financially dependent, or a breadwinner who feels everyone depends on them, this may take more courage than staying put. But in all cases, this is about being well and evolving our soul, not about avoiding conflict, helping other people feel superficially secure or happy, or finding an easy way out.

Lastly, one of the most obvious evidences of our spiritual progress is the strength of our character. Is our sense of peace easily upset? Are we easily dissuaded from what we know is a spiritually healthy course by someone else's advice? Do we have the flexibility of adjusting our approach to each new situation without losing our overall focus? Can we let go of our ego and our attachment to outcomes without losing our sense of alignment with a greater good? Can we be disciplined and moderate without being overly rigid and oppressive? If our character is strong, we can do all of these things. That is how our faith bears witness in us, when we truly believe.

> "The fulfillment of your dream does not depend on outside forces. It depends on your living willingly in the integrity and essence of who you are."
>
> Rabbi Shoni Labowitz, *Miraculous Living*

Creativity

> "Art is an affirmation of life, a rebuttal of death."
> Madeleine L'Engle, *Walking on Water*

All art speaks for itself, and aside from educating ourselves to better appreciate cultural tradition, a specific artist's technique, or the broader context of a work of art, creativity is like meditation for both the artist and audience. It is both intensely personal and profoundly universal. Creativity expresses all that is Divine in human nature, and whenever I find myself in the presence of creative genius, I experience the same qualities of mystical awe as when I stand on the rim of the Grand Canyon, am touched by some simple act of loving kindness, or am infused with a life-changing epiphany. In my worldview, true artists are the priests and priestesses of the mystic impulse, and their finest work connects us with ourselves and the shared understanding of the Universe in ancient and continually reinvented ways.

One of the greatest tragedies of modern U.S. culture is that artistic self-expression is either encouraged to conform to popular formats or discouraged and demeaned altogether by the mainstream. As with the commercialization and commoditization of many other things, art in the U.S. has often become a mediocre byproduct of assembly-line capitalism. There is excellence to be found, but artistic expression for mass consumption is inherently risk-averse, so the only excellence that survives is that which happens to resonate with opportunistic promoters, has a guaranteed avenue of broad distribution, or has enough mass-media traction to reap large profits. There are exceptions, of course, but they seem to be fewer and farther between of late. Meanwhile, parents returning home from the current hit movie may rave about the writing, acting, music and cinematography, but when their own child expresses a desire to be a writer, or an actor, or a musician, or cinematographer...what do the parents say? If the lopsided funding in public schools is any indication, they are saying: "You should be a scientist, a lawyer, a professional athlete, or maybe get an MBA...but don't even *think* about pursuing an artistic career!" I only hope that as more people discover and nurture their spiritual nature, the critical importance of creative expression will blossom out of the wonder in their hearts.

> "Is it not possible to conclude that if we make contact with our highest potential level of consciousness through the practice of high thought and dedicated, disciplined action, we find ourselves opening, like the lotus petals from the bud, giving forth our own special gift to life?"
>
> Edith Schlosser, from her essay "Creativity and the Mystical Experience" [46]

Our Freedom

I often use the word "choice." A choice to create our life, instead of submitting to a default condition of impulses, approval-seeking, herd instinct, delusion and egotism. A choice to be conscious, to awaken our heart to the world, and surge forth with audacity to meet the most worthwhile challenge of being authentically ourselves. Yet choosing to *be* ourselves requires that we first *know* ourselves, to love and honor our lonely soul, and that is much of what the path of spiritual evolution is all about. So the sooner we begin living a spiritual existence, the less effort we will expend being lost in distractions, and the sooner we can laugh aloud at all the silliness we once thought was so important.

Yet we humans are elaborately resourceful at constructing mazes for ourselves, confining our choices with layer upon layer of assumptions without ever questioning why. And – once again – asking *why* can be very useful in deconstructing those mazes. For instance, let's say someone dislikes their job. It's stressful, a little boring, and they feel intense hostility from an insecure boss. But they *can't* leave! Why? Because they have to make those house payments. Why? Because they have a six-year-old child, and a spouse who just

---

[46] From *The Silent Encounter: Reflections on Mysticism* by Virginia Hanson, Editor, Theosophical Publishing House, 1974

quit work to care for their long-awaited second child, and the whole family is expecting not only a nice home, but also the bigger second car, and then there will be the savings account for college, and decent clothes, and toys, and the trip to Disneyland....

Now, wait a minute.

Can you see the string of faulty assumptions, here? First of all, every single one of these "must haves" constitutes a choice. Marriage. Children. The nice house. The bigger car. The pre-paid college education. The toys and trips. Were all of them necessary? Was there some clear priority and life-plan involved here? Or do these choices represent societal expectations, pressure from relatives, the advice of friends, a marital spat which was never resolved, or just plain old ego? One of the first things most of our parents tried to teach us as children is the distinction between wants and needs, but how often we lose sight of that distinction when we become adults! In this example, a hoard of competing wants – all of which are being treated as *needs* of near-equal priority – have convinced this person to stay in a job they dislike.

> Don't try to put out a fire
> by throwing on more fire!
> Don't wash a wound with blood!
> No matter how fast you run,
> your shadow more than keeps up.
> Sometimes, it's in front!
>
> Rumi, *Enough Words?* [47]

The fallout from such lack of distinction and prioritization is predictable: we become miserable, and all of the precious objectives we were striving for are undermined by that misery. After all, what do children really need? Love and approval for who they are. Confidence. Resourcefulness. An understanding of boundaries and consequences. Some solid, fundamental life skills. A thoughtful head start on their spiritual journey. Opportunity. Are any of these

---

[47] From *The Essential Rumi* by Coleman Barks, Harper San Francisco, 1997

guaranteed by the maze our example breadwinner has put in place? Imagine a child who grows up with parents who are stressed-out and inattentive. Imagine the impact the child's resultant low self-esteem will have on personal achievements and relationships. Imagine, as that child emulates the parents' behavior, a series of poor choices based on confused priorities, which invariably lead them deeper into a miserable maze of their own! How meaningful will any money-bought opportunity be to such a misdirected soul?

And where is the end of the maze, anyway? What is the cheese? Generation after generation of unhappy families with stressful jobs, broken hearts, and just enough money to guarantee the next generation the same self-loathing? Not a very attractive outcome. But there is a remedy: we can break the cycle. We don't have to accept the default perpetuation of unhealthy lifestyle choices. We can reject the labyrinth of conformist assumptions that control the societal herd. We can be attentive and aware, careful about our goals and the rate and method of our consumption, and willing to find our own way out of the maze. And if our priorities are structured around spiritual evolution instead of primitive impulses, what an amazing array of options even our most fleeting wishes can provide!

> The intellect of man is forced to choose
> Perfection of the life, or of the work,
> And if it take the second must refuse
> A heavenly mansion, raging in the dark.
> When all that story's finished, what's the news?
> In luck or out the toil has left its mark:
> That old perplexity an empty purse,
> Or the day's vanity, the night's remorse.
>
> *The Choice*, by W.B.Yeats

Cecile Andrew's book *The Circle of Simplicity* is a valuable resource for examining and reshaping lifestyle choices.

The Long, Dark Night

Many mystics and writers about mysticism have offered their own interpretation of a condition which is reported in many spiritual traditions, but is perhaps most widely-documented in the writings of Christian mystics: the "long, dark night of the soul." I offer my own perspective within Lifestyle Choices because I believe this event in our spiritual development has important implications for how we choose to live. It is, in essence, a graduation into the beginnings of spiritual adulthood. Why the dark metaphor? Because it represents the ultimate separation from the initial object of our quest, that union with Divine energies that assures us we are not alone, and evidences a more mature understanding of the illusions we once maintained about ourselves and the Universe. For a seeker on the path of Love's Perfection, this can be agonizing, because the subjective experience is one of abandonment, isolation, and nothingness – a superficial but at first inexplicable contrast to the rapture of earlier transitions through gnosis. And yet, it is not really separation at all – other than from an earlier, incomplete understanding.

When we realize our purpose through mystical awareness, and begin to live in harmony with our Self, the Source of Life and Light, and an ever-increasing refinement of the golden intention, there are still a few attachments yet to relinquish. One of them is our delight in previous contemplative states, which is a particularly strong attachment if we associate them with spiritual accomplishment. Another is the differentiation between self, the Source and our actuation of intentions. For there is in truth no separation of identity, believing and doing – these are the vestiges of our childhood understanding, still orienting itself to externals: external definitions of self, external appreciation of Divinity, and external expression of will. And whenever we remain dependant on externals – even if it is only a conception of reality that is being externalized – we will eventually experience disappointment and despair. But in the highest contemplative states, the furthest emotional transformations, and the deepest spiritual gnosis, peace does not issue from spiritual accomplishment, or even an awareness of any of these separate things. There is no intellect, no heart, no spirit. There is no action.

What awaits us at the journey's end? Consider the possibility that there is no end; that there is only continuation, in being and forms and realms and relationships beyond our current comprehension; and that the answer for our questing soul is securely woven into that process of continuation and cannot be described in terms of arrival or conclusion. Think of a good friend, or life partner, or family member, and imagine asking them: "So…when do you suppose our relationship will reach its peak? When will the way we connect or communicate tomorrow threaten to be less than what we have attained right now, simply because there is no greater breadth or depth available?" For is love only won or lost, or is it an ever-changing landscape? Even as we become content with who we are and how we live, that does not mean the Universe is done with us. Even in the last hours of this earthly life we may witness new kinds of appreciation, interconnectedness, and depths of communication…if we are open to them.

And it is our openness which marks us as a *vital* mystic. To resist or avoid new spiritual horizons will only cause us pain, and although we may believe we have a formula for spiritual health and wealth – this book may itself sometimes stumble over that arrogant assertion – our assumptions will, in due course, be challenged. Noticing this, and embracing the challenges as they arrive, is our never-ending adventure and the true source of all deep and enduring contentment.

> "When we have mature understanding, partial understanding falls away. When I was young, I thought like a child and spoke like a child, but as an adult I have let go of childish ways. For now, we may only see an enigma in the mirror, but then we shall see face to face."
>
> 0New Testament, *1 Corinthians 13:10-12*

Chapter Questions

1. How have you defined success for yourself? What choices in your life have brought you closer to that success?
2. Do you believe that the Universe has a matching funds program for your dreams and aspirations?
3. What choices have you made during your life that you now regret? Why did you make them at the time? Why do you regret them now?
4. What will you do tomorrow to bring you closer to your dream?
5. Have you immersed yourself in artistic excellence recently?
6. What does "perfection" or "completion" mean to you?
7. Do you consider yourself "creative?" Why or why not?

Part Four: Navigating the Thorns

11. DISCERNMENT: the WALK, the WAY, the WARNING SIGNS

I suppose because of my own lingering discomfort with judgmental attitudes I have encountered both in myself and others, this is one of the more difficult chapters to write. There is fertile ground here for pride and self-righteousness to grow, blocking out the light of understanding and obscuring the path of self-discovery. But it is necessary to address this topic, if only to help maintain focus as we navigate the demands of each day. Early on in this book, I mentioned that I was distracted from my own path of mystical awareness, even after credible reinforcement from different sources that what I had mystically perceived and experienced in my life was valid. I rejected my own inherent spiritual intelligence, and chose the harder road of experimentation...and what a long road that was! Nearly ten years and a fair amount of suffering led me full circle to where I began. And that cycle of departure and return has repeated itself many times since.

This, then, is one approach to preserving priorities during our journey, even as the mystic impulse guides into deeper truths. I have learned not to regret what I call "lapses into existential futility," because I ultimately benefit from them, if only by their contrast to a more successful way of being. But if I can avoid such lapses in the future, and help others avoid – or at least recognize – these diversions, then perhaps I have done something useful and kind.

The Warning Signs

Here are some indications that we may be drifting out of the realm of spiritually healthy effort. Once again, we can certainly learn from everything we experience, but I believe there are real consequences for our attitudes and actions, and some of those consequences may be unfortunate for ourselves and others and far-reaching in effect. What are the warning signs? There are so many! Here is the beginning of a list which undoubtedly will require later additions:

Blindness. "When one eye is fixed constantly on your destination, there is only one eye left to find your way."[48] We may seek guidance, but miss the signs provided to us. We may experience the same events over and over, feeling like we are in a fixed orbit around our true destination, never able to reach a sense of purpose or peace. We may have repeated success in worldly achievement, but still feel empty. All of these are symptoms of the same illness: paying too much attention to our goals, and not fully experiencing the present moment. Have you ever met a young person who is anxious to grow up? To be able to drive a car, or be independent, or have their first intimate relationship? Western culture inundates children with images and ideas of how wonderful being *adult* is, while far too little celebrates the joy and importance of childhood. Then, as adults, those who have rushed to adulthood often look back on their youth as a missed opportunity for playful, carefree joy. This is an example of what blindness is. The pattern of always fixating on a place besides where we are is a malady which seldom dissipates with time; the child who strove to be grown up may now strive to attain some other *elsewhere* goal, and thereby trample blindly over the playful, carefree happiness of *right now*.

Dependence. "Learn about your inner self from those who know such things, but don't repeat verbatim what they say."[49] For much of my younger life, I longed for a mentor to guide me into All Truth.

---

[48] A Zen Buddhist teaching
[49] From *The Essential Rumi* by Coleman Barks, Harper San Francisco, 1997

This process may be different, I think, for the feminine and masculine in us, but a similar longing exists in most people at some point in their life: that a strong, centered, *powerful* being will provide the example and encouragement we need to spur us on. This could be a spiritual guide, an organization, financial security, an oracle, or even a mind-altering drug...it might, at different times, be all of these. This state of dependence is a natural step in our spiritual development, but it should only be a temporary milestone for us – eventually we must move on, and relinquish our reliance on externals. Why? Because this becomes habituation on power outside of ourselves for achieving well-being. As children, we expected to be fed. As adults, we must learn to feed ourselves. The deepest wisdom, after all, is continually being written in our own hearts.

Comparison. I remember a dear friend of mine once saying, "I want a wizard, too!" She was referring to the magical inner guide, complete with long white beard and majestic purple robes, whom someone she knew was consulting at that time. Another friend of mine would go to bed at night with a humble prayer for help in some area, only to have that prayer answered, consistently and powerfully, the very next morning! Did I wish such synchronicity for myself? Of course! This can happen to anyone, for the more conscious we become of the nature of things, the more we will see power manifested in others, and in the thriving of life in general. But love is not jealous. And that is the heart of it: close kin to dependence, the habit of comparing oneself to others is debilitating and self-limiting. The moment we let go of this habit is the moment we begin to express with our life the very things we so longed for. For a spiritual life is not about having or attainting, it is about effortlessly and unselfconsciously being.

Stubbornness. "By letting go, it all gets done. The world is won by those who let go! Though you keep trying, the world is beyond winning." [50] How easy it is to live the expression: "I'm beating my head against a wall!" And that's a sure sign that we are holding on

---

[50] *Tao te Ching*

too tightly to some idea, belief, or practice. Why does pride go before a fall? Because when we become overconfident and belligerent about our own choices and direction in life, we close ourselves to possibilities and insights that could heal us, help us, and enlighten us. "I don't want to!" is the child's plea to be free of obligation and responsibility. "This is new territory for me, but I will go forward out of love for myself and others..." is true freedom from oppressive attachments, because it shifts the focus away from the fortress of pride we have constructed to protect ourselves, and opens the gates of our heart to the lessons of the unknown. "We should make all spiritual talk simple today: God is trying to sell you something, but you don't want to buy. That is what your suffering is – your fantastic haggling, your manic screaming over the price!" [51]

Fear. I believe fear has an important place in our inventory of emotions: it is the "beginning of wisdom," as King Solomon said, and initially benefits us as a primitive self-preservation response. Without some healthy, rational fear, humans would quickly perish. But if we are continually experiencing an irrational or overwhelming fear as we move through the choices of our lives, it is unlikely we will take the risks necessary to flourish and grow. Research into emotions has shown that fear and excitement have very similar physiological components (adrenaline, increased heart rate, rapid breathing, etc.), and that the one main difference is what we expect the outcome to be. Have you ever seen Ron Howard's movie *Parenthood?* In it, the grandmother character talks about people who like the merry-go-round, which just goes round and round, and people who like roller coasters. "I like the roller coaster," she says. "You get more out of it. I always wanted to go again. You know, it was just so interesting to me that a ride could make me so frightened, so scared, so sick, so excited, and so thrilled all together!" If we transform a resisting, irrational fear to positive excitement, we can create space in our lives to welcome its surprises.

---

[51] From *I Heard God Laughing: Renderings of Hafiz* by Daniel Ladinsky, Sufism Reoriented, 1996

Joylessness. In nearly every spiritual tradition, the mark of a true believer is abiding joy. Such joy may be expressed differently in different cultures, or have different qualities during progressive stages of spiritual life. For one person, dancing in a circle and singing at the top of their lungs expresses glorious connection with the Divine. For another, quiet tears and gratitude evidence the soaring of their heart. I sometimes feel that profound joy is only a hair's breadth away from deepest sorrow. Hafiz says it this way: "What happens when your soul begins to awaken – your eyes and your heart and the cells of your body – to the great Journey of Love? First there is wonderful laughter, and probably precious tears, and a hundred sweet promises, and those heroic vows no one can ever keep...." [52] At the other extreme, we can lose our sense of humor, playfulness, gratitude or contentment altogether, and find our emotional latitude constricting to serious brooding. When abiding joy flees, we know something is amiss: either we are avoiding a necessary encounter in our spiritual path, or our self-nourishment is out of balance.

Chronic Illness. Our bodies have a deliberate way of reminding us when something is lacking in our lives: we get sick. For some diseases, there are genetic predispositions; for others, there are environmental factors which may be out of our control. But for many – perhaps a majority – of illnesses, we likely have a choice to be healthy that can only be exercised through maintaining our self-awareness and self-esteem. This is not, however, the sort of cause-and-effect I would wave in front of a critically ill patient, nor is this about feeling guilt or blame for health problems. But this *is* about taking responsibility for the quickest and surest way of managing our illness and ultimately being well. One example is Type II Diabetes. Regardless of how it is brought on, this disease can usually be managed with changes in diet and exercise – often to the point where no medication is required. But to change our attitudes and habits requires an investment in self, an investment that comes easily out of affection and compassion for who we are, but is very difficult if we

---

[52] From *I Heard God Laughing: Renderings of Hafiz* by Daniel Ladinsky, Sufism Reoriented, 1996

inhabit a space of perpetual unhappiness. Thus, it is much easier to arrive at wellness if we first arrive at happiness. This topic is discussed further in the chapter About Suffering.

Chronic Chaos. Are things in your life perpetually complicated? Are you always busy, always have demands on your time, or always engaged with other people's expectations? Do you find it difficult to say "no" to new activities or commitments? Do concerns about people, plans, schedules, and goals consume your every waking thought? These are signs of what I call *chaos-addiction*, a dependency on externally driven priorities to feel fulfilled, be stimulated, or approach satisfaction about our lives. I like the way Rabbi Shoni Labowitz speaks about this: "Your life has value; do not waste it in the fast-moving, eternally revolving door of illusion."[53] Concerned with chaos in my own life, I once participated in Cecille Andrews' Voluntary Simplicity workshops. What an eye-opening experience! Her book, *The Circle of Simplicity*, is a summary of her thinking on how we can simplify our lives, making them more purposeful and powerful in the process.

Acute Loneliness, Anxiety or Depression. Solitude can be an enriching experience, but acute loneliness, the kind that stings us to the core, is a corrective emotion. Like guilt or doubt, loneliness reminds us that some action or consideration needs to occur, and is not a condition we should suppress, ignore, or try to be comfortable with. Something in us wants tending – though what, exactly, may be less clear. Anxiety, free-floating or fixed obsessively on anything, is another corrective response: something in our patterns of thought or behavior has to be addressed. Depression is likewise a reminder that there are things to work through, and can rob of us the hope that inspires us to look for answers. Discovering what we are reacting to may require hours of deep meditation, a good therapist, or continuous prayer, but smothering our loneliness with relationships, blanketing our anxiety with stimulation, or medicating our depression into emotional disconnection will not nourish the part of

---

[53] From her book, *Miraculous Living*, Fireside, 1996

us that is reaching out for help. Whatever is triggering these emotions likely represents the next hurdle for our spiritual development; though the hike may be strenuous, the views will be spectacular.

Control Behavior. When we try to control our external environment, it is because we have unresolved chaos within. Each time we have an impulse to control, we should listen to our own heart and the murmuring of our spirit for the source of pain and disorder inside us. A focus on healing those internal hurts is the only thing that can calm the storm of controlling behaviors.

Feeling Overwhelmed. This is a sure sign of one of three things: a) we have overestimated our abilities and taken too much on; b) we are stubbornly refusing to learn some lesson; or c) we're about to reach a new plateau of understanding. Discernment and experience help us to see the source of the deluge. If we find ourselves in this space, however, it may be time to withdraw and reconsider the course we have chosen for our life – or at a minimum the course we have chosen for our day.

The more attuned we are to our inner world, the more easily we will recognize these and other conditions which alert us to a spiritual struggle. One of the most widely promoted ways of maintaining balance and nourishment is through a thoughtful and constantly renewed spiritual discipline. The chapters Self Awareness and Self Esteem and A Mystic's Way described aspects of this effort, as do the thoughts that follow.

The Walk: External Discipline and Internal Organization

> "Solid [spiritual] food is for the mature, who through practice have their senses trained to discern good from evil."
>
> New Testament, *Hebrews 5:14*

In short: self-control *matters*. By being disciplined, by practicing what we believe to be right even when it's hard – even when it requires sacrifice – enables us over time to mature reliable insight and discernment. If we intend to evolve, we learn how to order our existence even as that regimen changes over time. This is perhaps the one crucial instance where an external structure enables internal empowerment, at least initially. Some would argue that if we are truly motivated by love and compassion, we would not require strictures, boundaries, or any other controls on our behavior. This, it could be argued, lies at the heart of differing opinions about how to raise children, teach a class, manage people, or govern society: do you reward constructive behavior, punish unproductive behavior, or encourage development and direction through empowering the individual to govern themselves? The idea of discipline in itself doesn't answer this, for whether imposed from without or from within, discipline is represented in all of these models.

To answer this question, we must make certain assumptions about what motivates us to reach a specific goal. In the spiritual arena, what will inspire us to work towards our next stage of being? If we believe the ember of longing for a higher level awareness and a greater contribution to the good of All are native to every soul, then all anyone needs is a little encouragement to stay the course. We need only nurture that ember into a comforting flame, and trust that each new way of being is reinforced and rewarded from within. If, on the other hand, we believe the inspiration to spiritually evolve is beyond basic human nature or propensity, then employing some kind of behavioral conditioning from without seems a reasonable course. In the dualism inherent to many religions, the struggle between good and evil, darkness and light, and spirit and flesh often add a cosmic dimension to this dilemma, but the basic question of the most constructive way to motivate still goes unanswered.

Which is why we find concepts like obedience, submission, asceticism, and brokenness in many spiritual traditions, while at the same time encountering the seemingly conflicting ideas of unconditional forgiveness, being Divinely chosen, created in a Deity's image, having a spiritual nature or conscience, or having complete freedom in everything we do. Can such contradictions be objectively resolved? The premise of this book is that we advance through different stages of being, and that within these stages we tend to emphasize, react from, and operate according to the various levels of our Pyramid of Self. In this context, we will require different incentives and structure in our lives at different times. Just as when we were infants we benefited from parents restricting our unwise behavior, in our earliest stages of being we will likely benefit from externally imposed discipline – and perhaps even a little fear. As we mature, we shed these restrictions in favor of following our internal Light, effecting discipline inspired by love instead of fear.

I remember many years ago, while perusing the art museums of Paris, remarking to a friend: "What's the point of learning how to paint, if all you do with your skill is abandon it? I mean, anybody could do this, couldn't they?" I was referring to Jackson Pollock's work and some other, non-objective paint splattering in the Pompidou. My friend, who was a painter himself, replied, "This is significant exactly because the artist knew how to paint, and then went off in a new direction. Nobody had done it before." These painters knew exactly what they were doing. With this new understanding, I had a deeper appreciation for what I was seeing, and it got me thinking about other art forms. Rock musicians and Jazz composers who had labored through rigorous classical training. Or the first sculptor who said, after apprenticing for years under a stiffly stylizing master: "Let's make these warriors look *real and alive*!"

Such artists share a common language and frame of reference from which to advance their unique style of expression. They have earned the right to challenge tradition because they have mastered that tradition. This is yet another parallel of our natural development, from dependence on external structure and ritual when we are children, to emancipation from those externals as adults and an increasing reliance on internally developed sensibilities to navigate each moment. But most often we must first "learn the basics" before we can launch into the unknown. Any of my own early teachers would be shocked to hear me say this now, because I was constantly challenging the most insignificant precept they tried to convey; I just couldn't accept any teaching as factual until its worth and relevance had somehow been logically proven. Of course, the most difficult concepts of all are learned by accepting and doing, not by debating.

Discipleship

> The student asks, "What is the Tao?"
> The master answers, "Your ordinary mind is the Tao."
> "How can it be found?" the student asks.
> "If you intend to obtain it, then you cannot obtain it."
> "But if I give up my intention to obtain it, how can it be found?"
> "The Tao is beyond being lost or found, beyond knowing and unknowing. It doesn't belong to any specific category. It's impossible to know what it is, and folly to grasp it through unknowing. Understanding the Tao is like understanding the empty sky."
>
> Zen teaching from *The Gateless Gate* [54]

Many ancient traditions practice a special kind of teacher-student relationship, a companionship in spiritual practice where one person mentors another, usually one-on-one. I experienced this as discipleship in Christian ministry, but the same type of relationship exists between a Hindu guru and their disciples, a Wiccan High

---

[54] Paraphrasing of text quoted in *The Tao of Zen* by Ray Gigg, Alva Press, 1994

Priestess and her coven initiates, a Buddhist master and their students, soul-friends who mutually mentor each other, and even a spirit guide and a receptive mystic. This discipline often includes sharing certain routine practices – sometimes without a clear explanation or objective – which lead to new awareness and insight. You might call it spiritual homework, and it is really no different than, say, deciding to start a healthier diet or learn a foreign language: you can't know what the outcome of your effort will be until after you have maintained a steady discipline for some time.

There are four things happening in this process that make it so effective. The first is that the "disciple" is letting go of previous assumptions and their desire for control. This has obvious ancillary benefits in achieving a neutrality of personal will so necessary for spiritual growth. The second is a demonstrated openness to new ideas and a retraining of the heart to be receptive and pliable. The third is a conditioning or "firming" of the mind that occurs through newly formed, scrupulous and ordered habit. The fourth is the simplicity and clarity of being that repetition, concurrent with detachment, provide. In other words, discipleship strengthens the skills required for early contemplative states and emotional transformation. Of course, without *paying attention* to what we are doing, it is likely this process won't clarify our perceptions or reshape our heart at all – it is therefore the shared responsibility of teacher and student to maintain and encourage both constant attentiveness and healthy detachment. But at some point, when the disciple is listening to the birds singing in the garden (or whatever the seemingly inexplicable task may be) in just the way an instructor has invited them to do for countless weeks, sudden understanding dawns. That understanding, in turn, is what activates the first glimmers of self-sufficient discernment. I have not encountered anything yet that accelerates this kind of learning by rote, and few things are as effective for early spiritual progress.

What happens in discipleship is more than just behavioral conditioning. Perhaps it is reorganization of our energetic and neurological pathways, or overriding primitive or habitual patterns of thought and emotion within a spiritualized context. Just as with learning any new skill, new internal connections are being made which change how we process information, how we perceive and interpret our world. When we pray, meditate, recite mantras, balance our chakras, give money to charities, forgive our enemies, practice mindfulness, free ourselves from some destructive impulse, or anything that the great spiritual traditions of the world teach their disciples, we are stepping onto a road of consciousness that advances our spirit and heals us at the foundations of our psyche. Eventually, we emerge from the chrysalis of such conditioning into a more spontaneous, unregulated state; but we begin to grow our wisdom by acting without knowing, and learning by doing.

> "Have patience with everything unresolved in your heart and try to love the questions themselves, as if they were locked rooms or books written in a very foreign language. Don't search for the answers, which could not be given to you now, because you would not be able to live them...the point is to live everything. Live the questions now. Perhaps then, some day far in the future, you will gradually, without even noticing it, live your way into the answer."
>
> Rainer Maria Rilke, *Letters to a Young Poet*

The Way: Head Time, Heart Time and Spirit Time

Wherever we are in our spiritual journey, our next steps often traverse three different arenas of learning: Heart Time, Head Time and Spirit Time. Most of us live in Head Time, where we think about what we are going to do, and then act on our decisions. Our minds can quickly grasp the challenges before us: how to get to work on time, what we will do with our friends when we see them on the weekend, how we might lose weight, or what book we will buy our lover for their birthday. In Western society, particularly in the U.S., Head Time is wildly accelerated, with schedules and crises and people at work and home all vying for our attention. But we scurry to keep up because our heads tell us *we can do it*. And on a superficial level, our ability to accelerate Head Time, or intellectual processing of each moment, does allow us to "barely make it in time" with some frequency. But all too often, our minds get so far ahead of our ability to experience and process life spiritually and emotionally that we effectively decapitate ourselves on those levels. No matter how exciting it may feel to be "on top of our game," our spirits and hearts are running around with their head cut off.

Heart Time and Spirit Time can't be forced into tight schedules and hurried lifestyles. Even in cultures where Head Time is more reasonably paced, Heart Time will usually lag behind, and Spirit will trail even farther behind the Heart. I don't know why this is. Perhaps the whole of our being hasn't caught up with the complexity of the 21st century, or perhaps the way we have chosen to live and prioritize in modern times is essentially unhealthy. Whatever the case, there is no way to rush emotional understanding, mystical awareness, or spiritual epiphany. As frustrating as we may feel about it (a warning sign in itself), the less analytical parts of us operate completely independently of our rational mind, respond to different stimuli, and process and resolve life's conundrums in their own unique ways. This is why spiritual evolution takes a while, just like developing a satisfying friendship does, or healing from intense grief.

In summary, take time for your heart and your spirit. Be attentive to their progress. Celebrate the changes you experience in yourself, and be patient. Perhaps if we all lived in Heart Time, we would elicit greater synchronicity and enduring contentment in our lives. Perhaps if we structured our progress and plans around the Spirit, we would be more aware of the miracles unfolding constantly all around us.

The Confirmation of Synchronicity

At any given interval, one way we can test whether we are on the most appropriate path is by observing the *convergence of synchronicity* in our life. When we are in the flow – that is, aligned with the Source of Life and Light and fulfilling a purpose uniquely suitable to us at a given time – we begin to notice a confluence of fortuitous events that enhance our progress.   I referred to this earlier as a universal matching funds program, for that is exactly how it feels; opportunities and resources we could never have imagined appear with ease. In their excellent book, *The Power of Flow*, Charlene Belitz and Meg Lundstrom describe the phenomenon this way: "Flow is the natural, effortless unfolding of our lives in a way that leads us toward harmony and wholeness."   What we often don't realize, however, is that we have *created* this flow with the quality of our intentions; more than anything else, it is this quality which is being confirmed for us.

I have also noticed a sense of déjà vu when reaching a major milestone in my life.   At first, I doubted the significance, but sometimes the déjà vu was so overwhelming I could anticipate *exactly* what was going to happen next...right down to the words someone was about to speak.   Then I noticed something else: the images, sounds and other phenomena I was re-experiencing were uncannily similar to dreams from years earlier, dreams which were so vivid and detailed that I had written them down in my journal.   What was happening here? I wasn't sure, so I started tracking these incidents over time.   What has now become clear is that whenever I am arrested by an especially lucid déjà vu, I have almost certainly dreamt or intuited the moment previously, and it coincides with a decision or change along my path which, although I might not know why at first, is helpful to my spiritual progress.   This is the kind of encouragement the Universe offers us, if we choose to accept it.

But there is a caveat to this method of appreciating our development: if we begin obsessing over synchronistic moments and fortifying our self-esteem with them, a counterproductive state I'll call *dissonant spiritual feedback* is created.   The more we construct our confidence and security on the affirmations of fortuitous coincidence, the louder and more unbearable the squealing distortions of our own desires and spiritual awareness will become, like someone who turns up the volume too high on a lecture microphone. As a result, we will lose ourselves in needy self-obsession, and defeat our own progress. Perhaps this is one reason why spiritual masters have so disparaged people who demand they perform miraculous signs. Appreciating synchronicity isn't about *justifying* that we are good people, that our will is powerful, or that we are on the right evolutionary track; it is about celebration and gratitude when serendipity arrives, then being able to immediately let the moment go and flow onward. Ultimately, the greatest confirmation of our spiritual progress is not the miraculous or synchronistic, but the temperament of our heart, the clarity of our mind, and the tranquility of our spirit.

> "And even if angels were sent down to them, and the dead spoke to them, and all things were brought together before them, they would still not believe unless Allah willed it...."
>
> Qur'an, *Sura 6.111*

What to Trust When

1. **Pray or meditate over the situation.** Remain open, without forcing yourself to decide; just spend time with the question. Clarify in your innermost heart what it at stake, what your true motivations are, and identify all the contributing factors in the situation. Within contemplative silence, confusion will dissipate – though this doesn't always guarantee conclusive answers. In fact, our lesson may be something very different than what we at first supposed. Before meditating, I will frame my question as "What is the wisest course for the good of All in this situation?" Then I will relax into a *gnosis of specificity*, that is: I will relinquish any expectation of an answer, but remain open to what is often very explicit insight. Wishing without wanting again. This will sometimes be a separate mediation, but also can be incorporated into the sitting meditation already described. If a solution presents itself, I will write it down immediately and commit to following through.

2. **If answers are still illusive, try taking a break from your life and retreat into a quiet spot of nature.** Spend a day or two clearing your mind and heart, without trying to decide anything. At the end of such a respite, try prayer or meditation again.

3. **In especially chaotic, clouded or otherwise difficult situations, I will turn to divination.** For me, the Tarot is an extremely useful tool, opening doors into intuition and mystical awareness which I may have previously overlooked – or misinterpreted. I will again offer the question of "What is the wisest course for the good of All?" as I prepare the deck. Meditating on a Tarot spread, admitting its dynamic wisdom, and acting on what presents itself has resolved some extremely perplexing challenges in my life. Once again, the key is to trust that new understanding, and act on it.

4. **Should you still remain transfixed by the magnitude or complexity of your decision, it is probably time to let go.** Give it up to the Universe, realizing that you have done your best, and simply cannot decide. Things will take their course, and the regret, joy or consternation that greets you as a consequence of not deciding will grow your wisdom, and inform every other decision you make.

Along the mystic's way, we are left with the puzzle of acting in the moment with an understanding that stretches into the Infinite. Such deep mystical awareness tends to trivialize everything else. Although reconciling the material with the spiritual – the finite with the limitless – can seem impossible at first, it does become easier with practice. And as we learn to trust both our intuition and our indescribable gnosis, life begins to flow more easily in us and around us, and the nature of each choice becomes increasingly transparent. Yet there is a cost for this clarity, and that is a sense of accountability and responsibility. For as we spiritually mature we will be presented with "solid food," that is, the more difficult and life-changing truths which shape new directions for our life. In the end, intuition, discernment, faith, and wisdom no longer compete for our attention;

there is only *what is*, compelling us achieve through the golden intention alone what we never could have anticipated and what words cannot justify or describe.

Chapter Questions

1. Where do you go when you seek peace?
2. Who are the people in your life you can count on to remind you of what is important?
3. What spiritual warning signs have you experienced lately, and what have you done about them?
4. Is there one particular warning sign that keeps resurfacing in your life? Why do you think this happens?
5. What advantages and growth have you experienced through discipline?
6. Is your life a "natural, effortless unfolding?" Are you *in the flow*?
7. How can you create a lifestyle that is continuously synchronized with Heart Time, or consistently flows in Spirit Time?

12. WHAT REAL EVIL LOOKS LIKE

"Rust being born of iron destroys iron; so evil being born of man destroys man."

The Buddha

When people ask me if I believe in malevolent evil, I have to say that yes, I do. The truest forms of evil share this prime objective: to disparage, reject or undermine the good of All by denigrating the nobility of the soul, enlarging the ego, and crippling self-esteem. Denying the existence of spiritually counterproductive and destructive forces in ourselves and in the Universe is a fairly ineffective way of dealing with them – such denial only facilitates these antagonists. On the other hand, becoming paranoid and fearful of evil only furthers its cause. But what does evil look like? How does it manifest? Usually as conscious or unconscious influences that are spiritually unhealthy in the extreme. Observing these influences at work might provoke a sensitive and compassionate spirit to righteous indignation, and perhaps even protective or corrective action. Yet confrontationally opposing evil, although sometimes effective in the short run, does not address the underlying problems that incite evil and cause it to flourish. A more enduring solution is the subtle and persistent transformation of evil into good; that effort is, in fact, what every chapter in this book intends to facilitate and enhance.

Here are some broad categories of what could be defined as "evil." Each category describes a behavior pattern, but more important are the intentions behind that pattern. Such patterns and intentions do not enhance or support spiritual evolution, but rather seek to undermine and oppose it. We can observe these evidences in others or in ourselves, but observation and identification should not equate a judgmental attitude. These descriptions are not intended to condemn any individual or group; on the contrary, all souls struggle in their own way to understand themselves, and we all share equal potential for stumbling in the dark. In addition, some of these habits may indicate underlying physiological issues or mental illness. However, I believe whoever knowingly practices such destructive behaviors, or deliberately influences others to practice them, has set themselves against the Source of Life and Light and all that is good in the Universe. This can only lead to suffering.

Willful Ignorance. Perhaps the most common malady of humanity is to intentionally and stubbornly maintain ignorance. We will deny responsibility for our actions. We will strive and struggle and beat our heads against a wall, and never pause to consider if there is a better way. We will run away from every truth our heart tries to teach us. We will endlessly repeat the same mistakes and injuries, and insist that nothing is wrong. We will submit to every whim and impulse and never question why. We will forget completely who we are, and pile thick layers of hateful mud around the pleading screams of our own soul. We will expend all our energies in distraction and never relax into the present moment. There are many different circumstances and conditions that lead to this state, but the most common seems to be a strong attachment to pain, self-punishment and despair (the natural results of willful ignorance) because we have not learned compassion for ourselves or understood our purpose in this life.

Animalism. By this I mean a mistaken belief in the supremacy (as opposed to balanced integration) of the Animal[55] in human beings. That is, that the most basic and self-serving of impulses should be celebrated and satisfied above any other, regardless of the cost to

---

[55] See the *Pyramid of Self* in Chapter 2

ourselves or the well-being of those around us. For most, this attachment to insatiable desire is part of an initial stage of being; it is a natural part of our early development. And so we must have compassion for ourselves and for others who face the constant pull of primitive impulses. But much harm has come into the world through animalists who, even though they are cognizant of the destructiveness of their behavior, have no desire or intention to transcend it. Thus, although all animalists victimize themselves, they are usually eager to draw others down with them in order to validate their wanton pleasure-seeking. Evidences of animalism are responses like greed, self-serving ambition, covetousness, selfishness, uncontrollable lust, jealousy, destructive anger, aggressive competitiveness, inability to manage thoughtless impetus, and a generally unabashed abandonment, completely devoid of love, to the most primal aspects of self.

A classic examination of *Animalism* is William Golding's novel, *Lord of the Flies*.

Invalidation. Invalidators try to make other people wrong. This has many different forms, the more subtle of which are perhaps the most damaging. Invalidation seeks to undermine spiritual evolution by trivializing, criticizing, teasing, or otherwise trying to harass or control anyone who seeks a healthier and higher Self. The invalidator's unconscious objective is to hold someone back from further spiritual progress – or better yet, to lure them into reverting to a previous stage of being. Just as an injured or trapped animal may gnaw at its own leg and lash out at others who try to help it, so too invalidators are likely acting from deep hurt or despair, and irrationally justify – or are willfully unaware of – the damage they are wreaking on themselves and others. Thus, invalidators are first and foremost victimizing themselves, but also seek to dominate, control and tear other people down.

> "The mouth of the righteous is a fountain of life, but the mouth of the wicked conceals violence. Hatred stirs up strife, but love covers all transgressions."
>
> *Proverbs 10:11-12*

For an in-depth examination of Invalidation, try Jay Carter's book *Nasty People*.

Deceptive Manipulation. "Like a madman who throws firebrands, arrows and death, so is the man who deceives his neighbor, and says, 'Was I not joking?'"[56] Convincing oneself and others to feel good about destructive behaviors most often occurs with deliberate intent, but not always. Deceptive manipulation seeks to confuse what is spiritually healthy with what is spiritually unhealthy, so as to cause its victims to run in useless circles, going nowhere. Like invalidation, at its heart we find a dishonesty and pathology born of fear, self-loathing and lust for control. Once again, this behavior can be the unconscious byproduct of a deeper psychological disorder. Here is a disconcerting description of one kind of deceptive manipulation from William Blake's *Vala*:

> "Compel the poor to live upon a crust of bread, by soft mild arts.
> Smile when they frown, frown when they smile; and when a man looks pale
> With labor and abstinence, say he looks healthy and happy;
> And when his children sicken, let them die; there are enough
> Born, even too many, and our earth will be overrun
> Without these arts. If you would make the poor live with temper,
> With pomp give every crust of bread you give; with gracious cunning
> Magnify small gifts; reduce the man to want a gift, and then give with pomp.
> Say he smiles if you hear him sigh. If pale, say he is ruddy.
> Preach temperance: say he is overgorged and drowns his wit
> In strong drink, though you know that bread and water are all

---

[56] *Proverbs 26:18-19*

He can afford. Flatter his wife, pity his children, till we can
Reduce all to our will, as spaniels are taught with art."

Legalism. When malevolent intent is transparent, it is easiest to
identify and transform. But evil is more difficult to recognize when it
is hidden beneath apparent conformance and propriety, or within
actions that seem easily defended as being "within the law" or "in the
best interest of all," yet clearly lacking in any real empathy or
compassion. This outward conformance to what *seems* right is the
core of legalism. Legalism has reared its self-righteous head in nearly
every spiritual tradition introduced in human history. At some
point, the laudable intentions of a tradition's values are corrupted
into inflexible regulations and restrictive edicts, primarily so that a
select few in the hierarchy of that tradition can have power over
others. For that is what legalism is all about: creating and
maintaining power. Once again, this doesn't define those
unwittingly trapped in a rigid system of social, religious or political
rules as "evil," but anyone who is conscious of a systemic
compulsion to subjugate others, and happily operates within the
corrupt falsehood of legalism, is smothering the Divine Spark within.

> "Don't think we have revealed to you a mere code of laws. No,
> rather, we have unsealed the choicest wine with fingers of might
> and power."
>
> Baha'u'llah, *The Most Holy Book*

Empty Habit. Very subtle and easy to fall into, empty habit excises
all value and joy from spiritual practice, and eventually from life
itself. There are meditative states in which the goal is detachment,
and this can be very constructive as a conscious objective. But when
we detach from life because we have forgotten our purpose, become
emotionally shut down through inattentiveness, or withdraw into
ourselves because we have been wounded in some way, we create
empty habits. This is why constant renewal and mindful practice is
so important: to pay attention to what we are doing and why, every
day and with every breath, and to resist complacency and laziness in
our self-awareness. Sometimes, when we have fallen out of love-
consciousness, the momentum and structure of our spiritual practice

may still continue – even as we doubt there was ever any love in us or the Universe. At the darkest depths of empty habit, it might even appear that the power of our beliefs is but fantasy and delusion. Yet if such moments can be transformed into advanced contemplative states, we can begin again from the void of not-knowing, waiting with patience for renewed Light to shine out from our soul, and new meaning to blossom in our hearts.

For an entertaining read of the different manifestations of spiritual antagonism, albeit from a mainly Christian perspective, I recommend *The Screwtape Letters* by C.S. Lewis.

Our Best Response to Evil

For those who question why there is such evil in the world, communing with the Infinite through mystical practice can often provide surprising answers. I have my own understanding of why evil exists, and why spiritually counterproductive influences are, in fact, sometimes necessary in this realm of existence. However, I encourage you to find your own answers to this very old question. In one way, if we were to look at the most horrible wickedness in the world from Fred's perspective, from within his bubble of nothingness, it would have no meaning anymore (if you haven't yet read about Fred, he's in the Nature of Our Existence chapter). If we are brave enough to anticipate an ultimate outcome of good for every soul at the end of Time, despite all the morally jarring atrocities of the past, present and future, that too might soften our desire to rail against the very existence of evil. And if we assert the inability of violence, spiritual oppression, or even death to stop the evolution of a timeless soul, our capacity to endure the flaming arrows of iniquity might surpass acceptance and become compassion. Yet for someone who has witnessed pointless brutality first-hand, or feels trapped in an abusive situation, or anyone crushed beneath rampant disease or perpetual poverty, such intellectual abstractions may hold little comfort or validity. Pain is, after all, as potent a reality as joy. But I will hold to the assertion that even in the midst of our greatest suffering, *the meaning of evil is still not relevant*. All that truly matters is how we respond to it.

Our most primitive reflex is to react to evil as a lone animal struggling to survive: meeting anger with anger, hate with hate; "an eye for an eye." The next, more sophisticated response is also based on self-preservation, but hopes to be left alone by being passive, either in denial or resignation, and so "let sleeping dogs lie." At our next advancement of understanding, we anticipate the selfish benefits of cooperation and treat others as we would like to be treated, trusting they will see the mutual benefit of reciprocation, and likewise do good for us. Eventually, we arrive at a more spiritually edifying attitude: authentic agape, where we care deeply about the underlying suffering from which evil is born. In the following chapter, there is plentiful discussion of chronic illness, crippled self-esteem, codependence, and childhood abuse, all of which could be perceived as a kind of evil. In each case, the emphasis is on how to repair and replenish hearts, minds and spirits in order to transform these conditions, rather than control them. With a sincere readiness to help repair the brokenness which misdirects human will into spiritually destructive patterns, we become the agents of unconditional love, our will aligning with the Source of Life and Light to enhance positive change. Beginning with this intention, we require only discernment and wisdom as to how such healing can be achieved. Once again, understanding what evil looks like aids our efforts, but dwelling on explanations for the existence of evil does not. However, as mentioned earlier, I believe a fullness of knowledge about the whys and wherefores of malevolent destruction is available for anyone who seeks it.

Because all effective change must begin as a heartfelt desire for change, there is no way we can force, persuade or cajole ourselves or anyone else to be a better person. For children, we explain the consequences of negative actions and enforce them. For ourselves, we can set goals, be diligent and disciplined in our spiritual practice, and have faith that we will grow out of unhelpful patterns by developing more courage and an enveloping compassion for ourselves and others. For someone else, even someone close to us about whom we care deeply, the best spiritual exhortation is the example we set with our words and actions. Since every soul is accountable to itself, we can only create space for someone else to find their own way, offer the nourishment of our loving presence, the occasional gentle but honest opinion when we are asked, and then hope for the best. In the short run, we may acutely feel the antagonisms of spiritually counterproductive acts on the progress of our soul or the happiness of others, but like any negative experience, this should only spur us on to shine more brightly, develop judicious and resilient empathy, and pay closer attention to the joys and victories of each moment.

There remains the question of what to do when we have an opportunity to prevent a destructive act, or intervene in someone's suffering. To this end, I feel I have a responsibility to transform such evils in non-confrontational ways wherever possible. We can make a truth known without it being a demeaning accusation. We can speak in private, with a loving and sincere attitude, to someone who exhibits destructive behavior, and offer a means of healing if they are open to it. We can calmly refuse to cooperate with any harmful acts, and step between the evildoer and the victim, patiently explaining that there is another way to be. When necessary, we can call upon people in positions of influence or authority, in hopes that they will exercise these same compassionate approaches when ours have had no obvious effect. In the U.S., we are privileged to be able to influence society with how we spend our money, and with the people we vote into public office. And of course there are always the more indirect artifacts of will, tempered with the golden intention, which have far-reaching potential. It is really not such a lofty ideal to "love your enemies, and do good to those who hate you; bless anyone who curses you, and pray for those who mistreat you."[57] Certainly, if we can change the course of human history with a thought, all that remains is to be patient. But here is an adage I live by: a wise person

---

[57] New Testament, *Luke 6:27-28*

yearns for justice, but is cautious about being its instrument. We do not always know what lessons are being learned by everyone involved, or what the ultimate consequences of their situation will be. And what are our intentions? To arrogantly right a wrong, or humbly heal what is broken? That is why the shape and timing of appropriate action should be sought through careful reflection and spiritual discernment, and is always a matter of courage balanced with humility.

> "People exist for the sake of one another. Teach them then, or bear with them."

> From the *Meditations* of Marcus Aurelius

Chapter Questions

1. Is it possible to cultivate a life that is entirely free of any kind of evil?
2. When did you last observe something spiritually antagonistic in your life? How did you respond to it?
3. How do people tend to respond to the spiritual antagonisms described in this chapter? What does that indicate about the nature of evil?
4. How can we transform malevolent intentions in ourselves and others?
5. Is there such a thing as a *neutral* intention, an indifference that promotes neither the good of All, nor the destruction of what is good?
6. Do you believe there is such a thing as a "necessary evil?"

13. ABOUT SUFFERING

Illness

The object of all healing is happiness. Without a sense of joy pervading our life, we will get sick, and may even die from the natural consequences of our dis-ease. Stress, for example, is surely the number-one spiritual inhibitor, ailment-producer, and killer in the U.S. today. Is this an oversimplification? Consider a possibility: what if most – if not all – symptoms of illness could be correlated to specific emotional, spiritual or psychological issues which have not been resolved? What if injury or physical incapacitation is a result of diverting ourselves from our own spiritual evolution? Caroline Myss has explored aspects of this, and I recommend her *Anatomy of the Spirit* as a starting point in your investigation. At the same time, however, I must acknowledge that genetic predispositions, accidental injuries, and environmental factors do, of course, result in chronic or even terminal conditions. Yet even in these cases, the sickness or disability – like any other limitation – can be our teacher if we have the courage to listen.

I have had my own encounters with illness. Months of near-immobility from sickness and several years of a weakened immune system thereafter; multiple kidney stones; ulcers and other GI problems; two surgeries; debilitating allergies; depression; and most recently, a tumor! During my twenties, it seemed that as soon as I overcame one ailment, another reared its ugly head. Although it is tempting to find blame for these illnesses somewhere outside of myself, this is less important than understanding an appropriate and spiritually healthy response. As in so many other areas of our lives, the first step in facing our illness is acceptance. Without being flippant or trite, we can embrace our condition and have compassion for it without losing ourselves to either self-pity at one extreme, or denial at the other. Walking this razor's edge can be especially difficult when we're not feeling well, but it is the path we must walk to get better.

After acceptance comes compassion – toward ourselves first and foremost, and toward the circumstances that led to our illness if they are evident to us. Following sincere compassion, we arrive at personal responsibility. This is not about feeling guilty when we get sick, or judging someone else's illness as a manifestation of their inner turmoil. But when it comes to understanding our illness and encouraging rehabilitation and healing, we are the only ones who can do it. We alone are responsible for getting well. We may want to leave diagnosis and treatment to qualified practitioners – traditional or alternative – but any skilled and experienced practitioner should place the task of wellness right back in our hands.

Once again, this isn't about blame, it is about knowing where the wellsprings of true healing lie. I practice Reiki, and have seen Reiki perform amazing things in willing recipients, including myself. But that willingness to get well cannot be taken for granted. If some part of me wants to remain sick, no amount of treatment will deliver me from myself. I have seen people resist healing, or get better only to become sick again, because their underlying wellness is not intact. Much of modern medicine is about treating the symptoms and helping us *feel better*, without addressing the underlying issues that lead to those symptoms. But to be well means *being* well, not just *feeling* well.

The following is a real-life illustration of this principle from my own experience. An acquaintance of mine has a massive heart attack that requires a triple-bypass. He is initially frightened into changing his lifestyle, and during recovery he loses weight, begins exercising, quits smoking, and won't even think of eating fatty steaks. He is surprised how much better he feels, and begins to enjoy life in a way he never experienced before. Then he goes back to work, and some of his stress returns. He comes home tired, and now feels he doesn't have the time or energy to exercise. In the following weeks, stress at work increases, and he starts smoking again. Feeling sorry for himself, his old eating habits then resurface and he begins gaining weight. A mere four months after he nearly died, he is right back into his old lifestyle, and at a routine check-up, his doctor gives him the bad news: his damaged heart muscle is struggling to keep him alive, and he may not have long to live...unless he transforms his lifestyle back into something more sustainable.

I have seen this pattern mirrored by a hundred different people, in a hundred different ways. A recovering alcoholic who falls off the wagon over and over again. A fibromyalgia sufferer who frees herself from pain, only to spiral down into self-destructive addiction. A manic-depressive who won't take his medicine. Someone who narrowly escapes acquiring HIV, but continues to have unprotected and risky sex. How about a person with a history of kidney stones and ulcers who keeps drinking coffee – until recently, that was me! All of these are real life examples, and one doesn't have to look too deeply to find the recurring theme: unhappiness is undermining the possibility of wellness, manifesting as denial, or a new compulsion, or a new way to medicate the deeper emotional pain. The real healing, therefore, comes when we identify and treat the source of that underlying unhappiness.

I believe that, of necessity, our spiritual evolution will take us into the depths of our despair, and bring us face-to-face with our spiritual, emotional, and psychological antagonists. I discuss this further in The Roots of Us and in the next section on Grief and Loss. We will likely face many such challenges – life is change, after all, and the spiritual path will heighten our awareness of every change necessary for growth. Yet in my experience, the gifts we receive along the way far exceed our expectations. Once we create our own purpose, and through mystical practice begin to realize the dream called living joyfully, even the most debilitating illness will not keep us from our prize: the sense of satisfaction and fulfillment that true well-being brings. There are many kinds of pain and suffering, but none is as great as that of a lost soul gnashing its teeth in the darkness. Sickness may issue from that place of abandonment and despair, but we need not follow it back there. Realizing this is to understand the nature of true healing.

For more reading on the mind-body relationship and illness, I also recommend *Full Catastrophe Living*, by Dr. Jon Kabat-Zinn.

Consuming Carefully

For many years, I followed the "all things in moderation" guideline for my more overall lifestyle. But this begs the question of what *moderation* really is. For instance, as long as I exercise once or twice a month, don't binge constantly on any one food group, and keep my stress level below a nervous breakdown, am I being adequately moderate? Probably not. On the other hand, can we ever be truly objective about our own habits? Ongoing research seems to offer constant variations on "ideal" modes of exercise, nutrition, and overall lifestyle; so what is the answer? Let me propose this alternative: that pursing the mystic's way provides us with a host of tools to evaluate and enhance our life in the context of our spiritual journey, exploring the totality of who we are and what nourishes us on every level. We will discover what moderation means for our unique, individual selves because we are mindfully paying attention to our existence. And the confidence we have in every choice will be supported by self-esteem made healthier through mystical experience. By following the practices outlined in this book, it is my hope that you will benefit in such holistic, ever-expanding ways.

To be well, we must certainly evaluate diet and exercise; our news and entertainment choices; the air, water and energies permeating our environment; and the character of our interactions with others. At this point in my life, avoiding highly refined foods and stressful settings, being disciplined about daily exercise, and carefully choosing the mass media I am exposed to has done wonders for my energy and overall health. Yet even more than what I consume, I have also changed how I consume. At one time, I reveled in hurried meals with the TV or radio blaring in the background, late night feasts with friends I hadn't seen in months, and a couple of two-week vacations each year to cram in all my recreation and entertainment. As an outgrowth of my mystical practice, I tend to chew more slowly and thoughtfully at every meal, spend time in meditation and recreation every day, and create space for my friends each week. It took me years to realize how I could engineer these changes, but I am physically, emotionally and spiritually the healthiest I have ever been because of them. In essence, mysticism demands that we orient our lives to Heart Time and Spirit Time, and this alone provides us the space and balance to develop healthy habits, and make wiser choices.

The Power of Repression and Denial

Self-deception is a tricky thing, and very difficult for most people to identify in themselves. However, without exception, I have yet to witness someone suffering from chronic health problems escape its clutches. "Denial" in this context consists of a complex relationship between assumptions that undermine our well-being, our inability to perceive reality, and a strong desire to protect our ego. Much like the Fear Cycles described in Self-Awareness and Self-Esteem, the assumptions may be false, but the malady that results from them reinforces and validates the lie we have told ourselves. This is, in effect, an artifact of will, a confused intention that evolves into very real suffering. But once again, the relationship is complex, and rarely are cause-and-effect directly apparent.

Take the example of someone who once asked my advice about her chronic back problems. She indicated shooting pains down her leg, an inability to exercise consistently or sleep well, and an increasing frustration over her condition. I asked her how long this had been going on, and she said it had been an on-and-off issue for many years, but lately – since she moved in with her fiancé – it had gotten worse. On a hunch, I asked to see her bedroom, and found an ancient bed. I asked if she was comfortable sleeping in it. She immediately became defensive, her body rigid, and her hands jerked nervously while hurried and distracted sentiments poured forth. She explained how she and her fiancé would shop for new furniture – including a better bed – after they were married, when they bought their first house together. She added with evident worry that she didn't think that would occur until they started having children. When I asked if she thought a new bed would help her back pain, she responded with irritation that no, that wasn't the problem at all. She then changed the subject and moved away from her back problems to other ailments.

I believe what was really at issue here was an understandable anxiety over some major life events, surrounded by a set of inflexible, self-imposed dependencies for her progress and success in those areas. If the bed was in fact the *direct* cause of her back problems, this woman was denying herself the opportunity to get well by thinking that buying a new bed symbolized failure in some way – i.e., that she had not yet achieved a vitally important goal of motherhood she had set for herself. What does future childbearing have to do with sciatica? Directly, nothing...but indirectly, everything. This is how obscured repressive responses can become, and how easily they can end up correlating with physical symptoms. If you would like more examples of how convoluted such defense mechanisms can be, read some of Sigmund Freud writings on repression, denial and other types of defensive "forgetting."

> "We see then that something is forgotten for its own sake, and
> where this is not possible, the defensive tendency misses the
> target and causes something else to be forgotten – something less

significant, but which has fallen into associative connection with the disagreeable material."

> Sigmund Freud, from *Forgetting of Impressions and Resolutions*

If we have so much trouble observing denial in ourselves, how can we know if it's there? Improving self-esteem and introspective self-awareness through mystical practice helps. And sometimes an epiphany will plainly show us our true obstacles. An honest and insightful friend can also gently bring the issue to our attention. Of course, we will likely refuse to believe any of this – agreement would be inconsistent with our denial, after all. But the more we surround ourselves with sincere, caring people, and the emotional space and physical time to contemplate our life, the more likely it will be that we won't escape our truths for long. In the 12-Step system, there is a practice called intervention, where a group of family members and friends closest to a denial-sufferer will wake them up early in the morning and, with love and concern, confront them about their situation. This is a fairly extreme measure, but it often can break through years of self-deception to a muted core of honesty. However, out of fear of facing such honesty, I have seen people who have chosen to perpetuate their illness alienate everyone close to them, insulating themselves with shallow, easily manipulated acquaintances and ever-increasing isolation. These are severe warning signs, indicating a deep-seated injury to self-esteem and a long, dark road to recovery.

Abuse, Dysfunction and Recovery

Sexual, physical and emotional abuse, alcoholism, and mental illness have all left their mark on my family and me. In addition, whether as a consequence of the culture in which I was raised, or because of my own empathy for others with similar childhood experiences, a large number of the people I have known throughout my life have had dysfunctional relationships with their parents, and consequently an impaired relationship with Self. One definition for the pervasive outcomes of this kind of injury and dysfunction is codependence. Codependence is the exclusive reliance on external definitions of equilibrium or happiness for our own well-being. In other words, we can only feel good about ourselves if we maintain the illusion of control or influence over everyone and everything around us, usually suppressing our own emotions in the process. These codependent attitudes, beliefs and behaviors as an adult are most often the legacy of abuse we suffered during our early development. Pia Mellody, Andrea Wells Miller, and J. Keith Miller, in their book *Facing Codependence*, discuss in detail the dynamics and subtleties of childhood trauma and how those events shape our self-image and adaptive responses that become so self-limiting as adults. Some of what they have written is considered controversial, but my own experience and observations have testified to the accuracy of most of their assertions. The following table is an interpretation and expansion of the book's cogent observations about codependency's cause-and-effect.

Table 8: Impact of Childhood Abuse on Adult Behavior

Innate Characteristics of a Child	Occurrence of Physical, Emotional, Psychological, or Spiritual Abuse	Dysfunctional Childhood Survival Traits	Symptoms of Adult Codependence
Valuable, precious, with unlimited potential.		Defining self comparatively: as either less-than or better-than others, and using external measurements (wealth, success, power, etc.)	Crippled self-esteem and inability to nourish self, and a continuation of comparative, external definition of well-being.
Vulnerable and without protection or boundaries.		Perpetually vulnerable and insecure, without *any* boundaries. - or - Completely invulnerable, protecting self with walls of fear, anger, constant busyness, or withdrawal.	Continued difficulty setting physical and emotional boundaries, resulting in extremes like premature trust and intimacy on the one hand, or perpetual mistrust and rejection on the other.
Imperfect, emotive and expressive.		Rebellious and challenging of all constraints and authority: deliberately "bad." - or - Overly careful, self-oppressive conformity: striving to be perfect and "good" at all times.	Difficulty maintaining a realistic or honest self-awareness, or to accept responsibility for own actions and well-being.
Dependant, needy and demanding.		Too dependant, insecure and needy: cannot nourish self at all. - or - Emotionally shut-down, overconfident and "anti-dependent."	Difficulty nourishing and nurturing self, compounded by fear of becoming dependant on the one hand, or confusion of dysfunctional behaviors with nourishing oneself on the other (for instance, thinking that sex is the only avenue to emotional nurturing).
Immature and not very self-aware.		Chaotic and perpetually immature: out of control. - or - Rigid and controlling.	Still out-of-control or overly controlling of others: not able to live in balance or moderation, or develop adequate self-awareness.

Behind these symptoms, a cascade of attitudes and beliefs emerge to sabotage our adult relationships. The following are some examples of those, captured in classically "codependent" language:

- "Things have to be done a certain way, or everything will fall apart."

- "If you're not happy, I can't be happy. If I make you feel good, I'll feel better."

- "I never get what I really want. I would have to be selfish, and that's bad."

- "If you don't do as I say, I'm going to be angry."

- "You said you would be home at 8:00! Now it's 9:00. You're a liar. How can I ever trust you?"

- "If it's right, it's right. If it's wrong, it's wrong. There are no in-betweens, no gray areas. Period."

- "I have to be perfect! And I can't ever ask for help. If I show weakness or faults, no one will ever love me."

- "Everything bad that happens around me is because of me. I must be doing something wrong, and this is the result. I'm being punished."

- "It's not my fault, I can't help myself!"

- "If I get too close to anyone, I'll just get hurt."

- "I'm sure everyone knows when they hurt my feelings, they just don't admit it."

- "It's not necessary to discuss what I feel. It's not a problem, and even if it was, what's the point of talking about it?"

- "If you don't like what I'm doing, I'll do the opposite! There, how do you like *those* apples?"

In examining codependence, a common theme which underlies nearly all childhood abuse quickly appears: whoever the abuser is, they are demanding that a child fulfill an adult's desires – emotional, social, sexual – instead of being a nurturing presence for the child.

This behavior, in turn, is then emulated by victims of abuse. The end result is that we find, once again, a focus on external satisfaction or fulfillment being the root of all kinds of unhappiness, including the abuse of others. And that leaves us with the question of how to mend our codependence and keep it from perpetuating itself.

As with any illness, there are differing approaches, and out of necessity I have explored a few. For some, 12-Step programs like CoDA (*CoDependents Anonymous*) are a useful way to broaden perspective – that is, to realize that we are not alone, and others understand what we have gone through – and acquire some new survival tools. For others, the 12-Step system does not provide all of the essential building blocks for fundamental change in self-image and behavior. In addition to CoDA, cognitive-behavioral therapy – specifically, CBT with a therapist who is experienced with the origins and symptoms particular to codependency – as well as the practices outlined in Self-Awareness and Self-Esteem, will be indispensable aids to healing. But the single most helpful thing I have done for myself is embraced my own mystical proclivities: disciplining my mind for introspective contemplation, holding whatever I discover in gentle and compassionate arms, and engaging and nourishing the core of who I am.

At the heart of ongoing recovery is the practice of learning to nurture and nourish the self independently, especially in areas where we did not receive support and encouragement as a child. Once this is accomplished, we can begin to enter into more successful, intimate and healthy interdependencies with others. At a minimum we will want to dialogue with the child inside us who still hurts from old abuse, and to compassionately process the trauma we experienced when we were young. In addition to meditation, it may be helpful to regress back to our childhood, or replay the trauma in our imagination with our adult self present. I have also benefited from role-playing those experiences with a therapist. In fact, any of these approaches may require help from a professional, though a chief characteristic of the codependent is that we usually *detest* asking for such help.

But even cathartic encounters with our past to the exclusion of CBT, other cognitive help, or advanced skill with contemplative meditation, is not recommended. It may feel great in the moment, but won't address the years of living with that past. In the same vein, it is also unlikely that an occasional weekend seminar will reshape our thinking and behavior with sufficient depth, or for very long. Likewise, unless our condition is primarily biochemical, medication can offer only temporary – and incomplete – treatment. A balanced *combination* of such temporary remedies with cognitive-behavioral therapy and meditation can be extremely powerful. The key is to realize that even with a host of new tools and therapeutic practices, there are no quick fixes, and little success without sincere commitment and hard work. Healing is, after all, not only a matter of intellectual confidence, but of trying to live in Heart Time and Spirit Time. Returning once again to the areas of nourishment outlined in Self-Awareness and Self-Esteem: if we take the time and effort to enrich our lives with activities that engage our physical, mental, emotional and spiritual selves, our continuing attention and discipline will perfect in us a self-sufficiency founded on patience and compassion, and we can begin to dialogue with the child within – and the dysfunctional family of origin where it all began – from a place of safety, forgiveness, and humble empowerment.

For more information on cognitive-behavioral therapy, visit www.aabt.org, iacp.asu.edu/links.htm, or www.nacbt.org. For more information on CoDA, see www.coda.org. Another useful resource is www.adultchildren.org, a 12-Step site for adults who experienced a dysfunctional home environment while growing up. For suggested preparations and a list of questions with which to interview prospective therapists, see *Appendix C.* To try some exercises in dialoguing with your family of origin and your fearful child, see *Appendix E.* I also highly recommend the book *Facing Codependence* – if you experienced an abusive family environment as a child, you may find, as I did, that you will read this book many times over.

Grief and Loss

> Between extremities
> Man runs his course;
> A brand, or flaming breath,
> Comes to destroy
> All those antinomies
> Of day and night;
> The body calls it death,
> The heart remorse.
> But if these be right
> What is joy?
>
> *Vacillation*, W.B.Yeats

There are many kinds of grief, and many kinds of loss. A disappointment for one person may be devastation for another, and what one person associates with a life change or redefinition of identity may feel like chaos and death to someone else. So in discussing the grieving process, everything is filtered through the subjective, and there can be few hard and fast rules. What remain are some general observations and considerations that apply to any kind of loss. Our grief can come over any major life change: having a hope or expectation disappointed; losing a person, a relationship, a pet, or some other cherished thing; even something as natural as aging can produce grief. Since many excellent books have already been written about the grieving process itself, I want to focus on those of us who have had trouble completing our mourning and instead hold on to our pain. Why? Because I have observed this to be the source of many kinds of suffering, with mental, emotional and physical manifestations and profound spiritual implications. Though the symptoms are diverse and often understated, what is common to all arrested grief is that a tremendous loss was never fully understood or emotionally accepted.

To begin, here is a brief overview of the stages of mourning. How intense each stage will be for someone, or how long each stage takes, will always depend on the individual and the type of loss they have experienced. As one example from my own life, a divorce in my mid-twenties was so devastating it took me nearly six years to recover. Was my healing process and duration normal? For me, I am certain my recovery was delayed because I did not fully resolve my grief, and my interrupted mourning process had a deleterious effect on my quality of life for far too long. Yet for someone else, six years might be just the right amount of time to move through every stage of mourning – it is truly a different experience for everyone. However long it takes, and however varied or sporadic the intensity, the grieving process can be described as passing through the following five phases:[58]

1. **Initial shock, emptiness, and disorientation.** There may be disbelief, denial of what has happened, and emotional numbness. There may be anger and frustration over how incomprehensible and uncontrollable the loss is.
2. **An increasing panic over the reality of the loss.** To deal with feelings of helplessness, attempts may be made to postpone the inevitable or influence a different outcome by bargaining with people, with the Universe, or even with ourselves; "maybe if I do something drastic, I can change this awful situation..."
3. **Once the shock, denial and panic have subsided, there can be additional anger, guilt or regret, and often deepening depression.** These can be accompanied by listlessness, insomnia, health problems, emotional overreactions to normal events, and increasing disconnection from others.
4. **Eventually, acceptance and adjustment begin, and we are able to start taking responsibility for our well-being, emotionally reinvesting ourselves in the present. We begin allowing ourselves to move on, make plans, and set goals.** We may still struggle to fully understand our loss, but we have begun redefining our life without the constant shadow of the past.

---

[58] Gleaned from a survey of essays about grief by J. William Worden, Beverly Raphael, and Sharon L. Johnson.

5. **Ultimately we come to understand what the loss really means to us.** The lessons and importance of what we have experienced become clear, and we remember what is no longer in our life with an increasing sense of peace, and less pain.

In the end, we may still experience sadness over our loss, but it is softer now – not the gut-wrenching anguish we initially felt. In many cases, our grief is even transformed into joy at the loving memory of what we have let go. But some people may not reach this peaceful, accepting phase because their mourning process was never completed; they never fully experienced all the emotional dimensions of what happened to them. A man who is still confused over a parent's death he witnessed as a teenager; a parent who has never forgiven themselves for abusing their child; a chronic illness sufferer who is perpetually absorbed with their illness; or someone who hasn't recovered from a failed romantic relationship. All of these people find they can't move forward, and as a result there is perpetual conflict within. They may struggle to maintain healthy self-esteem, or have trouble creating mutually nourishing relationships, or be constantly depressed or unhappy, or even become debilitatingly ill. Over time, the grief-arrested start to feel like victims of life, and believe that their greatest achievement will just be to make the best of the poor hand they were dealt. Beneath an increasingly thick defensive skin – of anger, codependency, compulsive control behaviors, substance abuse, self-martyrdom, profound emotional unresponsiveness, pleasure-seeking, or other means of crippling their emotional and spiritual sensitivity – they are still waiting for their grief to heal, still struggling with the bitter bite of loss, defeat and sorrow, even if they do not consciously recognize this.

So *why* does this happen? How can we become so *stuck*? I believe there are most often two main reasons why we haven't resolved our grief: either we have protectively suppressed our pain, or we have deliberately perpetuated it. In order to address either condition, we can utilize stages of emotional transformation and progressive contemplative states as our model of exploration and healing.

Suppression

Suppression occurs out of protective reflex as we shut down whole parts of ourselves to avoid emotional chaos. It is natural to raise self-protective barriers during extreme hurt; both adults and children can forget the details of past traumatic events for this reason. In the same way, we can bury our injury and grief because we simply cannot process what has happened. And this response may be amplified by other factors. Overwhelming guilt, for instance, or social pressures and time constraints surrounding the initial crisis. Often, we may not have had the emotional tools or support at the time to cope with the loss, and this triggers our withdrawal. Unfortunately, when we suppress our pain, we inadvertently lose access to other emotions along with it: trust, love, courage, confidence, self-worth and excitement may become dim echoes of their former selves. In essence, we no longer believe we are safe to feel deeply, or fully be ourselves, and so cocoon ourselves away from other life experiences. The impact this has on our spiritual cognizance, and ability to advance to a new stage of being, is understandably severe.

Perpetuation

Others of us have arrested our mourning process not out of defensive reflex, but because a part of us believes we should never stop grieving. The reasons for this are complex, intricately bound up in self-esteem, self-image, and black-and-white ways of thinking. Frequently, it seems as if there is only one terrifying alternative to perpetuating our grief: to admit that the past loss, failure or emotional injury has no meaning at all. Yet this, in turn, seems like a betrayal, perhaps to ourselves, or to whatever and whomever we have lost. This possibility is especially disturbing because it challenges what has become a fixed identity for us. The prospect of creating meaning in the present *without the context of loss* is far more upsetting than living with the pain. In this way, we can become attached to our suffering, confining our self-image and purpose within the unbearable events of long ago. Consequently, we remain intimately connected with a past and continually recurring moment, which defines self as the center of calamity.

Resolution

I have not yet discovered a satisfactory answer for why some people tend to suppress or perpetuate their bereavement, while others free themselves to heal. Perhaps it has something to do with the lessons our soul is learning, the emotional skills we acquired early in our lives, or the natural neurological variations from one person to the next. Whatever the case, if we embrace our *arrested* emotional state as normal and correct, we create a negative identity that tends to resist positive change: a "victim-identity" which we then reinforce with self-defeating choices. How can we break free of this? How can we regain a healthy self? One very effective approach is to first recapture our sense of safety and stability, so that we become secure enough to begin feeling again. The following are some steps to achieve just that, and to reengage our grief wherever we left off. I recommend keeping a journal throughout this process, referring back to it often as you move forward. Since there is substantial overlap in working through both suppressed and perpetuated mourning, suggestions for both have been combined.

Our first step should be to find an empathetic, non-judgmental ear. This is not a journey we should take alone. Finding someone who can be there for us while we uncover buried feelings will be tremendously beneficial, and grief counseling or grief support groups are widely available for this purpose – sometimes free of charge. Our objective here is to create the place where we can really let go, where we can be *completely out of control* for a while as we discuss our pain. Yet this is not easy. For someone whose habit has been to suppress or extend some phase of their grief, this uncorking of the emotional bottle can feel close to insanity. Extreme mood swings, resurfacing of unwanted memories, powerful thoughts which seem to have a will of their own...all of this can be scary. However, creating a supportive environment, and feeling deeply what has long been denied, awakens the emotional honesty for which our heart longs.

(For Perpetuated Mourning) Recognize that self-victimization behavior is unhealthy. We should admit that someone who perpetuates a victim-identity for themselves is injuring their well-being, and that this isn't normal or constructive on any level. This doesn't mean we should judge ourselves, or feel guilty, or become angry. It means we are just observing a truth *in principle* about natural but unhealthy patterns of behavior.

Develop more honesty in self-awareness. We can begin by using the tools and approaches in the Self-Awareness and Self-Esteem chapter to build a more accurate picture of Self. The CBT-oriented steps to break fear cycles in Appendix E may be particularly worthwhile in improving our understanding of all the issues involved. For the mystic, reflective meditation will then bring us that much closer to our truths. Along the way, we may identify evidences of self-victimization in our own life: things like an inability to reach goals or commit to relationships; thrill-seeking or other risky behaviors; fear of abandonment; chronic or psychosomatic illness; unexplainable depression; or chronically low self-esteem. Yet even as we observe how our suffering may have been prolonged, we discover the possibility that, with a little guidance, we also have the capacity to heal ourselves.

Isolate the event(s) that caused emotional arrest. Can you easily identify the cataclysm where it all began? It may have been the experience of just one day, a week, or it may have been prolonged over a period of years. Such events may be uncomfortable to contemplate for long, as the mind is adept at protecting us from pain through distraction or redirection...but try. Spend some time with your past. If you are unable to identify the originating experience, you might want to attempt hypnotherapy or other regression technique to help you remember. It is also important to consider there may be more than one originating event, or that many similar experiences may be layered on top of each other. You may also want to review the previous Abuse, Dysfunction and Recovery section to evaluate other issues from childhood.

Write a letter about the event(s). Describe your feelings surrounding the loss. If the grief is over a loved one who is now gone, write them a letter. Tell them about your experience, and the depth of your emotion. Find an empty chair, imagine them sitting in it, and read the letter aloud to them. If you are mourning over childhood pain, try writing a letter to the person you turned to for support at that time, describing what is going on inside you now which you couldn't express then, and which they might not have known about. In some cases, this letter may be shared with a parent or sibling, but first try reading it aloud to an empty chair where you imagine them sitting...this can be hugely healing practice. Lastly, if there doesn't seem to be a particular audience for your loss, try writing a letter to the Universe, or the Deity you believe in, and imagine their representative in the empty chair, listening attentively to your heart-felt words.

Have compassion for yourself in your moment of pain. By practicing the self-nourishing mystical disciplines outlined throughout this book, you will fortify kindness toward yourself in a general way. Now, in the context of your greatest crisis and deepest anguish, it's time to be specific. Using your imagination to place yourself back in the moment, can you feel love and caring for yourself *at that time*? Can you forgive those you turned to for support and help, but who could not adequately comfort you? Can you forgive the person who hurt you the most? Can you forgive yourself sufficiently in the *past* to allow yourself to be vulnerable in the *present*? If you were not able to revisit your feelings before, you may now feel some intense emotions, beginning your mourning process wherever you left off. You may feel panic, anger, fear or overwhelming sorrow. It is now important to create space in your life to allow time alone with those emotions, letting them breathe.

Eventually, through a gentle cradling of the past self in the present, a *gradual* acceptance of what has happened emerges and equilibrium is recovered.

Exercise your freedom to move forward. As your sense of safety grows, so does your confidence that you can nourish and protect yourself. Inability to express your grief, and identification with being a victim of catastrophe, become part of the past, and you are ready to create new meaning and identity. When you relinquish those old attitudes and behaviors, you can start replacing them with a new, internally rich vision and daily practice for your life. This process of letting go and reinvesting is the heart of mystical practice. Increasingly, you can accept whatever comes (and whatever has been) without those old defenses, allowing yourself to experience strong emotions in a sense of safety you yourself maintain. Eventually, as you continue to evolve emotionally and spiritually, you will arrive at a place where rejoicing in the victory of life is an unaffected expression of who you are, and where each challenge you encounter becomes a time to rest and reflect sincerely, to fully feel and express all that you have become, and to once again learn to let go.

As with everything written in this book, I have both confidence in the effectiveness of these ideas, and humility in acknowledging that I have much to learn. I also know that none of the steps described here are easy or quick, and the longer we have lived in denial or suppression of a healthy Self, the harder it may be to break free of old attitudes and self-limiting behaviors. But we have the sovereignty to fashion whatever meaning we want for our life – for all of the highs and lows and in-betweens. We are not enslaved to failure, suffering or loss. We can allow ourselves to love, and to mourn. There is great hope in clarifying our perception, renewing our sense of purpose, and maturing a compassionate relationship with ourselves. As with so much in our existence, this is a matter of willingness and expectation, and of consciously choosing to grow and prosper each and every day.

"Suddenly, a day comes when we know it is safe to feel deeply again; the currents of our soul spring forth, and all the wonder of life seems miraculously paraded before our eyes."

Mark Helprin, *Memoirs from Antproof Case*

For a detailed discussion of many kinds of grief – including unresolved grief – and how to cope with them, please consider reading *The Mourning Handbook*, by Helen Fitzgerald.

Chapter Questions

1. How long have you, personally, felt intense and unrelenting pain for a deceased loved one, a debilitating illness, failed relationship, or other loss? Were you able to pass through all the stages of grief?
2. Do you think it possible for you to live a life where you never get sick?
3. What impact have anger or stress had on your health?
4. What is the first and most important step in any healing process?
5. What does the death of a loved one mean for those who go on living? Does that meaning change over time?
6. What are the underlying cause-and-effect dynamics of a dysfunctional family, and how can the cycle of abuse be broken?
7. What role does mystical practice play in ongoing health and emotional healing?

Conclusion

14. FIVE GUIDING PRINCIPLES

An acquaintance recently asked me, "Can you explain to me what you believe God is?" A wonderful question. For me, answering this begins with an experience of mystical awareness, and a willingness to arrive at decisions and actions without logical, or even definitive, conclusions. This approach, which has been a centerpiece of this book, is about emotionally and intellectually letting go – of ego, of black-and-white thinking, of all expectations and dependence on externals – and rediscovering the wisdom, freedom and transformative power innate to our being. Yet this can be very threatening to our habits, to our ways of coping with the experiences and perceptions we have collected over time, so it is only natural to resist it. But in order to access a deeper truth, we must continually discard the processes whereby we have reached past conclusions – whether an emotional sense of certainty, a logical progression from A to B to C, the advice of people we trust and admire, or even our last mystical epiphany. All of these sources are viable, and we may even fall back on them when we can't summon the courage to trust our newest spiritual insight, but to understand the true nature of things we must set comfortable habits aside and venture into the unknown.

And so we encounter change. Moving forward – growing spiritually – requires audacity, resolve, patience, and persistence. And once we reach a new level of understanding it is very difficult to turn aside from what we discover; even though we may sometimes fall back into old patterns, we will have a certain amount of guilt and pain over the tension between our reversion and what we know we should or could be doing. This is an instance where negative emotions can be constructive, for although guilt is not an ideal motivator, it can spur us on to positive actions, which in turn reinforce our growth in more uplifting ways. Still, it is perpetually difficult to modify our oldest habits! It is hard to set the old self aside and begin again.

So how can we overcome our resistance to progression through different stages of being? How can we keep taking one small step after another through a difficult journey of self-transformation? How can we maintain positive expectations? And how can we become ever-more intimate with the Sacred? Certainly, our rationale and modes of operation will change over time, and daily mystical practice as guided by the golden intention offers a continuously evolving support: an ever-expanding love-consciousness, a deepening trust in spiritual sensitivities, a clearer view of interdependencies in and around us, and much more. But what has also helped me overcome my own intermittent resistance to spiritual evolution are some basic assumptions: five guiding principles that are woven into the subtext of this book. More than anything, these are articles of faith, designed to align my inner world with constructive possibility. See what you think of them.

1. **Good succeeds over evil, wellness over disease, constructiveness over destructiveness.** In a short, compressed perspective, what we feel is negative or antagonizing sometimes appears to thrive. But the Source of Life and Light is a patient, enduring force: like a creeping glacier, or a tree reaching towards the sun, or a river carving canyons out of rock, influences for the good of All are persistent and inexorable, and will ultimately prevail – either in this life, or the next, or somewhere inconceivably distant in the ever-renewing cycles of time. All that is required of us, if we wish humanity to remain part of that victory, is to align ourselves with that prevailing force.

2. **When our heart is constantly filled to overflowing with compassion and loving kindness, and focused on the well-being of others as it coincides with the path of our own nourishment and peace, we will always be acting from a place of efficacy and noble purpose.** This does not mean the intended consequences of our actions are guaranteed, nor that we shouldn't try to be wise and discerning in our choices, but having such clear and honest intentions integrates us into the unstoppable forces of good in the world, and our progress is complimented by the overarching purpose of the Universe itself.

3. **Accepting whatever comes, and letting go of all need to control, we become miraculously powerful.** By relinquishing our ego, and simply acknowledging our wants without striving to indulge them – or trying to force the world to satisfy them – we open ourselves to the richest contentment and deepest sustenance. This applies especially to our understanding of Truth: to be wise is to let go of all wisdom.

4. **We have complete freedom, and that is a tremendous responsibility.** Every choice, and the meaning of every choice, belongs to us. Every consequence belongs to us. Our lives belong to us. This is our liberation from every confining regulation of the soul, from every angst-ridden directive we once adopted, while at the same time we choose to submit to the most rigorous law of all: the law of unconditional love. Without love and compassion, we may still consider ourselves free, but we are destined to repeat the same lessons over and over again, with no more meaning or purpose than dreamless, self-referential dust.

5. **Balance is achieved moment by moment, and begins and ends in our own mind and heart.** One instant we will integrate our intuition and mystical awareness fully into our intentions and actions. The next we may stumble into wanton desire. But always, if we remain attentive to what is happening inside us, we can approach the next moment with

humility and hope. With this continuous understanding, we never have to give in, or give up.

By holding principles like these in our heart, we can mature a faith that each successive step in our spiritual journey, however difficult it may appear, will eventually become easier, and that every impasse will ultimately be overcome. With this belief, we can fortify our hope in each successive moment, and our trust in a process and objective both inherent to and greater than ourselves.

15. TOOLS SUMMARY

After considering everything presented in *The Vital Mystic*, practicing believers of established traditions, aspiring mystics, and anyone who seeks to enhance their emotional strength and spiritual understanding should have the following tools at their disposal:

- Ways to evaluate relationships, work, health, and overall well-being in the context of spiritual evolution

- Exercises to develop intuition and awaken spiritual perception

- An explanation of profound mystical awareness and why it is a worthwhile pursuit.

- Different ways of achieving honesty in self-assessment

- Cognitive-behavioral tools to overcome fear and avoidance

- Techniques that enhance self-esteem and inspire compassion for others

- Insight into the language and power of the human will

- Ways to clarify thought and discern meaning from moment to moment

- A contemplative meditative practice that transforms intentions, invites synchronicity, and facilitates mystical understanding

For each of us, there are sure to be many questions left unanswered, but with patience and thoughtful diligence, the seemingly tangled riddles of life will surely unravel, and certainty declare itself. "The one who asks will always receive, the one who is searching will always find, and the door is opened to anyone who knocks."

Oak Leaf

What if
    fulfillment begins
    as we break free
    to see the world anew
    drifting weightless
    our future resting
    on a breezy whim?
What if
    all the spanning effort
    of our growth
    and breadth of our experience
    in leafy green
    only readies us
    for letting go?
And what if
    the shapely motion of our flight
    that hint of bliss in our descent
    is the greatest art
    our lives will ever know?

Thank you for spending time with these words.

Appendix A: Definitions and Concept Grouping

Inherent Components of Self

Soul
The spark of the Divine: the core of our true being, interconnected with all else, which exists in timeless continuity.

Spirit
Our life energy and soul-personality: that which animates and sustains us, and which communicates between the mind and soul.

Being
The combined whole of everything we innately are: *soul, spirit, mind, will and physicality*.

Will
The power of our being to influence our environment and perpetually create our existence.

Physicality
Our physical body, with all its instinctual desires for survival, and the most basic reasoning of the mind to facilitate that survival.

Volitional Expressions of Self

Identity
Our self-reflective *being*: how we interpret and express the assemblage of our *intentions, self-esteem, ego* and *wants* through self-awareness

Intentions
Our sincere expectations for our life and the outcome of our actions: how we motivate and direct our will.

Self-Esteem
Compassion for self, acceptance of our abilities and limitations, and appreciation and enjoyment of our identity.

Whims and Wishes
The desires that linger constantly below the surface of our thoughts, and which are a natural outgrowth of our identity.

Types of Perception
(Note: All but simple observation are aspects of "spiritual cognizance.")

Epiphany
A sudden and arresting insight which inspires us to move in a new life direction or operate with different assumptions.

Mystical Awareness
A profound and inexpressible connection culminating in a "gnosis of the Absolute:" a communion with the Divine, our own soul, with the All, with other spiritual intelligences, or with emptiness.

Intuition
A combination of experiential learning and the innate wisdom of our soul that operates apart from logic or conscious knowledge.

Discernment
The conscious insight that arrives through the ongoing practice of spiritually healthy attitudes and disciplines – such as intuition and mystical awareness.

Simple Observation
Observing the direct evidence of cause and effect.

Types of Certitude

Gnosis
Wisdom and direct knowledge (surpassing fundamental spiritual laws) beyond words or ideas and accessed through the quieting of ego and undistracted submersion in mystical awareness.

Shared Understanding
The *instinct of the spirit:* the fundamental spiritual laws our soul understands, but which our intellect may not fully grasp.

Faith
Confidence in a pragmatically adjusted ideal which does not stem from egoism or rationalization, but which is validated by the successes of living *in the flow* of good by aligning oneself with the Source of Life and Light.

Idealism
Seeded by hope and creative imagination, this is the beginning of faith, but is not yet adjusted by the realism and pragmatism of an informed spiritual practice.

Delusion
An ego-fortified rationalization of life choices and beliefs that endures even when contrary evidence invalidates it.

Types of Love

Agape
Boundless loving kindness that fervently desires the good of All, but is not attached to specific outcomes.

Compassion
Awareness and empathy for someone's suffering, and a devoted intention to relieve it.

Friendship and Fellowship
A joint commitment to mutual goodwill, cooperative effort, and interdependent nourishment.

Romance
An intoxicating convergence of emotional intimacy, the sharing of physical pleasure, and a desire for partnership.

Patience and Tolerance
Calm endurance of attitudes, behaviors and events which may at first seem inconvenient, unproductive or antagonistic.

Modes of Evolution

Harmonized Existence
Realization of the True Self – the Divine Spark within – and recognizing and uniting all aspects of self with the Source of Life and Light through persistent mystical awareness.

Alignment and Flow
A graceful continuity of events and intentions centered on spiritual evolution, in harmony with the Source of Life and Light and the good of All.

Transformation
Recognizing an opportunity for positive change, and activating our faith and focusing our intentions to that end.

Nourishment
Acknowledging the many facets of being, and making a conscious effort to heal, fortify and sustain them.

Discipline
Learning self-control, detachment, and a refining of character in order to develop clear

self-awareness and spiritual discernment.

States of Mind

Stillness or Emptiness
A quiet and receptive calm that relinquishes all meaning and purpose in the present moment, and expands an open and unknowing consciousness.

Mindful or Contemplative Attention
Being carefully and fully attentive to what is going on in and around us, without being attached to it. In *Suspension*, also diligently maintaining a neutrality of will.

Creative Imagination
The resourceful and original self-expression that results from an active coalescing of will, spirit, intellect and emotion.

Prayer
An intimate dialogue of heart and mind with the Sacred, characterized by humble, grateful and worshipful receptivity.

Opportunity Thinking
An optimistic attitude of openness and expectation, with a joyful readiness to act on whatever comes.

"External" Spiritual Information

Synchronicity
A coincidence of events and perceptions which tend to repeat and reinforce spiritual themes and personal lessons, providing insight into our life and our progression through stages of being.

Spirit Guides
Spiritual intelligences that inform and encourage our evolution with evocative images, ideas, discernment, promptings, dialogue or shared insight.

Mystical Dreams and Visions
Experiences unrelated to life events, and otherwise devoid of simple correlative meaning, which are so vivid and emotive we are certain of their spiritual relevance.

Divination
Accessing the soul's wisdom and the insight of spiritual intelligences using esoteric symbols and patterns, often to better understand personal development and life events.

Apophenia
Self-generated meaning and
pattern-creation where no meaning or patterns actually exist.

Appendix B: Measuring Insight and Esteem

As previously mentioned, there are very few scientifically validated ways of measuring self-awareness and self-esteem. This self-assessment has not been validated, and the following questions are therefore only an initial step to discovering your internal world, and your capacity to appreciate and care for yourself. The more self-aware you are, and the more honestly you answer each question, the more accurate the results are likely to be. Once you complete the questions, work through the Insight and Esteem Calculator that follows, and see if you agree with the analysis.[59]

For each question, decide whether you agree, disagree, or are not sure about the answer. Then, in the appropriate column, indicate how strongly you feel about your response. A **"1"** indicates you don't feel strongly about your answer, and a **"3"** indicates you feel very strongly about your answer. Be sure to only enter one number in only one of the columns for each question. For example, in response to "I dislike vegetables," I would put a **"2"** in the "I Disagree" column, because I *like* vegetables, but my feeling isn't especially strong. For the "Not Sure" column, simply put a check mark.

---

[59] Please note that there is now an Excel spreadsheet instrument downloadable from *www.searchforclarity.com* that contains the same questions and calculation methods as those written here.

Evaluation Questions: Insight and Esteem – p. 1	I Agree	I Disagree	Not Sure √
I really enjoy my time alone, and like to relax and be free of any specific plans or activities.			
Meeting people for the first time and making new friends is one of my favorite activities.			
I am very outspoken, and sometimes overly confident in my opinions.			
I am open to criticism, but if a person seems to be attacking me I may get defensive or stop listening.			
I rarely feel guilty about anything, even if someone else thinks I've done something wrong.			
I measure my success in life through what I have to show for it: my income, my position at work, my home, etc.			
I don't like conflict, and consciously try to avoid it.			
I'm comfortable with how I look, and feel I am an attractive person.			
I think it's reasonable to expect that people recognize and appreciate the effort I've taken to do something.			
I tend to be more critical of myself than of others.			
I feel close to my family, and believe we are generally open and accepting with each other.			
I believe I am fulfilling my purpose in life.			
I tend to lose myself and change a lot of my priorities when I'm in a romantic relationship.			
I don't mind at all when my routine is interrupted.			
If I had complete control of the world for a day, I think I could handle it just fine.			
I've always known my parents have loved me and have always wanted the best for me.			
I often end up being the center of attention in a gathering of my friends.			
I enjoy helping others, but generally don't ask for help myself.			
I'm often frustrated that others don't seem to share priorities or values that I feel are important.			
I think of myself as a good person.			

Evaluation Questions: Insight and Esteem – p.2	I Agree	I Disagree	Not Sure √
It is always best to clarify my position and finish an argument, rather than to leave things unclear or unresolved.			
If a close friend is suffering or grieving, a supportive thing I can do is find activities that divert them from their pain.			
I am seldom disappointed or jealous when someone I don't respect wins approval from someone I respect.			
When I'm angry, it's better for me to take a breather before making a decision about what to do next.			
When I fall in love with someone, I don't feel like have much choice about it.			
When I'm feeling insecure, I usually talk to someone I trust to work through why I'm feeling that way.			
When I'm feeling anxious, the best thing for me to do is ignore it, since it will eventually resolve itself.			
Humor is seldom the most productive way to diffuse a tense situation.			
I am able to make the best out of bad situations.			
Most unhappiness in the world is a result of trying to control things which can't be controlled.			
When my partner or lover is irritating me, a good way to bring it to their attention is to joke about it.			
I am rarely bored.			
I have no idea where shame comes from; it seems silly to be ashamed about anything.			
The best thing to do when someone is feeling uncomfortable is to find out what the problem is, and try to solve it.			
It is not very supportive to give a friend or partner "more space" when they are already acting distant or subdued.			
When I'm unhappy, I can nearly always quickly identify what is upsetting me.			
I'm comfortable displaying affection toward people I know well, as well as tell them when I'm upset.			
How others perceive me depends a lot on their emotional health.			
Remembering my mistakes helps keep me from repeating them.			
I often say things that I later regret.			

Insight and Esteem Calculator

Once results are calculated, you can then plot yourself in the **SASE Table.**

	SubTotals	Totals	Scores
Add up points in the **"I Agree"** column for questions 1,2,8,12,14,20,23,24,26,29,32,36,37&39	<u>ST-1</u>	<u>Total ST</u> (Add ST-1 and ST-2)	
Add up points in the **"I Disagree"** column for questions 3,4,5,6,7,10,13,15,17,18,19,21,25,27,33&40	<u>ST-2</u>		
Add up points in "**I Agree**" column for questions 11,16,30&38	<u>OA-1</u>	<u>Total OA</u> (Add OA-1 and OA-2)	
Add up points in "**I Disagree**" column for questions 9,22,28,31,34,35	<u>OA-2</u>		
Add up check marks in the **"Not Sure"** column, and <u>multiply by 2</u>	<u>U</u>		
Add up points in the **"I Agree"** column for questions 12,14,24,26,29,30,36,37,38,&39	<u>EA-1</u>	<u>Total EA</u> (Add E-1 and E-2)	
Add up points in the **"I Disagree"** column for questions 3,4,5,7,10,13,18,19,21,22,25,27,28,31,33,34 &35	<u>EA-2</u>		
Add up points in the **"I Agree"** column for questions 2,8,11,12,16&20	<u>SE-1</u>	<u>Total SE</u> (Add SE-1 and SE-2)	
Add up points in the **"I Disagree"** column for questions 3,6,7,9,17&19	<u>SE-2</u>		
SELF-AWARENESS = (Subtract **U** from **Total ST**) The ability to realistically assess and understand our strengths, abilities and limitations – on physical, mental, emotional and spiritual levels.			<u>Total SA</u>
SELF-ESTEEM = Total SE Our respect, appreciation and trust for every aspect of self.			<u>Total SE</u>
OTHER-AWARENESS = Total 0A The ability to assess, understand and react appropriately to those around us.			<u>Total 0A</u>
EMOTIONAL APTITUDE = Total EA The ability to manage and enhance **Self-Awareness** and **Self-Esteem**.			<u>Total EA</u>

		Self Awareness		
		Advanced	**Basic**	**Intermediate**
Self-Esteem	**Advanced**	I **Total SA** 64 – 87, and **Total SE** 27 – 36, and **U** is greater than 2	I **Total SA** 34 – 63, and **Total SE** 27 – 36, and **U** is greater than 2	II **Total SA** is less than 34 or greater than 87 (or if **U** is 2 or less), and **Total SE** 27 – 36
	Intermediate	I **Total SA** 64 – 87, and **Total SE** 14 – 26, and **U** is greater than 2	I **Total SA** 34 – 63, and **Total SE** 14 – 26, and **U** is greater than 2	II **Total SA** is less than 34 or greater than 87 (or if **U** is 2 or less), and **Total SE** 14 – 26, and
	Basic	III **Total SA** 64 – 87, and **Total SE** is less than 14, and **U** is greater than 2	III **Total SA** 34 – 63, and **Total SE** is less than 14, and **U** is greater than 2	IV **Total SA** is less than 34 or greater than 87 (or if **U** is 2 or less), and **Total SE** is less than 14

Emotional Aptitude *(Range **0-24** Basic; **25-58** Intermediate; and **59-81** Advanced)*

This suggests your ability to both adapt to the emotional dynamics of any given situation, and guide the course of your own evolution. The higher the value, the more able you are to recognize what requires healing or nourishment in yourself and others, as well as how to go about it. Whatever your SA and SE scores are initially, your

Emotional Aptitude can also aid your efforts to manage and improve your self-awareness and self-esteem.

Other-Awareness *(Range **0-10** Basic; **11-24** Intermediate; **25-30** Advanced)*

Your OA score suggests the experience and insight you have into other people, the nature of relationships, and ways to be a supportive, healing presence for others. Of all of the assessments, this seems to be the most readily learned. Combined with a high EA score, a solid Other-Awareness likely enhances our overall effectiveness in social situations.

Reflecting on these results, do they align with your self-image? How do they correspond with where you put yourself on the **SASE Table** initially? If the results seem inaccurate to you, why do you think that happened? Clearly, there are variations in how different people operate, regardless of how they scored on this questionnaire. Hopefully, this can be a useful starting point for you in your evaluation of what you would like to celebrate or improve, and which next steps may be the most helpful to you. By practicing what is offered in this book, it is my belief that you will not only make a strong placement in **Quadrant I**, but also refine your skills within that quadrant. To test this idea, try taking the assessment again after six months of mindful and diligent mystical effort.

	high **SELF-AWARENESS** ***low***	
high **SELF-**	I The healthiest state. A feeling of successful management of our internal and external life, with consistently renewed insight into how to maintain and improve this equilibrium. A solid and realistic understanding of our own capabilities and limitations, and a tendency to succeed and thrive. An easy integration into our community of peers, without suppressing or altering our identity or sense of self in unhealthy ways.	II Feeling confident and successful – and even achieving superficial success – without actually having a solid understanding of our own strengths and weaknesses. A tendency to *overestimate* our capabilities and ignore proven limitations. Unintentional alienation of peers, but with a disowning of responsibility for any negative outcomes of our actions. A strong sense of Self, but an unrealistic one.
ESTEEM ***low***	III A clear understanding of our own strengths and weaknesses, but a tenancy to feel insecure and unsuccessful even with this knowledge. Often, we sabotage our own plans, or alienate close friends, or isolate ourselves from supportive communities. We maintain a strong identity, but at great cost to well-being, contentment, and fulfillment of our dreams.	IV The least healthy state. Feelings of helplessness and not knowing how to free ourselves from victimizing situations. A tendency to *underestimate* our capabilities and assume limitations that are unproven. We will often subvert our identity to fit in with peers, with the potential of completely disconnecting from our True Self.

Appendix C: Therapy Recommendations

I am beginning with the assumption that someone trained in CBT (cognitive-behavioral therapy), and who preferably has a depth and breadth of experience in different techniques, is your best option for professional counseling. I also propose these objectives and milestones not as rigid metrics, but as helpful suggestions:

1. In the therapy session, interview the therapist to see if it's a good match (see Preparation below), then clearly identify your *main concerns*: your top priorities for personal healing and growth. One of the hallmarks of CBT is initial diagnostic testing to help you determine these issues.

2. You should make significant and measurable progress within the first 3-5 therapy sessions in understanding and addressing your main concerns. You should also be receiving lots of homework from your therapist to move the healing along on your own.

3. After 10 therapy sessions, you should have accumulated tools which are aiding your progress, and seen the potential (if not already evident) of the tools and therapy to make a noticeable difference in your life, and to gain a level of independence from your therapist in your healing and empowerment process.

4. After 15 therapy sessions, you should be able to either "graduate" from your therapist altogether regarding your primary concerns, have a sufficient foundation to continue on your own, or be able to branch out into other areas of concern using the same 1-5-10-15 milestones.

If you and your therapist are successful, you can always return at a later time with new issues to address. Like most health practitioners, the best therapists I have worked with have encouraged me to "do my homework" and be disciplined in using the tools and techniques they have provided to gain self-sufficiency, utilizing additional therapy as my support system only when I have new questions or a new area of concern to work through.

Preparation

Before you start looking for a therapist, know what you want to get out of it. Make a list of specific and detailed results you would like to aim for as "I want to..." statements. For example:

- "I want to feel better about myself."

- "I want to get out of this funk I'm in."

- "I want to reduce my level of anxiety when I am in large groups of people."

- "I want to mend my relationship with my mother."

- "I want to learn how avoid arguing or getting upset with people who challenge or contradict me."

- "I want to have more mutually nourishing relationships."

And so forth. It will be important to prioritize these for your therapist, and to let them know what are your top priorities.

The next step is to find a therapist with the appropriate training and experience. A quick phone call should discover all you need to know for an initial appointment.

1. Do they have CBT training and experience? What is their background?

2. How long have they been practicing in your area?

3. Do they use CBT methodologies exclusively, or combine them with other approaches?

4. Do they have experience and expertise in your specific area of need? (i.e. issues relating to childhood abuse, marital problems, sexual issues, anger management, specific anxieties or phobias, etc.)

You can also use some or all of the following questions in your first therapy session to "interview" your prospective therapist. Let them know ahead of time that you are "just shopping around," and will have a number of questions for them. Some of these may seem odd things to ask, but a therapist's responses to them can be revealing; also, there are no right or wrong answers, but there are certainly productive and counterproductive attitudes...and that is what you should be looking for. It is useful to ask these questions *before* you share the details of your own priorities:

1. What are their favored therapy approaches?

2. Why did they become a therapist?

3. How happy are they with their life right now? Why?

4. How long have they lived in the area, and will they be staying there...at least for the next year?

5. How long do their patients usually keep coming back to them?

6. What is the hardest thing they ever had to help someone through? Why was it hard? (No specifics necessary here, just generalities.)

7. How do they feel about spirituality?

8. Have they ever undergone therapy themselves? Was it successful? (It probably isn't appropriate for them to discuss specifics of their challenges or their past, nor should you ask them for these.)

9. Are they having a busy day? Why?

10. What is most important to them in their relationship with a patient?

Now you can give them your "I want to" list, and see what questions they have for you.

Assessment

Having good rapport with your therapist is important, if only to encourage trust and openness. However, it is not important that you like each other enough to become friends. This is a professional relationship, and should be treated as such; you are equals in this process, and should view each other with respect and appreciation. If you have trouble with emotional or physical boundaries, the therapist should clearly demonstrate their professionalism in your first meeting. For instance, if there is the slightest hint of sexual flirtation or a rush to physical contact (hugs, touching, etc.) initiated by the therapist, they likely have some issues of their own to work through and you shouldn't enter into a clinical relationship with them. Here are some questions to ask yourself when you get home from the initial interview:

- How did they answer your questions? Did you feel they were honest, or evasive?

- Did they belittle any questions or statements of yours, or in some way seem condescending or patronizing towards you?

- Did they seem negative or cynical, or were they joyful and optimistic?

- Were they receptive and attentive? For instance, did they spend all their time looking at their notepad, or did they make frequent eye-contact with you?

- Did they ask questions that helped you clarify your own priorities?

- Did they seem to understand your concerns?

- Did they seem tired and depressed, or warm and genuine?

- When you asked some of the "odder" questions, did they laugh, or become defensive or impatient?

- Did they seem more interested in you, or in discussing their experience and impressing you?

- Were they willing to be flexible? How did they respond, overall, to the idea of answering so many questions?

It is of course always useful to listen to your intuition. What was your impression of this person within the first few seconds of meeting them?   Did it change significantly after the first few minutes? Why? I myself would not hesitate to use the Tarot to help me decide, asking the cards "What is the wisest course of action with respect to this therapist?"   Then laying out the simplest of spreads. Whatever method you use to tune into your spiritual perception, use it to refine and clarify your choice.   Then, once you decide what to do, schedule your next session...with this therapist, or the next person on your list of prospects.

Appendix D: About Reiki

"Reiki" is a Japanese word that means "universal life energy." It is a hands-on healing practice that Dr. Mikao Usui brought to Japan in the late 1800s. Reiki is not a religion, nor does a person need to be religious to practice it. In fact, Reiki was designed specifically as a "lay" practice, so that anyone could achieve results through very simple training. It was brought to the U.S. by Hawayo Takata in 1937, and it is her tradition which is carried on in Usui Shiki Ryoho (which means: "Usui System of Natural Healing"). Reiki has flourished ever since, and is now practiced around the world.

A Reiki session consists of a series of specific hand positions – it isn't massage, the hands remain flat and still. A Reiki practitioner, who has received their training and symbolic attunements from a Reiki Master, simply places their hands on the person requesting treatment, and invites Reiki to begin. That's it. For such a simple practice, the results are astounding, healing the mind, body and spirit. The first session is often very relaxing, though it generally takes about three 45-minute sessions, over the course of a week or two, to notice significant changes or a promise of future results. The greatest benefit of being initiated as a Reiki practitioner, of course, is that you then can administer Reiki to yourself every day.

If you are interested in learning more about Reiki, or finding an Usui Shiki Ryoho teacher or practitioner, visit the website www.reikialliance.com.

Five Reiki Principles (as they were taught to me):

> Just for today, I will not worry.
> Just for today, I will not be angry.
> Just for today, I will give thanks for my many blessings.
> Just for today, I will do my work honestly.
> Just for today, I will be kind to every living thing.

Appendix E: Interrupting Fear Cycles with CBT

Although different techniques may be required for different kinds of fear, and a professional therapist may be helpful to assist you through this process, the following are some CBT-inspired steps to break the fear cycles described in the Overcoming Fear and Avoidance section. These exercises may take weeks or months to complete, and I recommend keeping a private journal as you work through the questions. Try to be thorough, giving yourself frequent breaks from the process, especially if you become frustrated or overwhelmed at any point. As with all healing, patience and persistence will be your greatest allies.

1. **Examine your primary fears, that is, the ones that you most frequently experience.** What are their qualities? Consider which one of the following best characterizes them:

    a. A free-floating anxiety about future uncertainties;

    b. A sense of futility, angst or uselessness;

    c. A phobia of specific objects, activities or environments that can't be explained or relieved in a rational way;

    d. A deep sense unease or panic that seems overly severe for the situation which triggers it;

    e. A replaying in your imagination of past or future events;

    f. A strong desire to avoid humiliation or embarrassment in specific situations;

    g. A consistent mistrust of others; or

    h. Sadness, grief or guilt over achieving success or happiness in some area of your life.

2. **What surface thoughts surround those feelings?** Take some time to listen to your internal dialogue, and note the ideas, words or phrases coursing through your head at different times throughout the day. Pay special attention to thoughts which seem to recur frequently, or come unbidden. What are you focused on most of the time?   What are you saying to yourself? Some examples:

   a. Do you find yourself frequently attaching meaning to what others do? Do you find your thoughts are critical of others, or forgiving?

   b. Are you negative about yourself, or supportive? Do you tend to judge yourself for something you feel, think or do, or are you accepting and patient with yourself?

   c. Do you find yourself curious about why encouraging or discouraging things happen to you, or do you believe you discern the underlying reasons for such events? Do you always know, or just some of the time?

   d. What about near-future events, how do you think about them? With joyful anticipation? With anxiety or nervousness?   Are you usually confident that things will work out for the best, or do you tend to expect the worst to happen? Do you find yourself saying, "What if...?" and then dreading the outcome?

   Write down some of this internal dialogue, and the feelings associated with it. Try keeping an ongoing log over several weeks. What patterns do you see?

3. **How do your primary fears manifest in your behavior?** See some of the examples in the Fear Cycles chart. What have the results of that behavior been? How does that make you feel? How do the feelings and consequences of your actions correspond to your internal dialogue? Do they reinforce your thoughts about yourself and your choices?   Do they contradict them?

4. **Now examine the underlying assumptions and beliefs that support your fears.** In addition to the examples in the chart, consider the following "downward arrow technique" for burrowing down to core of your thinking. Write down what you find.

   a. Think about any *result* you are afraid of, or nervous about, and ask, "Why is that so bad?"

   b. Now ask "What does this *mean* about me, about other people, or about the world in general? What does it mean about the nature of the Universe, or my relationship with the Divine? What conclusions do I arrive at because of this?"

   c. Keep asking "What does this mean?" and "Why is that so bad?" until you encounter the core belief that drives all of the assumptions behind your fear.

   Write down what you find, and reflect on it.

5. **Compare your beliefs about yourself with the beliefs you have about others.** If they are different, *why* are they different? Are you being fair and reasonable with yourself? With others? With the world in general? With the Universe and the Divine?

6. **Where did those beliefs come from?** Reflect on your past, especially your early childhood. Was there a pivotal moment or series of events that shaped your beliefs? A specific relationship that influenced your thinking? A recurring theme? A destructive or antagonizing environment? (In cases where you have trouble remembering the origin of your beliefs, review the sections Grief and Loss, as well as Abuse, Dysfunction and Recovery for other ways to explore your childhood.) Think about the last few interactions you had with a parent or sibling. What emotions did you feel? Did your interactions validate your positive beliefs about yourself and others, or did it reinforce negative beliefs?

7. **Begin a dialogue with your younger self, either in a journal or using your imagination, where you face the pivotal**

moments of your past *together*. In this exercise, your wiser "adult" self can support and comfort the younger one, offering some perspective, and hope. Consider writing a brief letter of friendship and encouragement to your younger self, offering love, support and guidance. Replay the events of conflict or trauma, applying what you know now to what you experienced at that time. Allow yourself to feel compassion and forgiveness in those moments of pain, shame or despondence that were so formative. Imagine being there to comfort your younger self, or be a protecting presence. If you find yourself becoming anxious, use relaxation techniques like mindful breathing, conceptual meditation, or contemplative prayer to return your calm. Try to accept the emotions for what they are in the moment: a strong reaction washing over you, and *eventually passing*. You may also find you want to grieve for a while over your revisited experiences, so make time and emotional space for that in your life.

8. **Recognize that although that younger self is still part of you, and deserves your compassion, it is not** *all* **of who you are, and cannot dictate your present or your future.** You may still be holding hands with the past, but your adult self takes the lead in the present, and has the tools to move forward. Have confidence in this.

9. **Consider a dialogue with your family of origin, where your original beliefs took shape.** Clear out the cobwebs of your childhood by courageously speaking about them in the present.

   a. Identify the key players during the most formative events of your past. Usually, these are parents and siblings. Sometimes they are peers, non-family caretakers, or early mentors.

   b. Decide what about these relationships could have been better in those early days. Could they have been more mutually accepting, honest and loving? Were there negative patterns you wish you could transform? What about in the present? Do you desire more acknowledgement over what happened in the past? Do you wish you could change current dynamics? Write down what you would like to see happen – in the past and the present – perhaps in the form of a letter.

c. Attempt a non-judgmental discussion with these key players, in your imagination first, and then in reality. Talk about your feelings – and actively try to understand their point of view – regarding what you have already identified as important events. Try pretending to *be* these people, walking through the past in their shoes; this can be an eye-opening experience. Take the letter you have written, and try reading it aloud to an empty chair, where you imagine them sitting and listening. If you decide you want to discuss this over the phone or in person, still try journaling or visualizing this interaction first, to understand what you really want to say, and to feel the depth of your emotions. If the key players who are accessible reject your gentle attempts to engage them, or if they are no longer living or able, your imagination will nonetheless be a helpful alternative for this dialogue.

d. Be sure to make time and space in your life (i.e. alone-time, freedom from commitments and demanding social interactions, and meditative stillness) for any anger, pain or grief these interactions may evoke, and support those emotions with the same compassion and forgiveness you offered your younger self, trying not to blame anyone involved – especially yourself.

e. With patience and persistence, begin to define a new, more accepting and positive interaction with your family of origin. Invite key players who are *able* to begin again to do so with you now; or, if they aren't able to engage you at this moment, leave the door open for future possibilities.

    f.   Write down your thoughts and feelings about all of these experiences, and be confident that you have done your best.

As thorny as this process may appear, lovingly healing and reinventing our primary family of origin relationships – in our imagination, via role-playing with a therapist, or in reality – is really a model for how we reinvent our beliefs and assumptions about ourselves, other people, the world in general, the Universe, and our relationship with the Sacred.

10. **Now it's time to confront and challenge the old, counterproductive patterns of thought and emotion you have identified.** Strongly question the validity of any self-limiting values and beliefs you may still hold. Are they really *always* true, *all* of the time? In your journal, try keeping a continuous record of every *positive* event, which demonstrates that those beliefs aren't always true. As the evidence mounts, permit that evidence to disconfirm those faulty assumptions. Continue to heap doubt and uncertainty on the old beliefs, and be increasingly comfortable with your questions about what really is, convinced that change is necessary.

11. **Decide that you want to replace old beliefs with open-minded ones, and consider what is truly important to you.** What kind of person you want to be? How do you want to live your life? What do you really want from other people? What do you want your life to look like a year from now? Five years? Ten? What do you really expect from the Universe? Write it down, mull it over for a while, and clarify a new vision of your life.

12. **Now choose values and beliefs that support your new goals.** These may come from your spiritual tradition, philosophic principles, or simply what makes sense for you. Be committed to these ideas; have faith in them. Write them in your journal, meditate on them, and make them part of you. (As an example, this is how the *Just for Today* meditations

were created.)

13. **Reinforce your new values and beliefs with *deliberately different* choices and actions than you have made in the past.** Say to yourself: "Because I believe *this*, I'm going to do *that*." And do it. Follow through. Experience some success in your new orientation, and start building confidence and trust that your new, "fear-free" beliefs are valid...*through living them.*

14. **Celebrate this new creation.** As you experience freedom from your fear, notice the fact and give thanks. Record every moment of victory in your journal, and cradle them in your heart.

I have found these exercises to be more than just a one-time adventure, and continually renew my practice of thoughtful self-examination by revisiting this process again and again. The results are always enriching, and often exceed my expectations.

Selected Bibliography

Almond, Philip C., *Mystical Experience and Religious Doctrine*, Walter de Gruyter & Co., 1982.

Barnhart, Bruno & Joseph Wong, Editors, *Purity of Heart and Contemplation*, Continuum, 2001.

Bharati, Agehananda, *The Light at the Center: Context and Pretext of Modern Mysticism*, 1976.

Cunningham, Lawrence S., *Thomas Merton: Spiritual Master*, Paulist Press, 1992.

Forman, Robert K.C., *Mysticism, Mind, Consciousness*, State University of New York Press, 1999.

Goldman, Daniel, *The Varieties of the Meditative Experience*, Irvington Publishers, 1977.

Hanh, Thich Nhat, *The Miracle of Mindfulness*, Beacon Press, 1996.

Hollenback, Jess Byron, *Mysticism, Experience, Response, & Empowerment*, Pennsylvania State University Press, 1996.

Idel, Moshe, and Bernard McGuinn, Editors, *Mystical Union in Judaism, Christianity, and Islam, An Ecumenical Dialogue*, Macmillan, 1989.

Jou, Tsung Hwa, *The Tao of Meditation Way to Enlightenment*, Tai Chi Foundation, 1983.

Merton, Thomas, *Mystics and Zen Masters*, Farrar, Straus & Giroux, 1967.

Sircar, Mahendranath, *Hindu Mysticism According to the Upanisads*, Paul, Trench, Trubner & Co., 1934.

Staal, Fritz, *Exploring Mysticism*, University of California Press, 1975.

Ullman, Robert , and Judyth Reichenberg-Ullman, *Moments of Enlightenment*, MJF Books, 2001.

Underhill, Evelyn, *Mysticism, A Study in the Nature and Development of Spiritual Consciousness*, E.P Dutton, 1930.

Wilhelm, Richard, *The Secret of the Golden Flower, A Chinese Book of Life*, Harcourt Brace, 1962.

Andresen, Jensine, Editor, *Cognitive Models and Spiritual Maps: Interdisciplinary Explorations of Religious Experience*, Imprint Academic, 2000.

Beck, Aaron, Arthur Freeman & Associates, *Cognitive Therapy of Personality Disorders*, Guilford Press, 1990.

Bookchin, Murray, *Re-Enchanting Humanity, A defense of the human spirit against anti-humanism, misanthropy, mysticism and primitivism*, Cassell, 1995.

Brill, A.A., Translator, *The Basic Writings of Sigmund Freud*, Random House, 1938.

Campbell, Joseph, Editor, *The Portable Jung*, Penguin, 1971.

Greenberger, Dennis, and Christine A. Padesky, *Mind over Mood*, Guilford Press, 1995.

Erikson, Erik H., *Identity and the Life Cycle*, International Universities Press, Inc., 1959.

Frazer, Sir James George, *The Golden Bough, A Study in Magic and Religion*, Macmillian, 1922.

Johnson, Sharon L., *Therapist's Guide to Clinical Intervention*, Elsevier Science, 1997.

Mellody, Pia, with Andrea Wells Miller and J.Keith Miller, *Facing Codependence*, Harper Collins, 1989.

Merrell-Wolff, Franklin, *Transformations in Consciousness, The Metaphysics and Epistemology*, State University of New Your Press, 1995.

Milne, Aileen, *Counselling*, Hodder Headline, Ltd., 1999.

Myers, David G., *Intuition*, Yale University Press, 2002.

Velmans, M., Editor, *Investigating Phenominal Consciousness*, Benjamin Publishers, 1999.

Varela, Francisco, *Neurophenomenology : A Methodological Remedy for the Hard Problem*, Article in *Journal of Consciousness Studies*, June, 1996.

Personal Healing & Development

Andrews, Cecile, *The Circle of Simplicity*, Harper Collins, 1997.

Belitz, Charlene, and Meg Lundstrom, *The Power of Flow*, Three Rivers Press, 1998.

Carter, Jay, *Nasty People, How to Stop Being Hurt by Them Without Becoming One of Them*, Dorset House Publishing, 1989.

Covey, Stephen R., *7 Habits of Highly Effective People*, Simon and Schuster, 1989.

Fields, Rick, Rex Weyler, Rick Ingrasci and Peggy Taylor, *Chop Wood Carry Water*, J.P.Tarcher, 1984.

Fitzgerald, Helen, *The Mourning Handbook*, Fireside, 1994.

Hendricks, Gay and Kathlyn Hendricks, *Conscious Loving*, Bantam Books, 1992.

Hendricks, Gay, *Conscious Living*, HarperCollins, 2000.

Kabat-Zinn, Jon, *Full Catastrophe Living*, Delta, 1990.

Labowitz , Rabbi Shoni, *Miraculous Living*, Fireside, 1996.

Myss, Caroline, *Anatomy of the Spirit,* Random House, 1996.

Roman, Sanaya, *Spiritual Growth, Being Your Higher Self*, H.J.Kramer, Inc., 1989.

Other References

Balthasar, Hans Urs von, *Prayer*, translated by A.V. Littledale, Sheed & Ward, 1961.

Bedi, Ashok, *Path to the Soul*, Samuel Weiser, 2000.

Blakney, R.B., Translator, *The Way of Life, Lao Tzu*, Mentor, 1955.

Bloom, Harold, *Kabbalah and Criticism*, Seabury Press, Inc., 1975.

Boehme, Jacob, *Six Theosophic Points and Other Writings,* University of Michigan Press, 1958.

Bonaventura, Saint, *The Mind's Road to God*, Liberal Arts Press, Inc., 1953.

Cicero, Chic, and Sandra Tabatha Cicero, *Self-Initiation into the Golden Dawn Tradition*, Llewellyn, 1998.

Ernst, Carl W., *The Shambhala Guide to Sufism*, Shambala, 1997.

Grigg, Ray, *The Tao of Zen*, Alva Press, 1994.

Gyatso, Tenzin, *Essence of the Heart Sutra,* Wisdom Publications, 2002.

James, William, *Essays on Faith and Morals*, Meridian, 1962.

Kraft, Norman R., *Ogdoadic Magick, Being a Year of Study with an Aurum Solis Commandery*, Red Wheel/Weiser, 2001.

L'Engle, Madeleine, *Walking on Water*, Bantam Books, 1983.

Morgan, Michelle, *A Magical Course in Tarot*, Conari, 2002.

Nicholson, Reynold A., *The Mystics of Islam*, G.Bell & Sons, Ltd., 1914.

Schaeffer, Franky, *Addicted to Mediocrity, 20th Century Christians and the Arts*, Crossway Books, 1981.

Zerner, Amy and Monte Farber, *The Enchanted Tarot*, St. Martins Press, 1990.

Spiritual Source Text Recommendations

Buddhist

> *Mahayana & Theravada Sutras*
>
> *Zen Koans*
>
> Goddard, Dwight, *A Buddhist Bible*, 1932.

Hindu

> *Bhagavad Gita* (Eknath Easwaran translation), *Upanishads*

Judeo-Christian

> *Proverbs, Ecclesiastes, Gospel of John, Romans, 1 Corinthians, Ephesians, Hebrews, and James* (New American Standard & Phillips translations.)
>
> Barnestone, Willis, Editor, *The Other Bible, Ancient Alternative Scriptures*, Harper Collins, 1984

Sufi

> Qur'an *Suras 3, 6, 13, 24, 30, 53, 64, 80, 86, 94, 97, 103*
>
> Hadith Qudsi (divine sayings)

Taoist

> *Tao te Ching* (Robert G. Henricks translation)
>
> *Chuang Tzu*
>
> *I Ching* (Jou, Tsung Hwa, *The Tao of I Ching*)

Wiccan

> Farrar, Janet and Stewart, *The Witches' Bible*, Phoenix Publishing, 1984.

Sampling of Mystical Writings

Note: Apart from the spiritual source material already listed, there is a vast, frequently cited body of mystical texts which has not been thoroughly represented in this bibliography. Instead, the following is a smattering of individual works and collections that reveal a small fraction of the many faces of mysticism.

Bach, Richard, *Illusions*, Delacorte Press, 1977.

Barks, Coleman, Translator, *The Essential Rumi*, Harper San Francisco, 1995.

Carroll, Lee, *The Journey Home*, Hay House, 1997.

De Mello, Anthony, *Song of the Bird*, Image Books, 1984.

Harvey, Andrew, *The Essential Mystics*, HarperCollins, 1996.

Hawken, Paul, *The Magic of Findhorn*, Harper & Row, 1975.

Ladinsky, Daniel, *I Heard God Laughing*, *Renderings of Hafiz*, Sufism Reoriented, 1996.

Ladinsky, Daniel, *Love Poems from God*, Penguin Compass, 2002.

Ladinsky, Daniel, *The Subject Tonight Is Love*, Pumpkin House Press, 1996.

Lee, A.H.E., Editor, *The Oxford Book of English Mystical Verse*, Acropolis Books, 1997.

For additional online resources, please visit
www.searchforclarity.com & www.integrallifework.com

www.ingramcontent.com/pod-product-compliance
Lightning Source LLC
Chambersburg PA
CBHW021043090426
42738CB00006B/162